Who's Your Father?

Returning to the
Love of the
Biblical God

ROBERT BERNECKER

Who's Your Father?

Copyright © 2013 by Robert Bernecker

All rights reserved. No part of this publication may be reproduced, stored in a retrieval system, or transmitted in any form by any means, electronic, mechanical, photocopy, recording, or otherwise without the prior permission of the author, except as provided by USA copyright law.

Italics in biblical quotations indicate emphasis added.

All Scripture quotations, unless otherwise indicated, are taken from *The Holy Bible, English Standard Version*. © Copyright 2000; 2001 by Crossway Bibles, a division of Good News Publishers. Used by permission. All rights reserved.

Scripture quotations denoted with "KJV" are taken from *The Holy Bible, King James Version*.

Scripture quotations denoted with "NASB" are taken from the *New American Standard Bible*, © Copyright 1960, 1962, 1963, 1968, 1971, 1972, 1973, 1975, 1977, 1995 by The Lockman Foundation. Used by permission.

Scripture quotations marked "NKJV" are taken from the *New King James Version*. Copyright © 1982 by Thomas Nelson, Inc. Used by permission. All rights reserved.

Scripture quotations denoted with "NIV" are taken from the *Holy Bible, New International Version*®. NIV®. Copyright © 1973, 1978, 1984, 2011 by International Bible Society. Used by permission of Zondervan. All rights reserved.

Scripture quotations marked (NLT) are taken from the *Holy Bible, New Living Translation*, Copyright © 1996. Used by permission of Tyndale House Publishers, Inc. Wheaton, IL 60189 USA. All rights reserved.

ISBN: 1482068389
ISBN 13: 9781482068382

Library of Congress Control Number: 2013901713
CreateSpace Independent Publishing Platform
North Charleston, South Carolina

CONTENTS

Preface	v
Learning from the Sparrows	1
The Illusion of a Gentleman God	19
Praying to a Gentleman God	37
The Big, the Small, and Our Present	53
Our Future Is Heading Our Way	67
Our Loving Father God, or the Great Puppeteer?	93
Fair Is Fair, or Is It?	129
Heavenly Robots	169
Unchanging Perfection	179
The God of Our Confidence	195
Notes	224

PREFACE

I never intended or planned to write this book, as unusual as that may seem. What started as a simple journal of God's incredible work in illuminating himself to my heart was transformed into a larger work when the message of this book flowed onto the pages with amazing ease. I have learned that to be correct merely for the sake of correctness is of very limited value, but a correct view of God can and will incredibly transform our walk with him—creating soaring worship and extreme gratitude in times of triumph and providing lasting comfort in times of sorrow. It is this proper, biblical concept of our God that this work attempts to describe. At its best, this book can only be an invitation into something deeper, an inducement into something wonderfully and immensely satisfying. The prospect that this book may perhaps be a signpost to point even a few readers toward this great treasure is reward enough for the labor.

My heart grieves that we have lost the sense of the true nature of God's immense love for us. We have replaced this reality with the notion of a God who conducts himself according to our own fallible standards of justness and fairness, and we mistakenly believe that our human choices determine God's purpose in our lives rather than relishing the precious reality that it is his perfect, divine choices that govern human actions. Perhaps unknowingly, until we form a correct concept of our loving heavenly Father, we allow such erroneous beliefs to deprive us of an astonishingly satisfying and previously unimaginable relationship with our loving Father.

I readily concede that this book dwells on the sovereignty of God without giving equal weight to each person's responsibility before our almighty God, and I am not at all oblivious to the fact that as many pages could be filled with a discussion of human responsibility as are filled here with a discussion on God's preeminence. Nevertheless, this writer feels that today's church is thoroughly immersed in teaching that accentuates human responsibility; therefore, little emphasis needed to be placed here on the matter of our responsibility before God for our choices and our actions. What is neglected by most Christians today is the comforting, awe-inspiring truth of our God's sovereignty, his great love for each of us, and the eminent trustworthiness of his eternal purpose, which includes each of us in infinite detail. This negligence robs us of our real joy and comfort in our Father who loves us, chooses us, redeems us, and perfects us. It is therefore my sincere desire that readers of this work will begin to critically think through the many false notions that we have formed about our God and allow his Word to form in their hearts a true perception of our almighty, predominant Father, from whom are all things, to whom are all things, and for whom are all things (Romans 11:36).

Sadly, this high view of God has apparently been lost in most of the church of our day. Readily found in the writings of great men and women of the faith from years past, what A. W. Tozer called a "lofty concept of God" now seems to have been discarded in favor of doctrines that are manifestly more appealing to human pride and egotism. I have therefore attempted to include many references from the enduring truth that was taught by these great people of God whose works have stood the test of time and remain as a ready source of spiritual guidance and encouragement still today. We need to return to our roots, so to speak, to the high view of God held by the Reformers and men such as Saint Augustine, William Tyndale, and Martin Luther. Great preachers and evangelists such as C. H. Spurgeon, George Whitefield, and Jonathan Edwards also taught us how this high view of God should be put into practice. More contemporary authors such as C. S. Lewis, A. W. Pink, J. I. Packer, A. W. Tozer, James Boice, and others are also referenced extensively to provide the reader with a generous diversity of solid, biblical teaching about the true nature of our loving Father.

Of greater importance, much Scripture is cited throughout this work, and it would be my hope that readers would digest this work with this book in one hand and God's Holy Word in the other. If a discrepancy is discovered, needless to say, anything I have to say should be discarded as stubble, and God's Word should be given the complete preeminence that it deserves and our Father demands. In the end, I pray that readers of this book will honestly and prayerfully reexamine their beliefs and emerge with a higher view of our God and a higher view of Scripture. The entire message of this book is indeed predicated on the belief that the Bible is our absolute point of reference, such that any conflicts between how we feel about a given issue and what the Bible states about that issue are resolved without question in favor of the Bible's authoritative teaching.

It is a basic rule of biblical hermeneutics that the most straightforward and simple meaning is usually the best meaning to ascribe to a particular Scripture being studied. As this book by a non-theologian layperson deals with weighty theological topics based on the straightforward message contained in God's Word, it will hopefully demonstrate the miraculous manner in which our incredible Father imparts truth to all of his chosen people through his powerful Word. Although many common doctrinal misconceptions are deliberately challenged, no attempt is made herein to develop a complete theological treatise, as that is not at all the purpose of this work. For the same reason, complicated, in-depth explorations of such topics as determinism, compatibilism, Socinianism, rationalism, or modernism are deliberately left for the theologians and the philosophers. It is instead hoped that the simple, commonsense style of this writing will by God's grace be able to communicate immense concepts in an uncomplicated, readable, and understandable manner. If this work were judged to be a practical book written by a common man for the edification of non-theologians, I would indeed consider that to be high praise.

Why my Father has chosen me to invest the time to elucidate these truths within this book is above my ability to understand. Nevertheless, I am quite confident that he has a purpose for this undertaking and that his leading will accomplish its intended purpose, whatever that may be. It is my prayer that God will cause the readers of these pages to find new encouragement and motivation to seek after God, explore his Word, and thereby partake in the wonderful blessings he sets before us. The biblical truth about our incredible Father will give readers of this book a new and lasting understanding of God's love, his purpose, and his power. This awareness cannot fail to lead them into a relationship with their loving Father that far exceeds anything that they could have formerly conceived. To God alone be the glory!

CHAPTER 1

LEARNING FROM THE SPARROWS

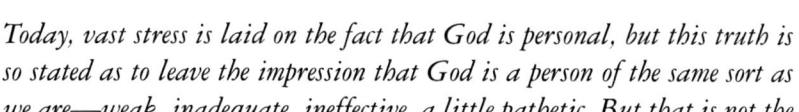

Today, vast stress is laid on the fact that God is personal, but this truth is so stated as to leave the impression that God is a person of the same sort as we are—weak, inadequate, ineffective, a little pathetic. But that is not the God of the Bible!

– J. I. Packer, Knowing God[1]

Our concept of God can be formed at a young age, and many of our understandings and perceptions are thereafter colored and shaped by these early foundational concepts. For me, one distinct example was the notion that God was an all-knowing and attentive God, but his involvement in any given event could not be taken for granted. Indeed, much of the world was presumed to be allowed to function on its own without any intervention from God. For example, rain is formed from moisture in the air that has evaporated from the surface of the ocean, and this process ostensibly could and would take place without God's control or direction. It was understood that the earth rotates on its axis and thereby causes the sun to rise each morning. It was observable that a man may jump off a cliff if he so desires, and he will certainly plunge downward and not accelerate upward. After all, God created nature, set the world in motion, and defined the law of gravity.

During this early period of my life, the church often sang a popular, old hymn that included these lyrics: "His eye is on the sparrow, and I know he watches me." This admittedly comforting phrase paints God as an attentive observer who constantly sees the activities of both sparrows and humans. We are taught that he may even be a potential benefactor if our choices and actions are pleasing to him. But is this really our God? Is he just a watchful, magnanimous old gentleman who sometimes chooses to extend kindness in our direction but most of the time allows evil to run its course? Is he either unable or unwilling to make circumstances or individuals different by interjecting his supposedly unlimited power and unlimited resources, even though he may be said to wish or desire they were different? Is a god that desires things to be different but is unwilling or unable to make them different really God at all?

In more recent years, during the pleasure of reading the Bible completely through many times in multiple translations, God began to form within me a completely different picture of himself. It turns out that the truth of the sparrows is much deeper than just God's awareness of when or where they may fall for any arbitrary reason. What Jesus himself actually said in Matthew was this:

> Are not two sparrows sold for a copper coin? And not one of them falls to the ground apart from your Father's will. (Matthew 10:29 NKJV)

Jesus' words point us to a dramatically different reality than the incomplete, erroneous concept that had been formed in my earlier years. God is not merely observing the sparrows; he is in control of their circumstances, and he is exercising his sovereignty and his will over those circumstances! Not just one particular sparrow, Jesus taught, but rather, God is in control of *all* of the sparrows' situations. How many billions of sparrows must this be? Yet, our God's providence guides each daily!

This may have come as a new realization to me, but it is by no means my own newly concocted understanding of this passage. One very popular old-time commentator, Albert Barnes, wrote the following concise, yet elucidating, statement about the sparrow we see in this verse: "That is, God, your Father, guides and directs its fall. It falls only with his permission, and where he chooses."[2] Barnes' view of this passage is neither unique nor novel; John Gill similarly expounded that "not one of them [the sparrows] is taken in a snare, or killed with a stone, or shot flying, or sitting, but by the will of God: from whence it may be strongly concluded, that nothing comes by chance; that there is no such thing as contingency with respect to God."[3] Adam Clarke also concurred with these views concerning Jesus' words in this passage, stating, "All things are ordered by the counsel of God." He adds, "The providence of God extends to the minutest things; everything is continually under the government and care of God, and nothing occurs without his will or permission; if then he regards sparrows, how much more man, and how much more still the soul that trusts in him."[4] Finally, John Wesley likewise noted that God's control and direction extend to the smallest of creatures, and this fact provides us the great assurance that he will do the same for us.[5]

If we give this passage a bit of thought, it becomes readily apparent that we can know with great certainty that Jesus did not mean to merely teach us that God is ever attentive—that a sparrow cannot fall to the ground without God noticing the event—because the thrust of Jesus' teaching in the surrounding verses is that we should not worry or fear about circumstances, events, or even what others may do to us since God is sovereign over all, including the sparrows. This teaching would completely fail to provide us with any reason to "fear not" (v. 31) if Jesus was instructing us merely that the sparrow may fall for any haphazard reason, and while God will surely notice such an event, it is not at all certain he will involve himself or impose his own will in the situation. Rather, the only credible reason we could have to "fear not" is that Jesus was teaching us plainly that nothing happens outside of God's sovereignty; if God involves himself in and controls the circumstances and details of the sparrow's lives, not to mention numbering the hairs on our head as well (v. 30), then he is most certainly controlling the circumstances and details of the lives of we whom he values much more than the sparrows.

As critically important as this realization may be, there is additional truth that we can learn from these sparrows to which Jesus referred. Jesus could have claimed his own sovereignty over the sparrows by saying that they could not fall to the ground apart from *his* will. However, he did not do so. Instead, as always, Jesus pointed us to the Father who is ultimately sovereign over all, which in this instance includes even the tiny sparrows (cf. John 8:28–29; 12:49; 14:10; 15:15; 17:7). Moreover, I believe there is a concept which is all the more marvelous that Jesus was trying to get us to see—a truth that I think we miss very easily in today's church because of the manner in which we have allowed our concept of God to become skewed. In my opinion, the greatest truth of this verse is that Jesus did not say that "his Father" is sovereign over the sparrows, even though he could have easily and correctly so asserted. Rather, he deliberately chose to assure each of us individually that it is "your Father" who is sovereign over the sparrows (cf. John 20:17).

This is amazing! Jesus is telling us that the ultimately perfect, all-knowing, completely sovereign over everything that exists, and all-powerful ruler of the universe is *our own* Father, not merely "the" Father! As a direct result of this great truth and, if one truly weighs and considers the matter, *only* as a result of this great truth, we should not worry because we are worth much more than many sparrows to him, and we know even the details of the sparrows' lives are included in his purpose and ultimate plan. *We must never miss the vital connection between God's love for us and God's purpose for us!* A full comprehension of this truth compels us to trust our Father audaciously, and it sets before us a feast of God's grace, goodness, and peace for our souls that cannot be otherwise experienced or understood.

Until we come to comprehend the infinite extents and depths to which this wonderful truth reaches, we may well refer to God as "our Father," but we fail to live and believe as if he is actually a loving Father that will always give us good gifts and not bad (Matthew 7:11), who loves us so much that he chooses us to be his own (Ephesians 1:4), who has the unlimited power and authority to back up his unlimited love (Psalm 136:12), and who is involved in everything that surrounds us every day, even the sparrows over our heads. It is God's power that enables him to subject *all things* to himself (Philippians 3:21), and it is the steadfastness of his love that gives us an unshakeable confidence in his purpose for each of us (Psalm 138:8; Ephesians 2:4–5). This, then, is our true Father; he is certainly not the detached ruler of the universe who will bring himself to tolerate us for Jesus' sake, nor is he a dispassionate benefactor who will even give us eternal life if someone happens to help him out by "pointing us to Christ" or manages to convince us that the Gospel is a good thing for us to "accept." Jesus' words eliminate any possibility of the truth of this latter assessment and instead direct us to be completely confident in both our Father's total sovereignty and his overwhelming love!

There is little confidence or faith that we can place in a God who is totally sovereign and infinitely powerful but who does not love or value us, a God who is not our own Father. Likewise, there is little confidence or faith we can place in a heavenly Father who either does not have the power and sovereignty to back up his love or who is not consistently willing to use his power and sovereignty on behalf of those he is said to love and value. Jesus, however, showed us that our God gives to us the perfect combination of unlimited love and unbounded sovereignty. We can, therefore, have a real and living faith, only because we can *know* that our loving Father exercises his sovereign purpose (his will) over *all* of the details in our lives!

It is not difficult for our finite, limited abilities and understandings to be overwhelmed by the seemingly infinite details of the circumstances and events of our lives. And yet, as I watch the many sparrows in my yard flit about, it staggers me to ponder that God, *my Father*, is directing each one of their situations every moment. They go up, and they go down, countless little birds making countless moves—and this just in my yard. Jesus said that all of these moves by these tiny creatures are God's will. If someone were to take up a rifle and freely choose to shoot one of these little creatures, making it fall to the ground permanently, that would have to be God's will. I certainly would not understand the purpose for such a senseless killing to be a part of God's providence, but Jesus' words would have to stand nonetheless. If it were *not* included in God's purpose for the sparrow to be killed, he would most certainly act by giving the individual a desire to *not* shoot the sparrow or perhaps by causing the shooter to miss the shot. It is an absolutely magnificent thing to know beyond a shadow of a doubt that God, my loving Father, is involved and in control of these minute details of life here on the earth! Our God is not a mere observer-god, but rather the sovereign, all-seeing, all-powerful, holy ruler of the earth who "subjects all things to himself" (Philippians 3:21). The apostle Paul summed up this incredibly wonderful truth in Ephesians 1:11, where he declared that God "works all things according to the counsel of his will." This sweeping and particularly unambiguous statement bestows to us no less than the most solid foundation imaginable upon which an enduring, unshakable faith can be built.

The fact that our own loving Father is not an observer-god at all should constantly flood our hearts with joy and peace. With Paul, we can rely upon the certainty that he is the omnipotent and omniscient God who is intrinsically involved in *everything* that happens here on this earth. All things are from him, through him, and to him (Romans 11:36); it is Christ who holds all things together (Colossians 1:17), and our loving Father indeed "makes everything to work out according to his plan" (Ephesians 1:11 NLT). We must ponder and absorb the magnitude of the powerful words found in Psalm 135:6, which makes this unconditional, all-encompassing declaration:

> Whatever the Lord pleases, he does, in heaven and on earth, in the seas and all deeps.

Assuming that God cares about us and about the sparrows as much as he says he does, this verse completely excludes the notion of a detached, hands-off observer-god. The natural and inevitable result of God's great love for us must be that what he pleases will also always be for our good (Romans 8:28; Matthew 7:11), and, just like the fall of the sparrow, his presence in everything that happens in our lives is thereby guaranteed. In fact, God says of himself in Jeremiah 23:23–24 that he is a God who is both near at hand and everywhere all at the same time—a fact of which David was fully cognizant as he exalted in Psalm 139 that there is absolutely no place where we can flee from God's constant presence, even if we should so desire. God said in Job 38:12 that it is he who commands the sun to rise each morning, and, according to Amos 4:13 and 5:8, it is God who turns daylight into darkness each evening. Our Father said in Job 38 that it is he who satisfies the young lions' appetites and that it is he who provides the prey for the young ravens. It is even God's command that causes the eagle to mount up and make its nest on high, a behavior that most today would wrongly ascribe instead to "Mother Nature" (Job 39:27).

Such an inconceivably intricate level of involvement and control is not only problematic for us to comprehend, it is also difficult for many of us to accept. By human standards, such behavior might even be negatively labeled "micromanagement." Nevertheless, God's Word provides us more than ample clarity, and we must realize that we too often unknowingly allow our perceptions of our infinitely capable Father to be shaped by the limitations of our own finiteness. Just as fish live their lives perpetually surrounded by water, so we as humans are constantly immersed in our own finiteness. For example, knowing that we have very limited abilities to give our attention to many things at once, we naturally try to automate as much as possible rather than attempting to control a multitude of details simultaneously. We would rather have a timer or photocell to turn on our outside lights every evening instead of trying to remember to do so ourselves, and we prefer to have a thermostat keep our house at a certain temperature instead of having to constantly pay attention to managing the temperature manually. We prefer not to control such things directly because we correctly discern that the fewer small details we have to manage, the more effective we can be in matters we judge to be of greater importance.

This is all well and good until we unintentionally transfer this same perspective to our understanding of our Father, and we thereby unconsciously dismiss the reality that God actually directly manages the smallest details of the universe. Because such a capacity is far beyond our comprehension and is precluded by our very frame of reference, we wrongly judge that God could not possibly actually actively manage all the sparrows in the universe while still maintaining full and undistracted control of the things that seem to us to be much more important. However, unlike us, God is infinite in his capabilities, and we unfortunately often fail to even attempt to understand the ramifications of this fact. When we do pause to contemplate this staggering concept, we still fall short of fully comprehending the ability to manage billions of intricate details simultaneously without having any less power or attention to devote to any other single detail. More importantly, our Father never has any less power or attention to devote to any of his chosen children, including all of our needs and prayers.

Because our Father is unlimited in perception, unlimited in power, unlimited in ability, unlimited in resources, and unlimited in wisdom, a billion sparrows can be micromanaged, a billion stars can be steered, uncounted eagles can be commanded to soar, and innumerable creatures and beasts governed and fed, and still it is as if he is not occupied with anything else at all as he relates to each of his children. If we can even begin to grasp this magnificent reality, such a realization can yield nothing less than unmitigated worship and adoration for our Father, who is sovereign over every detail in the universe and still chooses us to be his very own. We need to study and work diligently to develop this higher view of our God and make this high view an integral part of all that we think and do, indeed, an essential component of our very beings.

Daniel must have understood this concept as much as is humanly possible, and we can see his high view of God in his words describing the overarching preeminence of the Lord, which are found in Daniel 2:21 (NIV): "He *changes* times and seasons; he *sets up* kings and *deposes* them." It is vitally important that we understand that these are action verbs in this passage. God "changes," God "sets up," and God "deposes"; these verbs demand active participation and causation, not mere observation. This is well illustrated in 2 Samuel 7, where God told King David that it was he who had raised David up from tending sheep and caused David to ascend to the throne of Israel (v. 8). We should note well that this transformation of David's life was solely because of God's choice and the active hand of God, and it was not at all because of any other factor such as noble birth, David's skill as a warrior, or even blind luck. God was also clear when he told David that it had been God that had caused David's triumphs over his enemies (v. 9).

Our marvelous God next proceeded to give David a glimpse of the future, and in so doing God made it irrefutable that it was he who was going to divinely control this future and actively bring it to pass—once again we see action verbs used as God described the future. God would "give" David rest from his enemies (v. 11). God would "make" David's name great (v. 9). God would "make" him a house (v. 11). God would "raise up" Solomon (v. 12), and he would "establish" Solomon's throne forever (v 13). God would "make" David's house and throne sure forever (v. 16).

Our response to the loving, active, controlling hand of our Father in accomplishing his purpose in our lives should be the same as David's, who first humbly expressed his awe at being chosen by the God of the universe: "Who am I, O Lord God, and what is my house, that you have brought me thus far?" (v. 18). Moreover, David responded further with earnest praise for his glorious, preeminent God: "Therefore you are great, O Lord God. For there is none like you, and there is no God besides you" (v. 22). David also acknowledged that God had brought these things into being according to God's own perfect desires (v. 21). Finally, David walked in a confidence born of knowing that his destiny would unfold exactly as his loving Father had purposed and spoken: "For you, O Lord God, have spoken, and with your blessing shall the house of your servant be blessed forever" (v. 29). When we realize that the God of the universe chooses us just as he chose David (Ephesians 1:4-5) and promises to fulfill his purpose for us as well (Psalm 57:2; Philippians 1:6), we should follow in this same pattern of humble awe, earnest worship, and a confident walk. All three of these responses are rooted firmly in the glorious realization that our loving Father controls *all* of the details of his creation.

Indeed, there is nothing that is not under the umbrella of his sovereignty. Even the rain that I supposed was formed without divine supervision is created by God and under his direction and control (Zechariah 10:1; Psalm 147:8). It is God who causes it to rain on both the just and the unjust (Matthew 5:45; Acts 14:17), and according to Amos 5:8, even the evaporation of water from the ocean in order to form rain over land happens expressly at his direct command. At times, he directly sends rain to one city, while specifically withholding rain from another (Amos 4:7; 2 Chronicles 7:13). If our Father directly controls even the rain, should not we relish his control over everything else as well? Paul said in Acts 17 that God made every nation of men and that God (not humans) "determined the times set for them and the exact places where they should live" (v. 26 NIV). Every detail is included! Psalm 104:14 shows us that God "causes" even the grass to grow. The incredible breadth of this glorious truth is magnificently encapsulated in Psalm 119:91, which declares that *"all* things are his servants." Indeed, we should join with Paul in exalting our God who "works all things according to the counsel of his will!"

Because God's providence is consistent and reliable, the normal dependability of the natural order of things often causes us to fail to ascertain that our God is actually in control of all these details. God tells us that he makes the sun rise each morning (Job 38:12; Amos 5:8), but this particular providence is so predictable that we usually fail to offer him either credit or thanksgiving for this daily event. However, when what we perceive as the natural, expected order of nature is altered, we have little difficulty attributing what we term a miracle to the hand of God. When Jesus walked on the water, healed lepers, and changed ordinary water into superior wine, such actions defied the normal and are correctly recognized as miracles from the hand of God. Likewise, we also recognize the hand of God in miracles that we experience today. When sparrows fly overhead, however, we must know that this is no less from the hand of our God!

We make a great mistake when we attribute what we call miracles to God but deny his involvement in everything else in our lives. Our God is the author of both the miraculous and the mundane, and this is a realization that will revolutionize our walk with our Father. In fact, as far as it concerns God, there is little difference between the simple and the spectacular since he is in equal control of one as well as the other, both are integral parts of his purpose, and neither taxes his infinite abilities any more than the other. We rob ourselves of the security of our Father's love when go through life waiting and hoping for God to intervene with the supernatural yet fail to appreciate his hand in the details of our daily existence. It is common for people of our day to label an unusual event that they perceive to be a good thing as "a God thing." Doubtless there are indeed many "God things" in our lives. Our error is to attempt to compartmentalize those things that we will choose to allow to be "God things" while refusing to acknowledge God's involvement in those things we perceive as less than spectacular.

Too often do we hear people quote James 1:17 and claim that because "every good and perfect gift comes from above," we can therefore know that anything we humans consider or label "good" comes from God, and likewise anything we humans consider or label "bad" comes from Satan. Or, it may be suggested that the "bad" happened because God was either absent or uninvolved. However appealing it may seem at first glance, such reasoning is illusory for several reasons. Firstly, as C. S. Lewis masterfully and poignantly portrayed through the actions, attitudes, and words of the Green Lady character in his novel *Perelandra*, we humans actually have a tremendously flawed concept of what is "good" and what is "bad."[6] Indeed, we often may perceive a gift from our Father's hand as "bad" when it is actually his sovereign method of lovingly working for our own good.

Secondly, this is a shallow, ineffectual theology that strips God of his sovereignty and thereby robs us unnecessarily of our comfort and faith in troubled times. God refuted this poor theology directly in Isaiah 45:7, where he said, "I form light and create darkness, I make well-being and create calamity, I am the Lord, who does all these things." The psalmist exalted in the fact that our Father turns deserts into pools of water and at other times turns flowing springs into deserts (Psalms 107:33, 35). It is God who makes people to be mute, deaf, seeing, or blind, according to what he told Moses in Exodus 4:12, and it is he who both opens and closes women's wombs, thereby either creating life or not, according to his own purpose and timetable (Genesis 20:18; 29:31; 30:22; 1 Samuel 1:5–6). Moreover, in 2 Chronicles 15:6, God is said to "trouble them [the Israelites] with every kind of distress" or to "vex them with all adversity" (KJV), and he actually says that he may "send pestilence among his people" (2 Chronicles 7:13). This same concept is also clearly seen in Ecclesiastes 7:14, Micah 1:12, Job 42:11, Jeremiah 44:2 and 42:10, Hosea 5:14–15, and Isaiah 31:2 and 47:11. In fact, Amos 3:6 teaches us that calamity cannot come apart from the Lord's command: "Does disaster come to a city, unless the Lord has done it?" Jeremiah summarized this principle poetically in Lamentations 3:38 (NIV) with the following words: "Is it not from the mouth of the Most High that both calamities and good things come?"

We must not, therefore, attempt to remove from God his rightful glory and throne by suggesting that he must not be actively involved in governing our lives and circumstances merely because we feel that something that is happening to us is "bad" as judged by our limited, flawed perception. We can learn from Psalm 71:20, in which the psalmist pronounced: "You who have made me see many troubles and calamities will revive me again." This is a firm declaration that God is sovereign over our circumstances, and while he may well make us see trials for his purpose and our good, he nevertheless will certainly revive us. Here again, we must recognize that God "works all things according to the counsel of his will" and find great contentment and rest in this profound realization.

It may be derogatory to say of people that "they are in the habit of getting whatever they desire," but when this is said of the only holy, perfect, loving, omnipotent God of the universe—our Father—then it is no longer a detrimental attribute at all. Instead, it becomes a glorious tribute to the matchless power and unfailing faithfulness of our God. God gets what God wants! "Whatever the Lord pleases, he does!" This fundamental, basic truth about our Father from Psalm 135:6 could easily stand alone even if it were an isolated reference, but it is not; the Bible is filled with declarations of this powerful fact. If this maxim is given even a little serious thought, it quickly becomes evident that a god who does not get what he wants is not God at all. There would necessarily be some limitation to that supposed god's power, knowledge, resources, or abilities—otherwise that god would, in fact, be able to get what he wanted and to do exactly as he pleased. "A 'god' whose will is resisted, whose designs are frustrated, whose purpose is checkmated, possesses no title to Deity," said A. W. Pink, "and so far from being a fit object of worship, merits naught but contempt."[7]

But, our glorious God is not limited like this so-called god in any way at all. Praise, honor, and glory to him! Psalm 115:3 tells us that *"our God is in the heavens; he does all that he pleases."* It is inescapable that what our God pleases is what our God desires, and what God desires is what God pleases—and that is exactly what he does. Not some of the time, but all of the time. God made this declaration of himself through the prophet Isaiah: "My purpose *will* be established, and I *will* accomplish *all* my good pleasure" (Isaiah 46:10 NASB). What God says, that God *will* do (Numbers 23:19; 11:23; 1 Samuel 15:29; Ezekiel 39:8).

It is crucial to note that there is a huge difference between a God that simply foretells what he knows by seeing into the future (but supposedly does not control) and a God that brings to pass that which he wills and speaks. When God said to Abraham, in Genesis 17:5–7 (NASB), "I have made you the father of a multitude of nations, I will make you exceedingly fruitful," and "I will establish my covenant between me and you and your descendants after you," and again about Ishmael: "I will surely bless him," "I will make him fruitful," and "I will make him into a great nation" (Genesis 17:20 NIV), he was not just predicting the future; rather, he was unambiguously stating exactly what he already knew he was going to do. In fact, the phrase "I have made you the father of a multitude of nations" in 17:5 is incredibly revealing and must not be passed over lightly. At that point in human time, Abraham was not the father of many nations; he only had a single teenage son, Ishmael, and yet God stated Abraham's future in the present tense with as much certainly as if it had already come to pass.

This is indeed a powerful truth; our infinite, eternal God is outside of time, and to God the future is as if it is the present. What God knows he will do is in fact already done and not subject to being undone (Isaiah 45:23), and this knowledge is neither partial nor selective but is complete and all-encompassing. God said in Isaiah 46:11, "I have spoken, and I *will* bring it to pass; I have purposed, and I *will* do it." Here, and many other places (such as Isaiah 55:11 and Ezekiel 39:8), God told us directly that he *will* bring his purpose to pass. In another place, he said that he is "watching over his word *to perform it*" (Jeremiah 1:12). These many passages teach us emphatically that our magnificent God does not merely foresee the future; rather, he speaks of the future as it is included in his purpose, and then he acts and brings it to pass.

We can be certain his methods will vary; in this particular passage (Isaiah 46), he said that he may even call a bird of prey from the east or a man of counsel from a far country—but no matter what method he sovereignly chooses, we can know that God *will* bring to pass his purpose and his will. It is likely that God will most often use human choices, actions, and methods to accomplish his purpose rather than intervening with a lightning bolt from heaven or even a disembodied hand writing on a wall (cf. Daniel 5:5). It is up to us to properly recognize that God works his purpose through humans and not misattribute the work of his hand to others. Regardless of how God works, however, we may always be certain that "the Lord has both purposed and performed what He spoke" (Jeremiah 51:12 NASB).

If we are to properly know and worship our almighty Father, we must come to understand that he is not reacting to autonomous human choices as history unfolds and adapting his purpose accordingly. God's proclamation in Isaiah 37:26 provides us with a delightful insight upon which we can build this faith: "Have you not heard that I determined it long ago? I planned from days of old what now I bring to pass." It is altogether too easy to get the human cart before the divine horse, so to speak, and we are often guilty of this error in the teaching of our day. We would do well to realize, acknowledge, and meditate upon the fact that *God's words do not merely predict history, but rather the unfolding of history fulfills God's words.* If we have a proper view of God's sovereignty, this statement should not strike us as any great revelation. For example, at the very end of 2 Chronicles, after God had sovereignly brought calamity upon Judah, the few remaining people that survived this sword of judgment were exiled into Babylon (36:15–21). The chapter is quite clear that all of these things happened at the Lord's command, but the language of verse 21 is particularly revealing because there we are told very simply and directly *why* it all happened: "To fulfill the word of the Lord." We can thereby understand that this was not merely a particularly accurate divine prediction of human events; rather the Babylonian exile happened at God's specific command, in order to fulfill his own words.

Likewise, when God foretells the future, as he did in Amos 8:9–14, he is actually stating what it is that he will do in the future, not merely what will happen. In that particular passage in Amos, when God spoke of coming natural disaster, famine, mourning, and death to idolaters, he was stating what would certainly be brought to pass by his immutable (unchangeable) will, this enabled by his irresistible, infinite power. Logically, infinite power cannot be resisted or impeded by any finite resistance. Mount Everest is huge, but it is nevertheless finite and could therefore be flattened or removed by a single word from our infinite God if such a thing were ever his will (cf. Psalm 97:5). It is no different when finite human will or finite demonic power meets infinite divine will and infinite divine power—God's purpose will invariably be done.

God spoke of the absolute certainty of the accomplishment of his own purpose in Isaiah 14 by making this declaration:

> Surely, just as I have intended so it has happened, and just as I have planned so it will stand. For the Lord of hosts has planned, and who can frustrate it? And as for His stretched-out hand, who can turn it back? (Isaiah 14:24 and 27 NASB)

A striking example of this principle is seen in Ezekiel 21, where the Lord foretold the future of the Ammonites:

> And I will pour out my indignation upon you; I will blow upon you with the fire of my wrath, and I will deliver you into the hands of brutish men, skillful to destroy. You shall be fuel for the fire. Your blood shall be in the midst of the land. You shall be no more remembered, for I the Lord have spoken. (Ezekiel 21:31–32)

Here, God spoke his word, and that word foretold the future of the Ammonites. This was plainly not just a foreseen future, but rather a future that God himself would be bringing to pass. This future included sovereignly bringing in "brutish men" who would destroy the Ammonites, destroyers who supposed that they were acting of their own free will without realizing that they were in fact instruments of God's purpose. God stated very simply the reason why this prophecy would come to pass with utmost certainty: "For I the Lord have spoken."

We know, then, by these many passages, that God's word is *always* done, God *always* does what God desires, and God's purpose *will* be established. God is always sovereign. God will most certainly accomplish his good pleasure, which is his will and purpose (Isaiah 46:10). Our Father declared in Isaiah 55:11 that the word that goes out from his mouth will not return to him empty, but that "it shall accomplish that which I purpose, and shall succeed in the thing for which I sent it." Praise and glory to our Father! He will always accomplish his purpose and his desire. His word will invariably succeed in doing exactly what he intended it to do.

Even if God chooses *not* to do something, that lack of action is just as obviously what he desired. In other words, even if he did not do something, he *still* did exactly what pleased him most in that very act of doing nothing. We must additionally bear in mind that it is brashly presumptuous for us to ever assert God did "nothing" since such a judgment is only based on our flawed and limited human perception, and it is more likely than not incorrect. Moreover, although God certainly often does things in which it can be said he does not take pleasure, he nevertheless always maintains his sovereignty by doing exactly what he wills to do. For example, we know that God takes no pleasure in the death or punishment of the wicked (Ezekiel 18:23, 32; 33:11; Lamentations 3:33; Jonah 4:11), and yet the Bible is filled with examples of God willfully imposing death and punishment directly upon the wicked. The same God who said that he does not delight in the death of the wicked also said that he would take delight in bringing ruin and destruction upon Israel should they turn to wickedness (Deuteronomy 28:63). It would be fallacious and illogical to even consider that God could ever act against his own will, even when such actions definitely do not bring him pleasure (a being that could act against its own will would certainly not be a god and perhaps not even sane). We can instead rejoice that God, our Father, is not callous or sadistic in any way at all; rather, he is the completely just, completely loving, completely powerful, completely wise, and completely sovereign God who always acts according to his perfect will.

Simply put, God would not be God if ever a situation arose in which he did not do exactly what he most desired, what he pleased, and what he willed. He is not a disappointed, frustrated, thwarted, ineffectual God— that is not a god at all. Our God sees all, and nothing escapes his attention (Hebrews 4:12–13) or happens outside of his sovereignty and without his involvement (Psalm 139:1–18). As Amos said, "Does disaster come to a city, unless the Lord has done it?" God's will is done! Indeed, there is no biblical support for the all-too-common notion that the world is spinning out of control, but we should not fear because one day God will rouse himself and reel it all back in, somehow managing to restore order at the last possible moment. God has not abdicated his throne, nor will he. Because we know he truly reigns and that his reign is completely unbounded, we can possess a persevering peace and an indomitable confidence that cannot otherwise be realized.

David possessed an intimate understanding of God's supremacy over all his creation, as well as a keen awareness of God's loving involvement in the details of David's life, and he offered this astute exhortation in Psalm 27:14: "Wait for the Lord; be strong, and let your heart take courage; wait for the Lord!" It should be self-evident that waiting is just plain silly if one does not know or believe that someone is coming. If we believe our Father to be a disengaged God—a God who is either unwilling or unable to consistently involve himself in and exert sovereign influence upon human events or human will—then it becomes a ludicrous exercise to actually wait on that God. Given much of the teaching heard in so many of our modern churches, is it any wonder that the practice of actually waiting confidently on God is something that is rarely seen in our day?

Likewise, Paul's directives for us to give thanks "in all circumstances" and "for everything" (1 Thessalonians 5:18; Ephesians 5:20) are impossible admonitions if we have no confidence that God is in complete control or if we possess no certainty that our circumstances are ordered by our preeminent Father rather than by others. It is nearly irrational to suggest that we should, or could, give thanks to God for situations and things we believe to be outside his control and beyond the scope of his perfect purpose. We cannot realistically thank our God for all circumstances if we presume our circumstances to have possibly slipped past his only-occasional attention, authority, and administration—even if we believe that God may proceed to work as best as he can to help us in what we imagine to be circumstances that he failed to either foresee or prevent.

On the other hand, when we know that our sovereign Father is an involved God, a God that always hears, always works, always governs, and always fulfills his purpose, it then becomes much easier to wait, trust, and even give thanks for everything. We know that there are neither unforeseen nor uncontrolled circumstances for our God. This is a confidence from which true faith can spring up. We can joyfully identify with David's praise for our reliable, dependable, involved God: "The Lord is my strength and my shield; in him my heart trusts, and I am helped; my heart exults, and with my song I give thanks to him" (Psalm 28:7). Indeed, when we come to realize our God is truly a sovereign God, we too can experience the understanding deep in our souls that the fruit of his righteousness is real peace and a quietness born of an abiding trust (Isaiah 32:17).

"No people ever rise higher than their idea of God."[8] This discerning observation by James Boice neatly encapsulates why developing a biblically correct understanding of the supremacy of our loving Father is such an imperative matter. If we do not believe our God to be perfectly and completely effective in his detailed, wise, and holy administration of all things within his entire creation, we have created a God of our making who is in truth not God at all. From within a whirlwind, God gave Job an extended and forcefully direct declaration of his effectual sovereignty over all things (Job 38–41). None of us today are likely to experience such a dramatic personal discourse from God, but we would do well to learn from the individual who heard these words directly from the mouth of God. After this extraordinary experience, Job's words are both incredibly powerful and notably unambiguous: "I know that you can do all things, and that no purpose of yours can be thwarted" (Job 42:2). We must join Job in acknowledging God's sovereignty and giving him the glory he properly deserves, rejoicing always that no purpose of our Father can ever be thwarted in any way. Indeed, if we do not completely believe this eminently scriptural truth about our great God, then our God is not God at all.

Charles Spurgeon, often affectionately referred to as the "Prince of Preachers," perhaps summarized this best in a sermon in which he passionately asserted that we must totally believe that God's providence guides our path and our choices. He proceeded to eloquently describe how God is sovereignly in control of everything from the particles of dust that dance in a sunbeam to the insects creeping on a rosebud—as much in control of each falling autumn leaf as the tumbling of an avalanche. Spurgeon wrapped up these thoughts with these incisive words:

> He that believes in a God must believe this truth. There is no standing-point between this and atheism. There is no half way between a mighty God that worketh all things by the sovereign counsel of his will and no God at all. A God that can not do as he pleases—a God whose will is frustrated, is not a God, and can not be a God.[9]

CHAPTER 2

THE ILLUSION OF A GENTLEMAN GOD

How deeply do men err who conceive of God as subject to our human will or as standing respectfully to wait upon our human pleasure.

– A. W. Tozer, The Pursuit of Man[1]

In each of three separate books within the acclaimed *Chronicles of Narnia* series, C. S. Lewis' characters make the observation that "Aslan is not a tame lion."[2] Mr. Lewis's metaphor is quite accurate, of course. Our God is not tame; he does not answer to us (Daniel 4:35; Isaiah 40:13–14), nor is he our servant or our butler. These basic facts appear to be lost in today's church, where it seems normal for most Christians to casually believe that God indeed does our bidding. Moreover, very few are willing to dispute the common notions that "God is a gentleman" and "God will not interfere with a person's free will." While we may stop short of joining those who teach that humans may indeed become gods, we nonetheless embrace doctrines and teachings that strip sovereignty from God and hand it over to humans, thereby coming dangerously close to elevating the created above the Creator. A. W. Pink observed this trend back in 1918 and, perhaps somewhat prophetically, wrote the following:

> The trend of modern theology...is ever toward the deification of the creature rather than the glorification of the Creator, and the leaven of present-day Rationalism is rapidly permeating the whole of Christendom.[3]

In the preceding chapter, the resplendent principle of God's sovereignty over his entire creation was explored at length. While this tenet is truly magnificent and worthy of nothing less than our awe and worship, the fuller truth of God's loving sovereignty is deeper still and yet more precious. Indeed, we should rejoice that no matter how well we come to know our Father, because we are finite creatures, there will always remain a deeper and fuller truth about our infinite God for us to endeavor to comprehend and worship. We should therefore set our hearts to understand that our God is not a sovereign God who always fulfills his will for the universe but does so in an inscrutable manner while managing to leave humans alone to "do their own thing." Rather, our God is a personal God who exercises his sovereignty at the personal level. For example, Proverbs 21:1 teaches us that God works in human hearts to accomplish his divinely perfect purpose. The passage states that the "heart is like channels of water in the hand of the Lord; *He turns it wherever He wishes*" (**NASB**).

This dramatic statement is not some isolated assertion of a single Bible verse. It is a constant characteristic of a God who "fashions the hearts" of men and women (Psalm 33:15). This same attribute—that God moves, turns, and influences free hearts to accomplish *his* own purpose—is also seen throughout the entire Bible. In fact, any doctrine teaching God's unwillingness to interfere with each person's supposed free will runs head-on into a vast host of scriptural examples and teaching. To illustrate this fact, a partial list of such references is presented here:

Genesis 20:6	2 Kings 3:13	Jeremiah 1:15
Genesis 24:12–50	2 Kings 10:32	Jeremiah 32:39–40
Genesis 39:20–21	1 Chronicles 5:26	Jeremiah 51:1
Genesis 50:20	2 Chronicles 17:10	Jeremiah 51:11
Exodus 3:21	2 Chronicles 21:16	Ezekiel 23:22–23
Exodus 34:24	2 Chronicles 22:7	Ezekiel 36:22–29
Numbers 22:38	2 Chronicles 25:20	Ezekiel 38:10–11
Deuteronomy 2:30	2 Chronicles 36:22	Daniel 1:9
Joshua 11:20	Ezra 1:1	Zechariah 14:2
Joshua 24:10	Ezra 1:5–6	John 1:13
Judges 14:4	Ezra 7:27	Acts 2:23
1 Samuel 2:25	Psalm 105:17	Acts 4:28
2 Samuel 17:14	Psalm 105:25	2 Thess. 2:11–12
1 Kings 11:14	Isaiah 19:2	James 1:18
1 Kings 12:15	Isaiah 22:11	1 Peter 1:3
1 Kings 22:20	Isaiah 37:7	Revelation 17:17

This is not a complete list by any means. From Genesis to Revelation, God freely interferes with human will to accomplish his own eternal purpose. Even the great sinful rebellion seen in Revelation 17 is said "to carry out God's purpose" (v. 17). In regards to the choices and actions of the ten sinful, rebellious kings described in this passage, we are told explicitly that "God *put it into their hearts* to carry out his purpose" (v. 17), which in this case will be his inevitable conquering of these rebellious kings and people (v. 14).

The collective preponderance of these many Scriptures thoroughly dispels the notion that God is somehow a "gentleman" that is either unable or unwilling to turn the hearts and wills of humans (and thereby their choices) to accomplish his own purpose. In fact, Psalm 33:10 (NASB) teaches us the exact opposite: "The Lord nullifies the counsel of the nations; He frustrates the plans of the peoples." We do not read that the Lord honors the counsel of the nations and carefully respects the plans of the people. Instead, we are told, "The Lord reigns, let the people tremble!" (Psalm 99:1). We should learn from Jeremiah, who declared his awareness of this glorious truth in Jeremiah 10:23: "I know, O Lord, that the way of man is not in himself, that it is not in man who walks to direct his steps."

Contrary to much popular teaching of our day, our Father clearly can and regularly does interfere with human free will. To our great loss, we have drifted far from the historic confession of God's sovereign involvement in every facet of his creation. In fact, Augustine made no effort to conceal his disdain for any such suggestions that would artificially limit God's ascendancy, and he wrote bluntly that it was "blasphemous" and "foolish" to assert that God does not change the wills of men whenever and however he chooses.[4] We must repent of such foolishness, and we should instead praise our God that he does change our will! Many who profess that "God is a gentleman" have probably never considered the consequences of a world where God, for whatever reason they may assert, did not actually influence, change, and interfere with humanity's fallen will. How horrible indeed that would be!

We sing songs such as the popular "Our God Reigns" with great enthusiasm and joy, and then we turn right around and teach that God does not in fact reign over the wills of humans, perhaps even in the very same church service. Do we believe he reigns or do we not? Do we even realize how perilous it is to impudently suggest that our God's reign is somehow only partial? I suspect that for most of us this insolence is born of nothing more than having never actually reasoned the matter through completely. For example, we do not seem to have any difficulty accepting and rejoicing in the fact that God placed Esther as the queen of Persia "for such a time as this" in order to accomplish his purpose of saving the Jewish people (Esther 4:14), but we stumble when we fail to consider how this might actually have happened. Assuming it was not all just an auspicious accident by which the Israelites in exile were delivered from the total extermination threatened by the evil man Haman (Esther 3:8–9), did not God have to interfere with and influence the so-called free will of King Ahasuerus by causing him to find Esther pleasing (2:17) and then further causing the king to choose Esther to be the replacement for the previous queen Vashti?

The Illusion of a Gentleman God

For that matter, was even the banishment of Vashti just an unlikely but fortuitous accident that fell into God's lap and created a vacancy into which he could insert Esther? Are we to seriously believe God simply seized upon an opportune stroke of good luck when a drunken Ahasuerus just happened to call for Queen Vashti to put her on display (1:11), Vashti just happened to refuse because she was offended in her own pride (1:12), the king's counselors just happened to advise the king to banish her (1:19), and these same advisors later came up with an idea out of their own sinful hearts for the king to replace Vashti—a plan that would just happen to work out to a "gentleman" God's advantage? Such an assertion quite obviously strains credibility, and, worse yet, it also creates severely misplaced boundaries upon God's trustworthiness, omniscience, and faithfulness—boundaries that should not exist at all.

Is it not more likely by several orders of magnitude that this is a powerful example of how God exercises his sovereignty over human free will in order to accomplish his own purpose and that it also clearly demonstrates his willingness to do so? We should rejoice in the fact that God, human free will notwithstanding, invariably works out his "plans formed long ago with perfect faithfulness" (Isaiah 25:1 NASB).

There are many such examples of this same principle in Scripture, and one worthy of close examination is the account of Rehoboam's choice found in 2 Chronicles 10 and 1 Kings 12. In this vivid narrative, it is quite clear that Rehoboam certainly did have a choice. Following the death of King Solomon, the people of Israel had come to his son Rehoboam and offered to serve him faithfully if he would only reduce the heavy load that his father had placed upon them. Rehoboam gave this choice much deliberation. He asked the old men for advice regarding the choice before him, he asked the young men for advice about the choice, and he asked the people for three days in which to consider his choice. In the end, he decided to choose the way of the young men's advice, and he refused to lighten the burden on the people. The results were disastrous for Rehoboam. His subjects revolted, his kingdom was split into two separate kingdoms, and he lost ten of twelve tribes.

As tragic as Rehoboam's choice may have been, the story did not begin with the people approaching Rehoboam regarding the heavy load that Solomon had placed upon them. Instead, it had its beginning back in 1 Kings 11:26–43. We see there that Solomon's construction foreman,

Jeroboam, is given the ten northern tribes in advance and by the Lord through the words of the prophet Ahijah. This occurred while Solomon was still alive and still firmly king of all twelve tribes. We are told the Lord's reason and purpose in verses 31 to 33; it was because of Israel's idolatry and wickedness that the Lord was going to "tear the kingdom from the hand of Solomon" (as usual, human responsibility is not absent). In other words, long before Rehoboam ever had the opportunity to make his "free" choice between the counsel of the old men and that of the young men, God had already declared to Jeroboam in no uncertain terms that God's purpose would be fulfilled and thereby the kingdom would be split.

Here we see the paradox clearly; God uses human free will to accomplish his predetermined sovereign purpose. Rehoboam's choice was a real choice with real consequences—the Scripture is clear about that. He was presented with the wisdom of the old men (good advice) and the wisdom of the young men (bad advice), and he chose the latter to his own detriment. At the same time, Scripture is equally clear that he was *destined* to choose the latter, for God had already declared years before what Rehoboam's choice would be! The Puritans had a saying: "What God sovereignly decrees in eternity, man will always freely choose in time." As this saying would suggest, Rehoboam was free to choose either direction, but his destiny (decreed by God) was the latter choice, and there was no possibility that he would choose the former and thereby prove God wrong. It was not going to happen! He freely made the choice he was destined to make and thereby accomplished that which God himself was actually doing.

The pivotal question in the matter is whether God actually exerted his sovereignty over Rehoboam's free will or merely knew in advance which choice Rehoboam would make. Was the promise of the northern kingdom to Jeroboam simply God's opportunistic use of his eternal knowledge regarding Rehoboam's eventual decision? To accept the premise that it was mere foreknowledge rips sovereignty out of the hand of God and places it instead in the hands of men. At worst, this is heresy, and it is unscriptural at best. For example, God shared the future in Ezekiel 39, and then in verse 8 declared that "it is coming" and that "it *will* be brought about!" In Isaiah 25:1, we are told that God works with perfect faithfulness "plans formed long ago."

God did not look into the future, foresee Rehoboam's foolish choice, and then tell Jeroboam that Rehoboam would lose ten of twelve tribes of his kingdom because of this bad choice; rather, God spoke that he would *tear* the kingdom away from Solomon and Rehoboam and give it to Jeroboam instead! Not surprisingly, this is exactly what God made happen. The word *tear* is an action verb; the *tearing* of the kingdom from Rehoboam was an action of our eternal, unchanging God, not a result of an autonomous human choice. We can know, therefore, that God brought it about; it was not just happenstance. If God was involved in the split—and the Bible says that he was—then he had a single perfect plan for the split. If God had to change his plan to accommodate Rehoboam's choice, then the original plan was not perfect, and if God's plan is not perfect, then God is not God at all. If, on the other hand, the plan was perfect, then it was set in place long before the world began by our eternal God who stands outside of time. Therefore, Rehoboam could only have freely chosen one of the two choices. Indeed, just like us, *he freely chose what God had destined*.

Should there remain any doubt about Rehoboam's choice being inevitably what God had destined, then 1 Kings 12:15 (and 2 Chronicles 10:15 as well) dispels any such doubt. This Scripture plainly states, "The king did not listen to the people, for it was a turn of affairs brought about by the Lord that he might fulfill his word." This could not be clearer. This was not mere foreknowledge; rather, we are told directly that God brought about the outcome and that he did this so that his word would be fulfilled—as it always is and always will be! This inescapable conclusion is reinforced further by the prophet Shemaiah in 2 Chronicles 11:4, where Shemaiah gave the direct command of the Lord to Rehoboam to cease from his plans to fight against Jeroboam. God himself took direct credit for the series of events, stating that the split of the kingdom, which may have appeared on the surface to be a result of Rehoboam's poor choice, was actually his own sovereign work. He declared, "This is my doing" (NIV), "This thing is from me" (ESV), or "This thing is done of me" (KJV). Manifestly, there remains no room to doubt that God fulfilled his eternal, sovereign purpose, and he imposed his purpose on human free will in the process of so doing.

In his well-known 1754 treatise *The Freedom of the Will,* Jonathon Edwards famously and masterfully pointed out that humans are indeed free to choose what seems best to them.[5] But Edwards noted that Scripture is also clear that God can and does influence and determine what seems best to humans. As such, God influences human choices. A perfect example of this is found in 2 Samuel 17. Here, Absalom is given both what most would call "good" advice (it would have been better for him) and "bad" advice. He had a choice, and Absalom chose the "bad" advice of Hushai instead of the "good" advice of Ahithophel. Why would he do this? Was it just his bad luck or his bad judgment? Actually, it was neither. We are given the real reason in verse 14: "For the Lord had ordained to thwart the good counsel of Ahithophel, in order that the Lord might bring calamity on Absalom" (NASB). The Lord had willed (ordained) that Absalom would perish, and he influenced Absalom's free will by making the good counsel seem bad and the bad counsel seem good to Absalom, in order that Absalom would freely choose what the Lord had destined—thereby fulfilling God's divine purpose! We can praise our Father because he still works this way today and because his purposes are *always* fulfilled.

God's willingness and ability to sovereignly control what course of action humans perceive to be the best choice is also clearly exemplified in Genesis 34 and 35. In these chapters, when Jacob's sons slaughtered all the men of Shechem and plundered the city in retaliation for Shechem's defilement of their sister Dinah, Jacob accurately feared that he did not have the numbers or strength to defend his family should the other Canaanites and Perizzites seek revenge for this slaughter (34:30). Left to their own free will, there is little doubt that the remaining Canaanites and the Perizzites would have indeed pursued and killed Jacob and his family in revenge for the massacre at Shechem. However, we know that God's eternal purpose for Jacob was to bless him and make a mighty nation of him and his family, and God had previously promised to be with Jacob until God's purpose was fully accomplished (Genesis 28:13–15). It is therefore no surprise that God conspicuously interfered with the free will of the Canaanites and the Perizzites. According to Genesis 35:5, the people from the Canaanite cities freely chose not to pursue Jacob and his family as they fled to Bethel because God had sent a great terror into their wills. In other words, the people were caused to be unreasonably afraid to pursue Jacob when in actuality they possessed the superior strength to crush him. This divine interference with human free will allowed Jacob and his family to safely travel out of the area as God had instructed, and God's purpose was again accomplished.

It would be a great mistake to attempt to explain away these many accounts of God's interference with human free will and human desire as isolated incidents that are somehow not characteristic of God's dealing with the human race. We know that our God does not change, and we have no biblical suggestion that God will take on a role of less sovereignty in later ages than that which he clearly exhibited in earlier ages. It is tremendously more likely that we just do not notice God's hand most of the time, supposing him to be absent when he is not. For example, in Exodus 34:23–24, God told his people that all males, without exception, were to travel to the tabernacle three times a year to offer sacrifices, a command that was looking forward to the time when they possessed the Promised Land (also Deuteronomy 16:16). However, this command raised an obvious question—what would keep their enemies from attacking and plundering their families, their land, and their belongings while they were on these triannual pilgrimages? God's promise in this regard was unambiguous. He promised that no enemy would even desire to attack or plunder while the Israelites were away.

God's fulfillment of this promise would necessarily encompass countless nearby enemies who no doubt would quickly learn of these very predictable absences, if for no other reason than regularly observing a mass exodus of Israelites to the location of the tabernacle. Nevertheless, only as a result of divine interference with human will, it would never even enter into these enemies' minds to take advantage of these absences by attacking and plundering while all of the men of the entire nation were away from their lands offering sacrifices at the tabernacle. This divine interference with human free will is no isolated assertion of Scripture; we read in Proverbs 16:7 that God would indeed make the enemies of those who serve him to be at peace with them. Moreover, although the Bible does not state it directly, it seems nearly certain that these enemies would never realize that their desires, choices, and actions were being influenced by a sovereign God. It would therefore be reasonable for us to believe that our God always remains sovereign over all, and more often than not humans do not even realize that God's will is sovereignly influencing their own.

When the will of men conflicts with the purpose of the Lord, Scripture teaches us plainly that it is God's will that prevails. God does not respectfully acquiesce to the imagined sovereignty of man's free will, as some might suppose would be appropriate for a "gentleman" God. At the city that would come to be called Babel (Genesis 11), humans had decided of their own free will to create a name for themselves, and apparently a religion abhorrent to the Lord as well, by building a tower with which they supposed they might connect to the heavens. The desire of their human free will was readily apparent, but God's purpose was obviously quite different. As we all know, rather than respecting human free will, God confused their language in order to thwart and change their chosen course of action. It is noteworthy that God could have easily just spoken his command and instantly transported the tower builders to as many other places as he saw fit (à la Philip or Enoch), or he could have merely commanded the earth to open up and swallow them (à la Dathan and Korah in Numbers 16). Instead, God acted in a manner that resulted in the humans separating and going in different directions of their own free will. God made them freely *decide* to scatter—so off they went! According to Acts 17:26, we can know that they did not just wander off haphazardly (although it probably seemed that way to them); rather, they each went to the exact place that God had ordained by his sovereignty. It is quite likely that they did not realize at all that the change in their desires and free will was in fact the handiwork of the Lord; they merely chose what seemed best to them at the time, exactly as Edwards postulated. God interfered with and changed their free will, but, as is always the case, he did so using his own sovereignly chosen method.

Yet another illustration of how the Lord fulfills his purpose through human free choices and interferes with the human free will is found in 2 Chronicles 25. The king of Judah, Amaziah, received bad counsel (v. 17) and chose wrongly to pick a fight with Joash, the king of Israel. Joash attempted to talk Amaziah out of such a fight, but we are told very clearly in verse 20 that "Amaziah would not listen, for *it was from God*, that he might deliver them into the hand of Joash." Not surprisingly, that is exactly what God did. His purposes are always fulfilled. It is fascinating to ponder what would be written if the current events of our modern world were being recorded from a divinely inspired perspective such as this viewpoint in 2 Chronicles. Would not we fully expect to find that the same sorts of phrases such as "for it was from God" or "for the Lord fulfilled his purpose" would be used to describe our own lives and times? If not, are we foolish enough to believe that God has relinquished a degree of sovereignty that he routinely exercised in ancient times?

Most Christians today are confident when they are engaged in the act of prayer that God can answer that prayer. However, do they realize that such an answer often involves God interfering with human free will? In Genesis 24, for example, we see God answering prayer and doing so by imposing his will on human free will. Abraham, not wanting his son Isaac to take a Canaanite wife, had sent his servant back to Abraham's original homeland in order to find a suitable wife for Isaac. Abraham had asserted in faith that the Lord would send an angel before his servant and make the servant's efforts to secure a wife successful (v. 7). We should realize that an angel making these efforts successful would certainly involve God imposing his sovereign will on a number of human free wills. When the servant arrived in Mesopotamia at the city of Nahor, he prayed that the Lord would send the Lord's chosen wife for Isaac to the well to meet him and that the chosen wife would speak specific words in response to the servant's particular request for a drink of water (vv. 12–14, 42–44). He had hardly finished praying when Rebekah approached the well, ostensibly of her own free will (vv. 15–16, 45). When Abraham's servant asked her for a drink, she responded exactly as the servant had requested in his prayer by giving him a drink and offering to water his camels (vv. 18–20, 46). We see these choices and actions of her human will were quite obviously steered by the Lord.

Rebekah was a very attractive virgin who was also from Abraham's clan, quite the remarkable find if one were relying on a mere convergence of human free wills to produce such a result (v. 16). Moreover, in verses 50–51, Laban (Rebekah's brother) and Bethuel (Rebekah's father) recognized the Lord's purpose in the events of the day, and they properly acquiesced and offered Rebekah as Isaac's wife—this of their own free wills. In so doing, the actions of their wills were yet a further answer to the original prayer of Abraham, as well as his servant's prayer, and ultimately they were a fulfillment of God's eternal purpose. Christians who study this remarkable account today can choose to believe that our God was incredibly fortunate, that the people's choices, the circumstances, and the events in this narrative just worked out opportunistically with astounding accuracy and perfect timing, all because of the serendipitous decisions and attitudes of the many various free wills involved. Or, they can believe that our almighty God sovereignly influenced Rebekah's free will, as well as the other human wills involved, in order to accomplish his eternal purpose. It should be indisputably clear which of these two Gods is the real God of the Bible. The concept that should correctly emerge as we study this matter is that humans certainly make meaningful choices, and these choices have very real results and lasting consequences; nevertheless, God remains sovereign over all of these choices, the results and consequences of which all work together to accomplish his grand, eternal purpose.

Returning to Scripture, in another place we find a Benjamite man and his servant wandering about the countryside looking for donkeys that have supposedly just strayed away on their own (1 Samuel 9:1–27). After many days searching for these lost donkeys, Saul and his servant decide of their own free will, as a last-ditch effort, to seek out the man of God in nearby Zuph and inquire of this man of God (Samuel) as to the whereabouts of their lost donkeys. This might appear to be a normal, unremarkable series of events were it not for the fact that God was sovereignly working to accomplish his purpose. We can know this because in verse 15 we see that God had revealed to Samuel *in advance* that he was going to *send* a certain Benjamite man to Samuel, and Samuel was to anoint this man (Saul) as the person selected by God to be the first king of Israel. We are shown unmistakably, therefore, that the donkeys did not just happen to stray away, and Saul did not just wonder around the countryside of his own volition for several days before just happening to come near Zuph and luckily choosing to seek out Samuel.

This series of events was obviously not simply an opportune moment that fell into God's lap; it was God himself accomplishing his purpose by actively manipulating circumstances and choices—including both the actions of animals and the choices of humans! God told Samuel that it was he who *sent* Saul to him. The decision to pursue lost donkeys and the idea to visit Samuel did not originate in the mind of Saul or his servant, although it is highly probable that it seemed to Saul as if the idea and the choices were of his own making. Rather, the events and ensuing "free" choices clearly originated from the word of God in the unfolding of his own perfect purpose.

Examples such as these could easily fill an entire book, and it would require far too much space to individually examine all of the Scriptures listed at the beginning of this chapter in which God explicitly interfered with human free will. Despite these space limitations, the fact remains that the Bible palpably establishes that God is both willing and able to interfere regularly with human free will. This interference may be perceived by humans to be either "good" or "bad," or it may even go completely undetected. Human perception notwithstanding, it is God's prerogative to govern his own creation exactly as he sees fit (Isaiah 45:10; 10:15; Romans 9:21).

This divine prerogative is nevertheless often denied or ignored in much preaching and teaching of our day. Many profess, for example, that God is obligated to give undeserved mercy to all human beings and that he is never willing for any human to perish in their sin (perhaps by taking a passage such as 2 Peter 3:9 out of context). However, we read in Joshua 11:20 that God sovereignly chose *not* to show mercy to a large and varied group of undeserving, sinful people (just like us), and he instead set their hearts and their free wills to choose their inevitable death because it was undeniably his sovereign will that they perish:

> For it was of the Lord to harden their hearts, to meet Israel in battle in order that he might utterly destroy them, that they might receive no mercy, but that he might destroy them. (Joshua 11:20 NASB)

If we are willing to set aside the doctrinal prejudices that we carry and honestly seek after a correct understanding of the God of the Bible, we will inevitably discover a God that unhesitatingly exercises his right as the Creator to govern and manage his creation exactly as he sees fit according to his perfect wisdom and plan. God may sovereignly turn human free wills to hate his people (Egyptian hearts in Psalm 105:25), or he may just as easily turn human free wills to look favorably on his people (Egyptian hearts again, in Exodus 3:21 and 11:3). He may harden or blind human hearts (Romans 11:7; Matthew 11:25; Matthew 13:11; Lamentations 3:64–65; 2 Thessalonians 2:11–12), or he may soften hearts and give them understanding (Acts 16:14; Matthew 13:11; 1 Thessalonians 1:4; 1 Corinthians 1:23–24, 29–30). He may "make hearts obstinate" to the point of it resulting in their death (Deuteronomy 2:30), or he may give the grace necessary to enable belief in those hearts he has appointed (Acts 13:48). He may wound, or he may heal; he may kill, or he may make alive (Deuteronomy 32:39). He may stir up human will to accomplish his own purposes (Revelation 17:17; Ezra 1:1; Jeremiah 51:11). He may suppress an evil man's will or hatred for his enemies (Exodus 34:24; Psalm 105:14–15), or he may harden a man's heart and will against his enemies (Joshua 11:20). He may restrain humanity's natural will to sin (Genesis 20:6; Joshua 24:9–10), or he may influence human will in such a manner that it will lead to certain death (1 Samuel 2:22–25; Isaiah 37:7). He may well "allure" human hearts in order to turn them to himself (Hosea 2:14), or he may "hedge up" human ways to force them to follow his own purpose (Hosea 2:6). He may give people eyes that will not see and ears that will not hear (Romans 11:7; Isaiah 6:10; Mark 4:10–12; John 12:40; Deuteronomy 29:4), or he may give people eyes that see and ears that hear (Proverbs 20:12; Isaiah 32:3; 1 Thessalonians 2:13; 1:4). *But, no matter how he works, God's will and purpose is always accomplished.* He is God, and we are not! As for us, "who is there who speaks and it come to pass, unless the Lord has commanded it?" (Lamentations 3:37 NASB). As for God, he does indeed work *in* us, both to will and to do *his* good pleasure (Philippians 2:13).

The Bible, then, shows quite unmistakably that God is not a gentleman waiting on humans to will and to do the correct things, or combination of things, so that God's will can come to pass; rather, he is actively involved in steering the universe (including both sparrows and human hearts) in the direction he alone sees fit. Elihu (the fourth and final counselor of Job—the only one that was not rebuked by the Lord for speaking incorrectly) correctly asserted in Job 33:12 that "God is greater than man." He also pointed out that God often acts to influence human will, but often this action is not noticed by humans (v. 29, v. 14, vv. 15–20). The mechanism of God's influence is quite obviously beyond both our understanding and our revelation (Deuteronomy 29:29; Ecclesiastes 8:17; Romans 11:33–34; Isaiah 55:8–9), and it is just as obviously infinitely varied as appropriate for any given situation. While God may certainly take men and women by a "hook in the nose" (Isaiah 37:29), it seems likely that his influence more often goes initially unnoticed by humans—just as when God used Cyrus as his own instrument though Cyrus did not even know God (Isaiah 44:28; 45:5, 1–4, 13). God's reasons for using Cyrus in this manner are provided to us in this passage, and as we should expect, God was using Cyrus for his own glory (45:6), to accomplish his own righteous purpose (44:28; 45:13; see NLT), and to eventually reveal himself to Cyrus (45:3).

Moreover, our Father's total dominion over all of his creation runs deeper than just his transcendent influence upon our free wills. God forms the spirit within each of us before we are even born (Zechariah 12:1), and he does so with perfect foreknowledge. It is God "who fashions the hearts" of the inhabitants of the earth, and he "understands all their works," according to Psalm 33:15 (NASB). If "hearts" as used in this verse means the center of human desire and decision making, then it is God who fashions those hearts, good or bad, and only he who understands the particulars (what, when, how, and why) that will inevitably flow from his workmanship in that heart (Ephesians 2:10). If those works were not in accordance with his purpose, then he could have and would have fashioned the heart differently to begin with. God asserts that it is he himself who "puts wisdom in man's inner being" and "gives understanding to the mind" (Job 38:36), and it is this very inner being and understanding that drives human choices.

If we consider ourselves wise enough to understand perceptively, believe correctly, or choose judiciously, we would do well to remember that this very understanding and faith is a gift from God himself (Proverbs 2:6), and we have nothing at all that we did not receive from his hand, be it tangible or intangible (1 Corinthians 4:7). Further, we cannot choose to receive anything that we are not given from God as a result of his will (John 3:27), and it is God alone who gives us a heart to understand or eyes to see (Deuteronomy 29:4). God is the source of our decision-making capabilities; it is he who "gives wisdom to the wise and knowledge to the discerning" (Daniel 2:21 NIV; Proverbs 2:6). In short, there is no such thing as the so-called self-made man. All that we are, perceive, and believe must be correctly attributed to our sovereign Father.

If we were to be given a choice, it should be readily apparent that a truly sovereign God is far preferable to a "gentleman God" who rarely, if ever, interferes with the free wills and affairs of humans, even though we may fallaciously claim that such a God is also sovereign. Of course, we do not get to choose the truth about God; he is exactly who he is, and our misconceptions do not change him in any way, no matter how fervently we may declare them or how often we may repeat them. We must learn and accept the true God of the Bible if we desire a God who we can staunchly know to be our Rock, as David knew him to be (Psalm 18:2; 144:1–3). The alternative is a manmade, ineffective God who is surprised by and subservient to human choices, a God whom we portray as busily attempting to make as much good as possible out of all the unanticipated evil that is being done on the earth. R. K. Wright said, "Constructing a correct theology, a correct *theoria*, a correct 'beholding' of God, is the prerequisite for the body of Christ to worship God adequately. Otherwise, the word *God* tends to be the name of an idol we have made and does not refer to the Yahweh of the Bible."[6] When we come to understand the unlimited, boundless supremacy of the God of the Bible, however, our walk with him is transformed; the

Bible comes alive, difficult doctrines fall easily into place, and our faith and confidence in our loving Father are lifted to astounding new levels.

As a final, clinching example of God's repudiation of human free will and his disinclination to conduct himself as a "gentleman" according to our human terms, consider the example of King Saul that is recounted in 1 Samuel 19:18–24. Here we find King Saul traveling to Naioth in order to search out and kill David. Saul's free will was quite clear—he had chosen to kill David. However, God's will was equally clear—he had chosen David to be the next king. *Not surprisingly, it was God's free will and not man's free will that prevailed.* Apparently, God chose not to heed the theologians who would enthrone humanity by insisting that God must show the greatest respect for human free will and that he therefore must not interfere with Saul's choices, will, or selected course of action. Rather, in dramatic fashion, God proceeded to interfere in a manner that showed precious little respect for Saul's free will. Instead of capturing and killing David, Saul found himself "prophesying" (probably an intense worship) all the way to Naioth, and he then found himself stripping off his robes and worshipping on the floor all day and all night. It is not difficult to perceive that this was not at all what King Saul's free will had intended. God was hardly a "gentleman" with Saul. Instead, God's sovereignty was on brilliant display for all to see.

It is also interesting to wonder if this might have been a foreshadowing of the New Testament Saul, another Saul for whose free will God showed a notable lack of respect. This Saul was also on a journey to kill God's chosen, but he instead ended up blind and believing in God's Son, quite contrary to the initial desires of his own free will (Acts 9 and 22). Furthermore, God not only sovereignly changed Saul's will, he also sovereignly changed his name! God had a purpose for Paul, a purpose that was not going to be derailed or deterred by Saul's free will, and we are even today profoundly blessed by Paul's ministry and writings to the Gentiles. Paul himself stated that he had been set apart by God from birth and called according to God's grace (Galatians 1:15). In Ephesians 3:7–13, Paul added that his call and ministry to the Gentiles were by the *"effectual working of God's power"* (v. 7 KJV). This was clearly not according to Paul's will, but rather was "according to the eternal purpose" that God "carried out" (v. 11 NASB). Praise, glory, and honor belong to our nongentleman God! Our God works his effectual, mighty power within us to accomplish his eternal purpose.

If we reject this great truth, perhaps it might still be desirable to believe that a "gentleman" God, while unwilling to interfere with human free will or choices, nonetheless loves us and is working as best as he can for our good within these constraints; this is likely better than no God at all. However, this errant belief falls well short of realizing the magnitude, scope, and benefits of our Father's great love for us. Because we know that he is our sovereign, interfering Father and not a polite, uninvolved gentleman, we can be supremely confident in his great love for us. This wondrous love will unfailingly be demonstrated by his zealous determination and unlimited ability to fulfill his purpose for our lives, and this great realization cannot fail to give us immense comfort and unshakeable confidence.

We are taught the true basis for such confidence in Psalm 118:6: "The Lord is on my side; I will not fear. What can man do to me?" If we actually believe that God will not interfere freely and decisively with human free will, then it is irrational to claim that we need not fear what humans may do to us when we in fact have every reason in the world to fear what they may do. On the other hand, when we know with certainty that our Father is sovereign over the wills of humanity and effectually works to accomplish his purpose for his own glory and for our good, then, and only then, can we truly say with Paul, "If God be for us, who can be against us?" (Romans 8:31). We no longer have reason to fear the wills of men or women, and we know that our Father's purpose will be accomplished in and through those wills, be they evil or righteous. This is our real and lasting confidence!

CHAPTER 3

PRAYING TO A GENTLEMAN GOD

Free will I have often heard of, but I have never seen it. I have always met with will, and plenty of it, but it has either been led captive by sin or held in the blessed bonds of grace.

– C. H. Spurgeon[1]

Statements such as "God is a gentleman" may seem to be correct if for no other reason than having been repeated often, and misconceptions of this sort are only exposed if given careful scrutiny. As a result, it is far too easy for Christians to unwittingly embrace contradictory beliefs. Such is the case when Christians pray to the "gentleman God" of their own making. If we are truly convinced that "God is a gentleman," and he therefore will not change or otherwise interfere with a human's free will, then why would anyone who truly believes this speciousness engage in earnest prayer that God would do exactly the thing that they assert he will not do?

For example, we pray that God will save a person who as a matter of free choice has no interest at all in being saved, and rightly do we so pray because God most certainly can do just that and move to save the person for whom we are praying—even when that person's free will is completely opposed to God and everything pertaining to God. We pray that God will "draw" a person to church when the person clearly has no desire to come by his or her own free will, and we rightly believe that God can and will answer that prayer, even though the answer will involve God interfering with that person's free will. We pray that God will "make the person want to do so-and-so" by removing the person's blindness, thereby causing the person's free will to desire something entirely different than it did when it was blinded. All of these prayers conspicuously and unequivocally involve asking God to impose his own will on that person's free will, a free will that quite obviously does not want anything to do with God, and to thereby override that person's flawed free will. Whether we realize it or not, we are actually praying that God would move sovereignly to liberate that person's free will from bondage. We should praise God that it is his nature to do exactly that even while many today are claiming it is not.

If we say that God will only "woo" by creating circumstances that would point a person toward himself to be saved, then is not that exactly the same thing as God changing that person's free will using whatever method or circumstance that God sees fit? How is it any different if God creates circumstances that change a person's free will than if he just speaks that person's free will to be something different? Either way, it is God's work of intervening and imposing his purpose upon that person's free will; it is God sovereignly giving sight to the spiritually blind (2 Corinthians 4:4; 1 Corinthians 2:14; Ephesians 4:18). This is not somehow a bad thing! Rather, we should praise him and worship him because he *does* do exactly this. If we truly believe that God is always good and that he always loves his chosen (as in Romans 8:28–29 or Romans 11:5–7), would not we welcome him to interfere with our free will as often and as much as he likes? Would not that be a good thing and not a bad thing? More specifically, would it not be absolutely the most loving thing that he could do?

As a simple illustration of this concept, consider the possible actions of a righteous king who knows for certain that a city will be destroyed, and all of his family within that city will undoubtedly perish as a result. Is it more loving for the king to send messengers to merely warn and invite his children living in that city to flee, or should the king send his soldiers to compel his children to leave, thereby saving their lives? It should be obvious that it is far more loving for the king to act out of his own power to save his children's lives, and it should be equally obvious that when the city is in fact destroyed, the children will be eternally grateful to their father for having saved their lives by compelling them to escape the inevitable destruction. How then have we ever come to characterize God's interference with human free will as unloving and disrespectful—something a gentleman supposedly would not do?

Some may respond to this reasoning by saying that while God may "woo," he never compels, and the difference is that the right and ability to say no to this wooing always remains with the human will. However appealing this may initially seem, this is also a specious argument. Closer examination reveals that if this supposition is true, it allows for the unbiblical possibility that God could fail at anything he sets out to do, and it puts the one engaged in intercessory prayer in a very peculiar position. The prayer would necessarily go something like this: "Oh, Lord, please woo Sam to yourself, but don't make it so effective and convincing that it will overcome his free will. Please don't woo him enough that he will turn to you as a result of your wooing, only just woo him enough that he will turn to you as a result of his free will." This bizarre prayer borders on absurdity. We are actually praying that God will work ineffectually! If God were to work effectually, it would violate Sam's free will, and that just would not do. This is like saying, "Oh, God, may Sam make the right decision on his own, without you doing anything to interfere with his free will; may he just suddenly somehow decide to choose you for some unknown reason—any reason at all other than the unacceptable reason of you making him want to choose you."

No rational person would pray this way, of course, so we must therefore realize that in actuality it is God's sovereignty over the human will upon which we rely when we intercede in prayer. The prolific author Jerry Bridges summed up this concept quite nicely: "Prayer assumes the sovereignty of God. If God is not sovereign, we have no assurance that he is able to answer our prayers. God's sovereignty, along with his wisdom and love, is the foundation of our trust in him; prayer is the expression of that trust.

God's sovereignty does not negate our responsibility to pray, but rather makes it possible to pray with confidence."[2]

Additionally, and even more to the point, if we really believe that God will not change a person's free will, why would we take it upon ourselves to go and do it for him? Why evangelize? If sinful humans already have the natural, moral ability to choose God, and if, as is often preached in many of today's churches, God "has already done his part" and "has done all he can to save us," then what could we as humans possibly add to that? If God has done all he can do, then what is left to do? Why would we attempt and strive to talk people into believing (thereby changing their free will) if this is something that God himself is too much of a "gentleman" to do? Is it not much more likely that God is quite pleased when we are not "gentlemen," and we are used by him to change someone's free will (by his power alone, of course) such that they are brought to salvation? If so, do we really believe that we, as human servants and his creatures, just accomplished something that God could not or would not have done except with our assistance? Or, by so doing, did not we just accomplish that which was God's purpose all along? (Ephesians 1:4). Let us never be guilty of painting God as a benevolent ruler who is constantly doing all he can to save people but failing at it most of the time, a ruler who could really use all the help and "service" that we can manage to give him. That is *not* the God of the Bible. "Nor is he served by human hands, as though he needed anything, since he himself gives to all mankind life and breath and everything" (Acts 17:25).

It is quite possible that some readers may think that the glory and sovereignty of our God in the matter of humanity's salvation is a relatively small aspect of God's overall sovereignty, and they may feel that perhaps this particular point is being given undue emphasis. However, I believe completely that this particular point is a crucial one, a fundamental building block in a correct perception of our loving Father and his role in our lives. Our faith rests not in the wisdom of men, but in the power of God (1 Corinthians 2:5). When God's sovereign grace is given the preeminence that it rightfully demands, then God's proper place in all else will necessarily and inevitably fall right into place. Salvation seems to be the line that humans draw in the sand, in effect saying to God, "You may come this far, but you will not encroach further on our freedom." This sophistic line is drawn at the whim of human arrogance rather than on the authority of Holy Scripture.

"Whatever the Lord pleases, he does, in heaven and on earth, in the seas and all deeps." This verse, Psalm 135:6, was considered at length in the first chapter. However, this verse is extraordinary in that while it is exceedingly unambiguous in its meaning (along with Psalm 115:3), a remarkable number of Christians today do not seem to flinch at all when they assert, in effect, that this verse is categorically false and that God often does not (or cannot) do what he pleases. It has become quite acceptable, it seems, to portray our God as sadly settling for many things that would turn out completely different if he could only do as he pleased—a disappointed, frustrated God. As a single example, it is suggested that it would please God to save many people, or even all people, but he cannot manage to do so because of their free will or, worse, because he is unable to round up enough human help for this endeavor. This viewpoint turns these two verses inside out and suggests the rather fantastic notion that God has turned his throne over to humans, whereby it is humans who do as they please in heaven and on earth while God is subservient to those "free" actions.

Instead of falling victim to the whimsical conception of a disappointed, heartbroken God whose wishes and desires are being constantly stymied by the uncontrollable free will of humans, we must instead realize that human will is no match for divine purpose. God steers even the most powerful of human hearts as he pleases (Proverbs 21:1). Shocking as it may seem to some, an atheist can only remain an atheist because, for whatever perfect reason God wills, it does not please God to reveal himself to that particular atheist in a forceful enough fashion to change the atheist's will. Certainly the atheist is guilty even without such a compelling revelation (Romans 1 and 2), but we can never be so arrogant as to assert that God is not well capable of an irresistible revelation of himself to anyone if he so pleases—just ask Paul about his road trip to Damascus. If God does not do so, then we can be certain it does not please him to do so, and thereby we can also know that it is his will not to do everything within his power to save that atheist.

This irrefutable conclusion may well take many by surprise, but if we are to understand its ramifications, we must be certain to understand that the question examined here is not whether the atheist is guilty of rejecting God out of his or her own fallen free will; that can be readily observed to be true. Rather, the question is if we really understand that the omnipotent, omniscient Creator can never be resisted in any way by his own creation unless the Creator willingly allows such a resistance to take place, this according to his own good pleasure. The incontrovertible, yet magnificent, fact is that there exists no will that God cannot conquer, be it human, angelic, or demonic. To allow any other possibility is to say that God actually does not do all that he pleases in heaven and on the earth, that these verses in Psalms are completely false, and that God is less than God—a liar, in fact. If we believe that God does not do as he pleases with the human will, then we have allowed our own "futile thinking" to make God lower than humans—the Creator subservient to his own creation (Romans 1:25, 21). When we make this error, there remains no true foundation for even a shred of confidence in any prayer at all.

Many would try to escape this inescapable truth by asserting that while God obviously has the capability to conquer any human will, he respects human free will so much that he freely chooses not to interfere with human will. However, if this were true, the advocates of such a belief would also thereby have to acknowledge that God, by freely choosing not to interfere with and conquer the free will of some (or all), when he could easily do so if he so willed, is therefore obviously quite willing for these people to perish eternally. One cannot be true without the other being true, even if the adherents to such a doctrine find the latter distasteful. In other words, because the human will cannot resist the Holy Spirit unless it is God's will to allow it to do so, this fact means that the whole matter actually always unfolds exactly as God plans and wishes. We should rejoice in the great truth that God does sovereignly conquer human will as he pleases, and this fact is what enables us to pray with confidence.

To suggest otherwise borders on outright nonsense. Horatius Bonar was a Scottish clergyman noted for being a prolific author, hymn writer, and poet, and he strongly criticized the notion that God is unable to save any sinner whom God desires to save. Bonar rightly pointed out that such an assertion is tantamount to saying, "Because the Spirit has attempted a work beyond His power, He fails in His efforts. The sinner has overpowered Him and proved stronger than He. The sinner is able to overcome the Spirit, but the Spirit is not able to overcome the sinner. The Spirit has done His utmost and has failed."[3] Bonar pointed out that unless one is willing to assert that the creature is mightier than the Creator and is thereby able to resist and even overcome divine omnipotence (an assertion he correctly labeled a "profanity"), then one must concede that God is not willing to do everything within his power to save all humans. On the other hand, when God does decide to save his chosen, he will inevitably conquer human will, and by his grace he will create a new, divinely-originated desire to seek after God. It is God who "opens our minds" to understand the Gospel message (Luke 24:45).

This momentous reality is demonstrated clearly in Ezekiel chapters 34, 35, 36, and 37, which provide yet another wondrous example of God interfering with human free will and imposing his own sovereign, perfect will for his own purposes. In 34:11, we see that God will seek out and find his chosen people, his sheep. This incredibly beautiful work of grace is described further in verse 12: "As a shepherd seeks out his flock when he is among his sheep that have been scattered, so will I seek out my sheep, and I will rescue them from all places where they have been scattered." There is no mention that his sheep were first seeking him or that they must be seeking God in order to either motivate or enable him to seek them out. Instead, it is clear in verses 15 and 16 that this glorious deliverance is a work of God's grace alone: "I myself will be the shepherd of my sheep, and I myself will make them lie down, declares the Lord God. I will seek the lost, and I will bring back the strayed." We should be careful not to overlook that the party doing the seeking, saving, shepherding, and strengthening is the sovereign Lord, not the sheep.

In this same marvelous manner, God said in chapter 36 that he will cleanse his chosen people, remove their iniquities, put his spirit within them, and *give them a heart to seek him and obey him* (vv. 22–27; see also Ezekiel 11:14–20). God did not say that they deserved this wondrous rescue of mercy and grace because of any decision of their own, any state of their heart, or even because they had turned to him—in fact, he said the exact opposite. He said that they *do not* deserve it and that he will act for his own purpose and glory! (vv. 22–23, 32). He freely changes fallen human free wills and said that he will "cause" his chosen people to obey him righteously (v. 27). Our Father is clear that the "heart to seek him" is not something that people muster up by themselves after hearing some good preaching, but rather it is solely a gift from himself.

In Ezekiel chapter 37, God used the imagery of dry bones to represent those who are dead in sin, cut off from God (v. 11), and in need of redemption. God rhetorically asked Ezekiel in verse 3, "Can these bones live?" Ezekiel saw immediately that such a miraculous transformation can only happen according to the divine will of God (v. 3), and he answered, "O Lord God, you know." In this prophetic passage, God revealed to us that he will put his Spirit within the people represented by the imagery of the dry bones, and *then* they shall live (vv. 5–6, 14). God also made it clear that it is he who will "*cause* breath to enter them, and they shall live" (v. 5). The magnificent truth being illustrated so dramatically here is that fallen human free wills are like dry bones, and lifeless, decaying bones obviously cannot seek or choose God. The resurrection of a fallen, sinful will from a figurative grave (v. 13) is not a human choice or action; rather, it is both the purpose and result of the powerful grace from the hand of our sovereign, loving God! It is God who says he will "*cause* us to come up out of our [spiritual] graves" (v. 12 KJV).

Because of this great truth, we are left with absolutely nothing about which we may boast or for which we may take the slightest credit, save the cross of Christ and the loving grace of our Father in heaven! This was the message Paul preached in 1 Corinthians 1 and Romans 3:27. According to Paul, it is "*because* of him [God] that you are in Christ Jesus" (1 Corinthians 1:30), and boasting of any human contribution or wisdom of choice is thereby precluded (1:29, 31, 18, 20–22). The New American Standard Version translation of verse 30 is even more direct: "But by His doing you are in Christ Jesus." This is a vital concept that we too often neglect or, worse yet, outright deny.

This truth is not difficult to understand when we begin to grasp the unavoidable ramifications of Paul's teachings in Romans 3:10–12, where he forcefully declared that not even one human will ever seek God of his or her own free will. Instead, God is "found by those who did not seek" him, Paul said in Romans 10:20, and God shows and reveals himself "to those who did not ask for me [God]." This is our Father's mercy and grace in action! This is God imposing his will upon our free will and doing so for our great gain. As a result, we can join with David's praise in Psalm 62:5–7 by declaring joyfully that on God alone rests our salvation and our glory.

Paul told the Philippians that the gift of being able to believe was something "granted" to them from God (Philippians 1:29). Faith is said to be something that is "received" in 2 Peter 1:1 (NASB, NIV), and as the "gift of God," its origin is from God and not from humans, according to Ephesians 2:8. In the same way, repentance itself is also a gift from God, Paul said, something that is "granted by" the Lord (2 Timothy 2:25). In

Acts 5:31, Peter too declared that repentance was "given" by God, and the apostles and brothers in Acts 11 also recognized repentance as a gift granted from God. They rejoiced that God had "granted even the Gentiles repentance unto life" (v. 18 NIV) because they knew that this repentance must necessarily be God's power and choice at work and could never have resulted from the Gentiles somehow coming to their senses and repenting of their own free will.

Paul made this same point powerfully and unmistakably in 1 Thessalonians 1:4–5. According to Paul, if and when the Gospel is perceived as more than just mere empty words (or viewed as other than foolishness, as in 1 Corinthians 1:18) and instead comes to us with power and is received with conviction from the Holy Spirit, the very fact that we are able to receive it and believe is the proof that God has chosen us because of his great love for us. We can rest in the certainty that God's loving choice is always implemented by God's infinite power. As a matter of fact, Peter stated in 2 Peter 1:3–4 that it is God's "divine power" that "grants" us *all things* that pertain to eternal life and godliness, "through the knowledge of him who called us." By its very nature, this divine power can be nothing less than absolutely unlimited, completely effectual, and perfectly timed. God's perfect power cannot fail to succeed completely at anything that God directs it to accomplish. In other words, when God chooses us as the Bible says he does (Colossians 3:12; Ephesians 1:4; 1 Thessalonians 1:4–5; Mark 13:20), we can therefore be certain that his choice will never be wasted or in vain. If this is not true, then our God is not God at all.

We often make the mistake of viewing salvation as the gift and belief as our own contribution when in fact belief itself is also a gift from God. Peter did not say that God's power grants us only some of the things that pertain to eternal life and that we must contribute the remaining things in order to somehow activate God's divine power. Rather, belief is itself "through grace," and it is therefore unmerited and undeserved (Acts 18:27). In other words, seeking God with our heart that did not previously want to seek him (Ezekiel 36; Jeremiah 24:7), finding God when not seeking him (Romans 10:20), and thereby being able to choose to believe (faith) is "not of ourselves"; rather, it is "the gift of God" (Ephesians 2:8 KJV), and this can only be a result of God's willingness to powerfully interfere with our free wills. We should never resent this incredible, loving conquest of our wills as the act of a God who we think should really conduct himself more in keeping with our concept of a gentleman. Rather, we should glory in this willingness of our loving Father to free our enslaved, rebellious wills by a sovereign act of his grace. Paul made it quite clear who must receive the credit and glory for this changed heart: "But thanks be to God, that you who were once slaves of sin have become obedient from the heart" (Romans 6:17).

There are many, however, who contend that while salvation is indeed by grace and not by works, humans must still "accept the free gift of salvation" by their own free will. The fallacy of this position is that it necessarily requires that God's work of grace is a result of the preceding human choice instead of the correct view that the human choice is a result of God's preceding work of grace. Even those individuals that hold such a view acknowledge that a human work cannot contribute to salvation based on the incontrovertible teaching of passages such as 2 Timothy 1:9, Ephesians 2:9, Romans 3:20 and 28, and Galatians 2:16. In order for this human choice not to be considered a virtuous work upon which salvation depends (which would be contradictory to these many Scriptures), the choice is instead spuriously labeled an "act of the human will."

However, even if this erroneous recharacterization of what is unmistakably a human contribution (a work) is granted, Romans 9:16 still leaves no room for such a contortion by ruling out this possibility as plainly as could be imagined: "It depends *not on human will* or exertion, but on God, who has mercy." Praise to our God! According to Paul's epistle, salvation is neither by works nor by an act of human will. It is not our own will that somehow musters up enough belief; it is God's will that provides this belief to us and his mercy that *"caused* us to be born again" (1 Peter 1:3). As it is stated plainly in John 1:13, we are reborn "not of blood, nor of the will of the flesh, nor of the will of man, but of God." Were it otherwise, grace would no longer be grace (Romans 11:5–6), and we would indeed have something about which we could boast (Ephesians 2:9).

When this glorious truth permeates deep into our beings, and, contrary to much of today's teaching, the Creator is exalted and the creation is abased, then our relationship with our loving Father will inevitably flourish. It is the humility that comes of acknowledging our Father's work in our hearts as his own that is the catalyst that transforms our understanding of his great love for us and thereby propels our faith and our love for our Father to new heights. Consider our Father's words: "All these things my hand has made, and so all these things came to be, declares the Lord. But this is the one to whom I will look: he who is humble and contrite in spirit and trembles at my word" (Isaiah 66:2).

If a person has always believed that salvation was a work of grace, it may well be possible to fail to comprehend the critical distinction that was made in the preceding paragraphs and thereby dismiss the potential transforming benefits of such a realization. Indeed, in most of today's churches, we do not seem to have any problem professing that salvation is by grace alone (Ephesians 2:8; 2 Timothy 1:9; Romans 3:24; Acts 15:11). However, the problem mentioned previously shows up in too many of these same churches as they attempt to add to the absolute truth of salvation by grace alone by asserting that the "choosing" is nevertheless a person's necessary contribution to the matter.

While it is certainly true that it is necessary for humans to choose to believe, it is vital to discern both the true source of this choice and the actual result of this choice. In his writing *Against Two Letters of the Pelagians*, Augustine pointed out that if the gift of grace is given as a result of a person's choice to believe, then in that case, grace is rendered as something due, rather than as a gift—and so "grace is no longer grace."[4] Augustine further pointed out that the church had correctly condemned any teaching that "the grace of God is given according to our virtues," which would necessarily include the virtuous action of choosing God. Augustine correctly contended that the transformation of an "unwilling and resisting man" into one "consenting to the good and willing the good" could not possibly originate in the person, but rather is solely a work of God's grace.

A. W. Tozer understood this truth well. In his book *The Set of the Sail*, he wrote that John 6 teaches us clearly that "the ability to come to Christ is a gift of the Father." Tozer added these powerful comments:

> It is not surprising that upon hearing these words [John 6] many of our Lord's disciples went back and walked no more with him. Such teaching cannot but be deeply disturbing to the natural mind. It takes from sinful men much of the power of self-determination upon which they had prided themselves so inordinately. It cuts the ground out from under their self-help and throws them back upon the sovereign good pleasure of God, and that is precisely where they do not want to be. *They are willing to be saved by grace, but to preserve their self-esteem they must hold that the desire to be saved originated with them*; this desire is their contribution to the whole thing, their offering of the fruit of the ground, and it keeps salvation in their hands where in truth it is not and never can be.[5] (emphasis added)

C. H. Spurgeon also preached this same truth: "God is always first in the matter of salvation. He is before our convictions, before our desires, before our fears, before our hopes. All that is good or ever will be good in us is preceded by the Grace of God and is the effect of a Divine cause within."[6] The veracity of this discerning comment effectively removes any grounds at all for the belief in a human contribution to God's sovereign work of grace. If we are willing to give up our pride and be honest with ourselves, we can be certain that the good that enables us to choose to believe in the Gospel could not possibly have originated within ourselves, since Paul points out in Romans 7:18 that there is no good at all to be found in our sinful natures. Boasting is excluded (Romans 3:22–27), and our Father alone is glorified.

A very practical illustration of this concept is found in the book *Whatever Happened to the Gospel of Grace?* by James Montgomery Boice. In this excellent book, Boice points out that because we all know Ephesians 2:9 quite well, we understand that God will not have boasting in heaven.[7] However, he continues, if what makes the ultimate difference between one person who is saved and another who is not saved is the human ability to choose God—call it "free will," "faith," or whatever—then boasting is not excluded and all glory cannot honestly be given to God alone. As a further illustration, Boice proposes the imaginary scenario of a saved person in heaven who believes that he or she accepted God as the result of a good choice made of his or her own free will. If someone should happen to ask that saved person in heaven why he or she is there and another person who heard the Gospel and rejected it is not there, the saved person would have to reply, "Well, I hate to say this in heaven, because we are supposed to be spending our time here glorifying and praising God, but since you ask, I have to reply that the reason I am here and that the other person is not is that I had faith and he did not. I chose to believe. I, by my own power, received Jesus Christ as my Savior."

It is this very basis for boasting which Paul so completely precludes in Ephesians 2:8–9, 1 Corinthians 1:28–30, Romans 11:5–6 and 3:27, 2 Timothy 1:9, and Titus 3:5. We should never resent this truth; rather, we must come to delight in the incredible realization that the God of the universe first chose us and turned our hearts to desire him! It is this confidence that fundamentally changes our relationship with our loving Father. We come to realize that our salvation was never a business deal where we chose to do our part and God fulfilled his promised end of the bargain or,

Praying to a Gentleman God

worse yet, a somewhat tentative experiment of sorts in which we decided to "give Christ a chance." When we instead realize that we are nothing and that God chose us to be his own for his own good pleasure by absolutely no merit or act of our own, the result can only be heights of gratitude, worship, awe, love, peace, and a daily personal relationship with our Father such as can never be experienced when we mistakenly view the whole matter as a favorable contractual deal we were wise enough to choose to accept.

This personal relationship thrives in prayer, so it is vital to possess a correct concept of the God to whom we are praying. As we pray, there are three distinct possibilities. We can pray to a God we believe to be incapable of interfering with human free will, but such prayers would be virtually hopeless, if not outright lunacy. The next alternative is to pray to a God we believe to be well capable of conquering human free will but who we believe chooses to refrain from doing so because he is a "gentleman." Such prayers might be offered in the hope that we could somehow talk God into making some sort of a special exception in response to our prayers if we are fervent enough or perhaps get enough people presenting the same prayers simultaneously. However, if we are brutally honest about prayers to such a God, we are forced to admit that these prayers would also be virtually useless. At best, they would be prayers in which we could have no real confidence. The final alternative is that we can pray to a God who we are completely confident will sovereignly exercise his unlimited power and unlimited knowledge to change human free will however he sees fit to accomplish his own perfect purposes. We pray with great confidence, knowing that our prayers are also a part of his perfect purpose and that God will indeed act, interfere, steer, permit, block, or enable as will be perfectly appropriate for his will in every situation.

It should be plain which of these three concepts of our Father would be the most desirable if we were given a choice between them. The God we would desire to serve would obviously be the God described (only partially) in the third concept above. Our great blessing is that the God that we would most desire is also the true God of the Bible! Our prayers are effective and meaningful because our infinitely capable God reigns; he freely exercises his supremacy to accomplish his eternal purpose on the earth, and he sovereignly turns human hearts to himself.

This blessed reality can be clearly seen in 1 Kings 18, where God chose to turn the hearts of his people back to himself by setting up a confrontation between Elijah and the prophets of Baal on Mount Carmel. This wonderful passage is often referenced by those who would hold a lower view of God and limit his sovereignty. They cite verses 20–21 where Elijah exhorted the people to make a choice between the Lord and Baal, to no longer "hesitate between two opinions" (NASB). The Israelites under Ahab, they say, were called on to "make a choice." However, in my experience, this group tends to ignore or fails to see the truth of the matter contained in Elijah's prayer in verses 36 and 37 of the same chapter. In these verses, Elijah confirmed that indeed *all* that was done that day was done at the word of the Lord (v. 36). He went on to clearly state in no uncertain terms that it was God who had "turned their hearts back" (v. 37), thereby enabling them to make the choice to follow the true God. The truth is palpable here; the people were neither seeking God nor repenting of their double-mindedness until after God himself had set up the entire situation (not before—see v. 21: "the people did not answer him a word"). God sovereignly used the circumstances he had created to turn the people's hearts back to himself.

In the New Testament, Jesus confirmed this great truth by simply stating, "No one can come to me unless the Father who sent me draws him, and I will raise him up on the last day" (John 6:44). The initial action here is clearly God's, which is the drawing of the human heart. This drawing, by definition, is inevitably a divine interference and imposition upon the enslaved, sinful human free will. It is vitally important to note that those to whom this great mercy of the drawing of their hearts is shown are the very same individuals whom Jesus says he "will raise up on the last day." Furthermore, noted author R. C. Sproul pointed out that we too easily miss the real meaning of this passage, in that the Greek word that is translated here as "draw" (*helkō*) means "to compel" or "to drag" as Strong's lexicon indicates, not the impotent "woo" that some would assert today.[8] The same Greek word is used in Acts 16:19, where we read: "They seized Paul and Silas and *dragged* them into the marketplace to face the authorities," and again in James 2:6 where it is asked: "Are not the rich the ones that oppress you, and the ones who drag (*helkō*) you into court?"

In the classic book *The Pursuit of Man*, A. W. Tozer wrote of our Father's initiating love with great insight: "Salvation is from our side a choice, from the divine side it is a seizing upon, an apprehending, a conquest of the Most High God. Our 'accepting' and 'willing' are reactions rather than actions. The right of determination must always remain with God."[9] It is indeed a glorious revelation when we comprehend that we are no different than the original disciples; we did not choose him, but rather he chose us (John 15:16). This realization not only strips us of any grounds for boasting, it also creates a true revelation of our Father's great love for us that cannot otherwise exist. When our minds are infused with this amazing truth, suddenly our hearts explode with a reciprocal love, and the words "We love him, because he first loved us" (1 John 4:19) become exceedingly precious to us, now immeasurably more profound and meaningful than words that were once merely the simple lyrics of a cute children's Sunday school song we learned to sing by rote.

CHAPTER 4

THE BIG, THE SMALL, AND OUR PRESENT

The church has surrendered her once lofty concept of God and has substituted for it one so low, so ignoble, as to be utterly unworthy of thinking, worshiping men. This she has done not deliberately, but little by little and without her knowledge; and her very unawareness only makes her situation all the more tragic. This low view of God entertained almost universally among Christians is the cause of a hundred lesser evils everywhere among us. A whole new philosophy of the Christian life has resulted from this one basic error in our religious thinking.

– A. W. Tozer, The Knowledge of the Holy[1]

In the previous chapter, we examined passages such as Ezekiel 36, 1 Kings 18, John 6:44, and Romans 10:20 that clearly speak of God sovereignly changing human hearts and wills towards himself even when they are not seeking God by their own wills. We can see that same principle at work in chapters 24, 29, and 32 of Jeremiah as well. However, if we are to correctly understand and appreciate the supremacy of our Father over his entire creation, we must not unduly limit our perceptions of his actions in the hearts of mankind to solely that of drawing his chosen people to himself. In fact, God's purpose is inevitably accomplished in all our choices and actions. It is the very depth of our Father's wise involvement in the affairs on the earth and the unlimited extent to which he exercises his strong right arm to accomplish his purpose that are the true sources of our confidence and trust. As we begin to better understand the true God of the Bible, we will assuredly also begin to better fathom his great love for each of us.

Our Father's broad purview over human activities is vividly demonstrated in a series of events that are recounted in 1 Kings 22. In this intriguing account, we are shown decisively God's willingness and ability to interfere with human will in order to accomplish his purpose, even when his eternal will includes that certain humans perish. We are also treated to a rare and provoking glimpse into the operation of God in heaven. In this passage, as well as in 2 Chronicles 18, Scripture tells us that it was God's will that King Ahab perish. Therefore, God asked the "host of heaven" that was gathered about him who would go and "entice Ahab" to his death (vv. 19–20). One particular spirit volunteered to entice Ahab, and God selected and sent this lying spirit to fill the mouth of Ahab's prophet Zedekiah with falsehoods (v. 22). This spirit caused Zedekiah to proclaim that Ahab would surely be successful in battle against the Syrians. This lie led inevitably to Ahab being killed in battle—exactly as God had purposed and spoken (vv. 20, 37–38).

We can be certain that God's word will always accomplish that for which he sends it out and never return to him empty (Isaiah 55:11), and in this case God sent the spirit and told it, "You are to entice him [Ahab], and you shall succeed; go out and do so." Clearly, God interfered with human free will and human choice in order to impose his own will of judgment (death) upon a sinner. In so doing, God also steered the course of human history. If we are willing to set aside our preconceived notions, we can learn much from the principle that is clearly exemplified in this narrative: Ahab freely chose to go into battle, but it was the Lord's purpose that prevailed.

Indeed, Proverbs 19:21 declares, "Many are the plans in a man's heart, but it is the Lord's purpose that prevails." What a powerful and descriptive statement of how God works through humans to accomplish his purpose! This Scripture is teaching us that we are certainly free to plan, choose, and act; but no matter, we can be even more certain that it will be the Lord's purpose that will prevail in these plans, choices, and actions. This is not by any means a sporadic or atypical tenet of Scripture; rather, it is an underlying and recurring theme of both Testaments. Proverbs 16:9 expands and elucidates this foundational principle:

> In his heart, a man plans his course, but the Lord determines his steps.

Here again, the Bible is plainly teaching us that even as humans are planning and making choices, it is ultimately the sovereign Lord that determines both the outcome and what the steps will actually be. Lamentations 3:37 states this truth palpably with the following rhetorical question: "Who has spoken and it come to pass, unless the Lord has commanded it?" Humans will never be able to alter or undo God's perfect purpose with their actions, as Solomon pointed out in Ecclesiastes 7:13: "Consider the work of God: who can make straight what he has made crooked?" He added in Ecclesiastes 9:1 (NASB), "Righteous men, wise men, and their deeds are in the hand of God."

Our Father reminded us of the supremacy of his will and purpose over the actions of humans when he said in Isaiah 43:13 (NASB): "I act, and who can reverse it?" Similarly, the people of Jerusalem seen in Isaiah 22:9–11 freely chose to busy themselves repairing walls and building reservoirs to defend against imminent attack, all the while oblivious to the fact that their circumstances were from God—that it was God who really "did it" and had "planned it long ago" (v. 11). Contrary to the currently popular notion that humans may freely choose to do or achieve anything they set their minds to do, John the Baptist preached that "a person cannot receive even one thing unless it is given him from heaven" (John 3:27). This magnificent truth that God directs the details of human lives is encapsulated and forcefully echoed yet again in the prayer of Jeremiah found in Jeremiah 10:23:

> I know, O Lord, that the way of man is not in himself, that it is not in man who walks to direct his steps.

This is an essential concept we must neither dismiss nor disregard if we are to truly understand and treasure the love of our Father and his wonderful role in our lives as he continually works for the good of his children (Romans 8:32, 28; Matthew 7:9–11). It is one thing to be earnestly and worriedly searching for just the right steps to earn our Father's involvement and his blessing, and it is quite another to walk in the confidence of knowing that our loving Father is directing our steps.

The far-reaching implications of Jeremiah's confession of faith notwithstanding, we are all human, and we tend to have a built-in urge to unduly elevate our own perceived sovereignty over ourselves and even over others. For example, we think that we can freely decide to go to McDonald's and eat a cheeseburger tomorrow afternoon. Or, we may freely decide that we will take a job in a different city next month. These seem to us to be common choices we are free to make in one way or the other. In a sense, we are certainly free to make such choices, but that freedom can never usurp God's sovereignty—whether we are aware of that sovereignty in action or not. The foolishness of believing that it is our own human plans that will prevail apart from God's will is explained clearly in James 4:13–16, but we often skim right past the real heart and message of this passage. Here is the quotation:

> Come now, you who say, "Today or tomorrow we will go to such and such a city, and spend a year there and engage in business and make a profit." Yet you do not know what your life will be like tomorrow. You are just a vapor that appears for a little while and then vanishes away. Instead, you ought to say, "If the Lord wills, we will live and also do this or that." But as it is, you boast in your arrogance; all such boasting is evil. (James 4:13–16 NASB)

This Scripture is actually teaching that it is sinful arrogance (a usurping of God's sovereignty) to believe that it is our own will that determines "what our life will be like tomorrow," be it going to McDonald's or going to "such and such a city." Instead, we should be humbly acknowledging that "if the Lord wills" we will first and foremost even draw our next breath ("If the Lord wills, we will live," v. 15) and after that also "do this or that" if he so wills. If we do not want to be guilty of sinful arrogance by boasting that we control our own destiny, we must actually accept and live as if we believe the simple truth that is taught here: If the Lord wills it, we will do it; if he does not will it, we will not do it. Paul understood this quite well, and we see this truth manifested in his farewell to the Ephesians in Acts 18:21. He told them plainly, "I will return to you if God wills" (cf. Romans 1:10). Indeed, we honor the Lord when we humble ourselves and acknowledge this fact!

> Who can speak and have it happen if the Lord has not decreed it? (Lamentations 3:37 NIV)

> The God in whose hand is your breath, and whose are all your ways, you have not honored. (Daniel 5:23)

We also like to believe, it seems, that we make our own destiny, but Scripture destroys that notion as well. Hannah offered an inspired prayer in 1 Samuel 2 after the Lord had fulfilled his purpose by bringing the mighty prophet Samuel into being through her and her prayers, having previously sovereignly closed her womb. In her prayer (vv. 6–7 NIV), she echoed the song of Moses (Deuteronomy 32:39) and emphatically declared that "the Lord brings death and makes alive; he brings down to the grave and raises up. The Lord sends poverty and wealth; he humbles and exalts." Hannah realized that what we tend to attribute to luck, hard work, or even being a "self-made man" would in fact be more properly attributed to the Lord's action in accomplishing his own purpose. It is the Lord's purpose that will prevail, not a destiny of our own making.

In his farewell address to the people of Israel, Moses emphatically declared that it is God alone who "gives us the power to be successful," and he noted that we must never think or say, "I have achieved this wealth with my own strength and energy" (Deuteronomy 8:17–18 NLT). Notwithstanding this plain truth, it seems that more often than not we choose to teach that it is one's efforts that bring about one's destiny. This teaching runs headlong into Psalm 127:1, which declares, "Unless the Lord watches over the city, the watchman stays awake in vain." We often skim past this verse by assuming that it merely means that we need the Lord's help to be effective in our efforts. However, the full truth is much deeper.

We must carefully discern what constitutes the determining and necessary ingredient if the protection of this hypothetical city is to be effected. The verse is teaching clearly that the skill, alertness, or earnest efforts of the watchman, or even an entire host of watchmen, will accomplish absolutely nothing toward the protection of the city if it is not the Lord's will to protect the city. Likewise, we know that if the Lord is protecting the city, and it is his will that the city be protected, then unskilled, slumbering, slothful watchmen will not be able to prevent the city from being protected. Clearly, the necessary, critical, and determining ingredient is the Lord's purpose, not human effort. This verse is teaching us that we must realize that successes or failures that seem to us to be a result of human effort, ability, and choice (in this case, the protection of a city) are in reality brought about by the Lord's will and his purpose.

The poignant truth laid out by this multitude of Scriptures is indeed an affront to our natural human desire to be in total control of our own destiny. The modern notion that God is a God that is reacting to and confronting our choices as we make them rather than a God that exerts his sovereign rule over everything is both invalidated and precluded by these many passages. Charles Spurgeon spoke of our human resistance to God's preeminence over all things:

> Men have no objection to a god who is really no God; I mean by this, a god who shall be the subject of their caprice, who shall be a lackey to their will, who shall be under their control! They have no objection to such a being as that; but a God who speaks, and it is done, who commands, and it stands fast, a God who has no respect for their persons, but doeth as he will among the armies of heaven and among the inhabitants of this lower world, such a God as this they cannot endure. And yet, is it not essential to the very being of God that he should be absolute and supreme? Certainly, to the Scriptural conception of God, sovereignty is an absolute necessity.[2]

Our desire to reign notwithstanding, Psalm 103:19 (NASB) makes it clear that "the Lord has established His throne in the heavens, and His sovereignty rules over *all*." If we are to begin to truly know our Father, we must learn that this "all" includes the big, the small, and our present. On the grandest of scales, Isaiah 40:26 reveals to us that God brings out the stars by number by the greatness of his might, calling them by name—and "not one is missing." God's purpose for the entire universe is perfect; we as humans do not even know how many stars exist because such an inventory remains far beyond our capabilities. Because our Father is sovereign, we can nevertheless know for certain that the number of stars in the universe is perfect, and there is not even one too many or one too few.

It is somehow quite easy for most of us to picture God as being in control of the vast universe; we have no problem with him steering stars around or even with him accurately predicting future events and times in a manner inclusive of the smallest of details (as in Daniel and Revelation, for example). In the same manner, we do not seem to have any problem with him raising up and tearing down nations or determining their exact times and places (Acts 17:26; Daniel 2:21). We read the book of Jonah, and we are quite comfortable with God's displayed sovereignty over humans, storms, the sea, great fish, gourd plants, and even worms. Likewise, we do not seem to have any issue with him exercising his will, control, and provision for sparrows (as in Matthew), eagles, or mountain goats (as he declares of himself in Job), and we can even accept that it is he who has begotten each and every drop of dew in history (Job 38:28). It would appear, therefore, we can accept and be quite comfortable with God being in control of both the so-called big things and the small things. The difficulty seems to arise when we are forced to acknowledge the reality that God is sovereign over not only the big things and the small things, but he is equally sovereign over the middle ground that is our present!

Human pride and arrogance inevitably rise up and take exception to this latter assessment. Such pride notwithstanding, the big, the small, and our present are actually integral parts of our Father's single complete reality and are, as such, quite inseparable. If one gives the matter more than superficial thought, the easily observable and unavoidable conclusion quickly emerges that the entire course and outcome of the big things, such as the history and end of humankind and the earth, could be totally dependent and steered by the smallest of things or events, be it a rainstorm at just the right time or even a sparrow at a critical place in a critical moment. Those who would attempt to evade the reality of God's supremacy and involvement in every detail by asserting that "God only is sovereign over the final outcome" are therefore forced to admit that this assertion cannot be true unless he is also sovereign over the smallest and tiniest of details.

John Wesley, a leading proponent of human free will, preached a sermon titled "Divine Providence" in which he powerfully pointed out that God's providence (sovereignty) over the largest of things must necessarily include direct control over the smallest of things and that, in fact, there can be neither large nor small with God. The sermon is quite lengthy, but a few cogent excerpts are more than worthy of inclusion here:

> You say, "You allow a *general* providence, but deny a *particular* one." And what is a general, of whatever kind it be, that includes no particulars? Is not every general necessarily made up of its several particulars? Can you instance in any general that is not? Tell me any genus, if you can, that contains no species? What is it that constitutes a genus, but so many species added together? What, I pray, is a whole that contains no parts? Mere nonsense and contradiction! Every whole must, in the nature of things, be made up of its several parts; insomuch that if there be no parts, there can be no whole.
>
> Do you mean (for we would fain find out your meaning, if you have any meaning at all) that the providence of God does indeed extend to all parts of the earth, with regard to great and singular events, such as the rise and fall of empires; but that the little concerns of this or that man are beneath the notice of the Almighty? Then you do not consider that *great* and *little* are merely relative terms, which have place only with respect to men. With regard to the Most High, man and all the concerns of men are nothing, less than nothing, before him. And nothing is small in his sight that in any degree affects the welfare of any that fear God and work righteousness. What becomes, then, of your general providence, exclusive of a particle? Let it be forever rejected by all rational men, as absurd, self-contradictory nonsense. We may then sum up the whole scriptural doctrine of providence in that fine saying of St. Austin [Augustine], *Ita praesidet singulis sicut universis, et universis sicut singulis!* [He rules over particulars as over universals, and over universals as over particulars.] [3]

This brilliant teaching by Wesley presents virtually no difficulty to most Christians until it actually applies to their own lives or situations. Indeed, we seem to have little problem with God's sovereignty over either the big (the universals) or the small (the particulars). However, when we begin to realize that the same God who controls the big and the small also controls the middle ground of the everyday circumstances of our lives, we abruptly begin to characterize God with the Deists as an uninvolved

The Big, the Small, and Our Present

God who is "hands-off," as a "gentleman" who will not interfere with our choices and the outcomes of those choices. We have no problem with the concept of God calling the stars by name, but we cannot seem to accept that he calls his chosen by name. We are quite willing to acquiesce to the reality of God feeding the sparrows, clothing the flowers, commanding the eagles, and even placing each individual drop of dew in our yard each morning, but when it comes to our own circumstances, we unaccountably choose to believe that our fancied free will effectively fences God out from being directly involved in our situation, our surroundings, our thoughts, our feelings, and even our choices. We are not willing to give up the feeling of dignity and pride that comes from supposedly being in charge of our own destiny.

We will not admit to believing like the Deists, yet we will not embrace the scriptural teachings that God is sovereign over the big, the small, and everything in between! Wesley's words preclude us from even suggesting that God can be sovereign over "the world" while at the same time being anything but completely sovereign over the details of our lives. We are the "particulars" in the "universal" of the entire creation that God is steering to its perfect culmination, and Wesley correctly teaches us that these are inseparable. We must not fail to acknowledge that God, by his power, brings "everything" under his control (Philippians 3:21). We should learn to exalt with David that God is the ruler and head over everything, that any strength, honor, wealth, wisdom, or power that we may possess comes from him, and that everything in our lives comes from his hand (1 Chronicles 29:10–14).

Rather than adopting this scriptural view, we seem to desire instead to view God's influence as limited. We read in Romans 11:36 that *all things* are from him, *all things* are through him, and *all things* are to him, and then inexplicably we immediately begin to build a list of *some things* that we will choose to exclude from the *all things* that we will allow as being included in the scope of this all-inclusive description of our God's sovereignty. This impertinence is either the peak of human arrogance before our Creator or the pinnacle of human folly—perhaps even both.

For example, on the big end of the scale, it is no longer "politically correct" to admit that it was God's will for a hurricane, tornado, or even the 9/11 bombers to strike a city. Many have difficulty even admitting that God, in fact, must have at least allowed such a thing. And yet, there is no room for equivocation or ambiguity in the teaching of Amos 3:6: "Does disaster come to a city, unless the Lord has done it?" Likewise, we inevitably view war as a bad thing—a tragic result of sinful human nature. There is truth within this view, of course, but we cannot also dismiss our Father's sovereignty in any war. For example, we read of the Israelites engaged in a war in 1 Chronicles 5:22, and we are told directly that "the war was of God." Is it not arrogance and usurpation for us to assume the authority to judge to exclude things, be they big or little, from the "all things" that are "from him," "through him," and "to him" in Romans 11:36?

The real problem here is not that the Scriptures are not exceedingly clear; rather they are just not the way we as humans would have them to be—the way we would write them if we were doing the writing. As a result, we ignore them or rationalize them away, always magnifying and elevating humanity at the expense of diminishing the sovereign ruler of the universe. To borrow from David's piercing words in Psalm 4:2, how long will we obscure God's glory and honor, and how long will we love vanity and seek after a lie? Why should we not rather embrace Psalm 119:91, which reminds us yet again that *all* things are his servants? Do we, or can we, really believe that *all* things and not just some things are from God, through God, and for God's sovereign purpose? (Hebrews 2:10; Proverbs 16:4).

This is not just a mere theological abstraction. Rather, this is the very heart of the matter, the real thrust and driving truth that motivates the writing of this book. Whether we realize it or not, we are limited by our concept of our God, and our relationship with our Father is defined thereby. Our Father's unqualified, absolute sovereignty is not just a nice, but mostly inconsequential, fact; instead, it must be the very lynchpin of our faith! *Our view of the extent of God's sovereignty is the underlying and governing factor in how we view the Father and how we perceive his love for us.*

For example, Jesus told us that we should not worry or be anxious (Matthew 6; Luke 12), and he assured us that our Father knows exactly what we need. If we do not accept that God is sovereign and that he does in fact intervene in human events and human will—thereby working all things according to his purpose—then there is, in fact, little comfort in knowing that God knows what we need. After all, we are taught God will not interfere with the free will of humans or involve himself in the details of our daily lives, so we are forced to worry if God is free to intervene in our current need or has somehow limited himself from doing so. Little wonder, then, that we worry so much and are so anxious! Martin Luther wrote astutely about this very thing:

> For if you hesitate to believe, or are too proud to acknowledge, that God foreknows and wills all things, not contingently, but necessarily and immutably, how can you believe, trust, and rely on His promises? When He makes promises, you ought to be out of doubt that He knows, and can and will perform, what He promises; otherwise, you will be accounting Him neither true nor faithful, which is unbelief, and the height of irreverence, and a denial of the most high God! And how can you be thus sure and certain, unless you know that certainly, infallibly, immutably and necessarily, He knows, wills and will perform what He promises?...If, then, we are taught and believe that we ought to be ignorant of the necessary foreknowledge of God and the necessity of events, Christian faith is utterly destroyed, and the promises of God and the whole Gospel fall to the ground completely; *For the Christian's chief and only comfort in every adversity lies in knowing that God does not lie, but brings all things to pass immutably, and that His will cannot be resisted, altered or impeded.*[4] (emphasis added)

Indeed, how can we ever truly "Be still and know that I am God" (Psalm 46:10) if we do not actually believe that God is sovereign over every single thing, and instead we are left to hope that maybe, just maybe, God will choose to intervene, break his own rules, and work in the details of any particular pain or trial? Our lasting stillness and confidence can come only from knowing and understanding that "all things are his servants" (Psalm 119:91). As such, Paul could encourage the believers at Thessalonica by teaching them that their current sufferings had been "destined" (or "appointed," KJV), and they should therefore not be "moved by these afflictions" (1 Thessalonians 3:3–4).

Many individuals believe that God is good and that God is powerful, but he is not completely sovereign. As a result of this flawed concept, they can have no true confidence that God will see that his will is done in their lives, and they go about their lives worried that they must strive to convince God to get involved, help them out, and "bless their efforts." This is misplaced anxiety; God wants our trust, not our striving. Only when we fully accept that God's purpose will always be done and that our God is sovereign over all (including ourselves, our neighbors, Satan, our circumstances—everything) can we come to the blessed point of truly being still and knowing that he is God.

We are assured in Proverbs 16:4 that "the Lord works out everything for his own ends—even the wicked for a day of disaster." As humans, we have a natural desire to control and to understand our own way, but we run headlong into Proverbs 20:24, a Scripture that confronts us with this clear statement: "A man's steps are directed by the Lord. How then can anyone understand his own way?" Can we actually accept these scriptural teachings that our choices and our plans, both big and small, are directed by the Lord at a level beyond human understanding? This passage is in no way specific to godly people making godly choices, nor is it limited to humans who are Jews or Christians; rather, it is speaking of God's absolute sovereignty over human choices. There are no scriptural grounds to suggest that God waives his sovereignty and just "puts up with" and "deals with" evil men that happen to just appear on the earth as the result of biological processes in which God is uninvolved and who are somehow outside of God's original, eternal purpose—that sort of thinking, when broken down, borders on outright blasphemy.

In fact, some have gone so far as to suggest that God in some manner waives his sovereignty and will not interfere with our free will because if he were to impose himself on human will, then God could not possibly be glorified by such a thing. The speciousness of this position should be quickly revealed by even a cursory reading of the account of Paul's Damascus road experience in either Acts 9 or Acts 22, in which Paul's free will is trampled underfoot to God's everlasting glory. In fact, we are given a Bible full of examples of God's intervention in human free will and choices, a direct statement in the Psalms that God "frustrates the plans" of humans, and a declaration in Nahum 1:9 that God will make a complete end of any human's schemes or plots against him. We know for certain, then, that God intervened in human free will in the *past* to accomplish his purposes.

Paul also made it exceedingly clear that God will most certainly interfere with human free will in the *future* in order to accomplish his purpose. In Philippians 2:9–11, Paul told us that God has exalted Christ so that "at the name of Jesus every knee should bow, in heaven and on earth and under the earth, and every tongue confess that Jesus Christ is Lord, to the glory of God the Father." This statement is absolutely remarkable! Assuming that "every knee" does not exclude any human knees, whether they be in heaven, earth, or hell (under the earth), then we can be quite certain that God will indeed impose himself on the will of every single human being that has ever lived, including those who have not even an inkling of a free will desire to acknowledge him, much less worship him! All will bow, and all will confess their belief that Jesus is Lord, free will or not.

More remarkably still, Paul declared in verse 11 that this very act of irresistible, uninvited imposition upon the free will of humans by God will be done for the explicitly stated reason of bringing glory to God the Father. According to this Scripture, when God exercises his sovereignty over the free will of humans, we can know categorically that God does in fact bring glory to himself by so doing. This is notably contrary to the notion that God is not or could not be glorified by forcibly imposing himself on the free will of humans. Indeed, we are told in Revelation 5:13 that the day will come when every single created being (without any exception—all "free wills" shall choose to participate) will together offer praise, honor, and glory to God and the Lamb, and the same universal eventuality is also mentioned in Psalm 22:27–29 and Isaiah 45:23. This astounding fact unavoidably leads us to a powerful, confidence-inspiring conclusion that is eminently relevant to each of us today: if we see in Scripture that God certainly imposed himself upon human free will in the past and that he will certainly do so in the future (always to bring glory to himself and to accomplish his eternal purpose), why would we not also joyfully conclude that he does exactly the same at the present time in each of our lives?

CHAPTER 5

OUR FUTURE IS HEADING OUR WAY

I am immortal until the will of God for me is accomplished.

— David Livingston[1]

Many are offended by the fact that their destiny is from the Lord rather than being afforded the fancied opportunity to "make their own" destiny. While it is quite understandable that humans initially desire to feel as if they are making their own destiny, I have come to understand that it is far preferable to know that we are *living* our own destiny, a destiny which was authored by God, our Father. This fact can only fill us with joy when we come to realize that he loves us more perfectly than we could ever imagine, has completely unlimited resources and power at his disposal to accomplish his plan, and tells us imperatively that his plan for us is for our good, not evil. Stated simply, it only makes sense that God can do a better job of making our destiny than we can, so why should we prefer the inferior above the superior?

Before John the Baptist was ever born, God declared John's destiny to his father Zechariah (Luke 1:11–20). The angel that God sent to Zechariah proclaimed that John would "be filled with the Holy Spirit, even from his mother's womb" (v. 15). Dare we assert that it was unfair that God did not give John a choice in this matter? Moreover, the angel stated conclusively that this as yet unborn child would "be great before the Lord," would "turn many of the children of Israel to the Lord their God," and would minister "in the spirit and power of Elijah." As such, John would inevitably fulfill the antecedent prophecies of both Isaiah and Malachi by preparing the way for Jesus (Isaiah 40:3–5; Malachi 4:5; Matthew 3:3; 11:10, 14; 17:12–13; Mark 1:3). John's ministry was to be a glorious part of God's eternal purpose, and we see here that John's destiny was clearly written for him by his loving heavenly Father before he was even conceived.

Immediately after John's birth, Zechariah was filled with the Holy Spirit (Luke 1:67). He proceeded to prophesy that his newborn son John would be "called the prophet of the Most High" and that John would "give the knowledge of salvation" to the Jews. The infallible accuracy of Zechariah's inspired prophecy did not allow for the possibility that John might grow up and invalidate God's previous words by failing to make the correct free choices. It should not surprise us, then, that John the Baptist actually did exercise his free will to choose and live the single destiny that God had authored for him before the foundation of the world.

As another simple, biblical example of the fact that God authors destinies, we should notice that God chose the Promised Land for Abraham and later for the nation of Israel. He did not ask them what particular land they wanted to inherit, nor did he offer to give them the land of their own choosing; rather, he simply told them what they were going to inherit, and he proceeded to make it happen according to his decree. He did not give them the opportunity or the supposed right to choose Mount Seir instead of Mount Zion (Deuteronomy 2:5) or to choose the plains of Ammon instead of the plains of Jericho (Deuteronomy 2:19). Did the Israelites resent this divine imposition upon their opportunity to determine their own destiny or this supernatural restriction of their freedom of choice? The answer is found in Psalm 47:4; we read there a beautiful song of praise that celebrates the fact that God had *lovingly* chosen their inheritance: "He chose our inheritance for us, the pride of Jacob, *whom he loved*" (NIV). What may be the chorus is found in verse 6: "Sing praises to God, sing praises; sing praises to our King, sing praises." We should likewise learn to glory in the destiny that God has authored for us. Instead of resentment, the only proper response is to offer much continuing praise to our preeminent Father for the destiny (inheritance) he lovingly gives to us as his chosen people.

This concept that we are living the destiny that God has authored for each of us is not my own original thought by any means; in past years this was a commonly held tenet of faith. However, I am quite certain that many, if not most, in today's church would take exception to this creed. It would seem that this belief encroaches entirely too far on the supposed supremacy of the human will for the approval of many. Nonetheless, those that would have a negative knee-jerk reaction to this assertion may have failed to thoroughly and carefully think through this issue and consider the implications of their own foundational beliefs.

A foundational belief professed by all Christians that I have met, for example, is that God is both omniscient (all-knowing) and immutable (unchangeable). God obviously cannot be perfect without being omniscient, and Psalm 147:5 declares that the understanding of our perfect God is indeed infinite. It is inescapable that a perfect being (God being the only one that will ever exist!) can never learn anything that he does not already know, or he would have been less than perfect before acquiring that new knowledge. Quite obviously, this is why God is also immutable—he is already perfect, was always perfect, and will always continue to be perfect. Any change at all would require that he be less than perfect either before or after the change.

If it is possible to know the future at all, a capability the Bible unambiguously and repeatedly demonstrates that God indeed possesses, then God is not God unless he possesses a perfect knowledge of the future that includes the smallest of details—and has always had that exact knowledge. Furthermore, according to Isaiah 45:20–21, it is this ability to know the future that distinguishes our great God from the false gods. We must therefore incontrovertibly conclude that our prescient Father knows in advance all of the free choices each of us will make in the future. This fact is confirmed by Revelation 13:8, which assures us that the names of the redeemed (those individuals that were to choose God in the future) were written in the Book of Life *before* the foundation of the world. God knows our present and our future thoughts (Ezekiel 38:10–11; 11:5; Psalm 94:11), and he knows the words we will speak *before* we speak them (Psalm 139:2–4). He even knows the thoughts and deeds of our heart that we may believe to be secret and unknowable (Psalm 90:8). Indeed, our Father knows *all* things (1 John 3:20), and he has always known these things—long before we ever think them, do them, or speak them. He looks into the future and proclaims, "Behold it is coming, and it will be brought about" (Ezekiel 39:8). Moreover, God also affirmed his ability to foresee and control the future when he said of himself in Isaiah 46:10 that from the beginning he has declared the end, and he told us in the same verse that he declares from ancient times things "not yet done." According to this passage, our Father tells us directly that what he refers to as "the end" is already fixed and certain, having been decreed from the beginning.

We are told plainly in John 18:4 that Jesus knew in advance "all that would happen to him." If we correctly believe that Jesus was both perfect and divine, then we have absolutely no rational basis upon which we may propose to limit his knowledge of the future merely to the events of his crucifixion. Indeed, Jesus knew the entire future—including all that will happen to each of us—just as much as he knew all that would happen to him on the cross. Jesus himself provided us one of the key reasons why God sometimes reveals a small portion of his perfect knowledge of the future to humans, and this may be found in John 14:29. Here, Jesus said, "I have told you before it takes place, so that when it does take place you may believe." Indeed, when we come to understand and trust that our God knows and controls the future, this fact becomes a strong foundation upon which we may build unwavering belief.

Our God's unlimited ability to foresee and control every detail in the future is also illustrated unmistakably in 1 Samuel 10:1–8, where the prophet Samuel relayed to Saul a direct "message from God" (1 Samuel 9:27). In this detailed account, God shared his complete knowledge of the future in amazing detail, including such things as exactly when and where Saul would meet certain men, exactly how many men Saul would meet, and exactly what those men would choose to say to Saul. God's revelation of the future continued, and Saul was told that he would meet another three men (not two, not four) by a specific tree in a specific location. God next told him what each of the three men would be carrying in incredible detail: three goats, three loaves of bread, and a skin of wine. Is it even remotely conceivable that all this was just a series of remarkable coincidences? God also told Saul that the men would offer Saul two (not one, not three) loaves of bread, thereby demonstrating God's ability to foresee and control humans' future thoughts and decisions. Finally, God told Saul that he would subsequently encounter a band of prophets coming down from a high place near Gibeah, that Saul would also prophesy, and that Saul would be sovereignly "changed into another person" (v. 6 NIV). God thereby demonstrated his sovereign ability not only to wholly foresee the future choices and actions of humans but also to change human hearts for his own purpose! We proceed at our own great peril if and when we foolishly and arrogantly assert that this is an ability the God of the universe possesses only occasionally.

If there could remain any shred of doubt about our almighty God's ability to foresee and foreknow the future, we should consider that Scripture states clearly and unequivocally that we who believe were chosen by God before the foundation of the world (Ephesians 1:4; 2 Timothy 1:9; 2 Thessalonians 2:13; 1 Thessalonians 1:4; 1 Peter 5:13; Romans 8:29–30; Romans 11:5, 11:7; Acts 15:17–18; John 15:16; 1 Peter 2:9). Therefore, God must have known about each of us in much detail before the foundation of the world. He knew that we would in fact exist, he knew when and how he would create us, and he knew when and how we would be born. It would be an absurdity to say that he made a choice before the foundation of the world about individuals that did not yet exist if he did not already know that they were going to exist! Furthermore, how could he know we would exist if he did not also have full and complete knowledge of the choices and actions of our mothers and fathers (and their parents too, and so on) as well as a perfect purpose for how these innumerable choices and actions would inevitably culminate in him creating blessed offspring from their union that he had chosen before the beginning of time?

The unavoidable conclusion is that because we know God chose us before the foundation of the world (Scripture tells us that repeatedly), we can also know that God knew exactly when, where, and how we would come to exist. "Known unto God are all his works from the beginning of the world," according to Acts 15:18 (KJV). Moreover, Romans 8:29 (NLT) states plainly that he "knew his people in advance," and this is clearly a relational and proactive foreknowledge carrying a profusely deeper meaning than that of merely knowing of our future existence or even our future deeds or choices. With this magnificent truth in view, that fact that our incredible God foreknows the future perfectly is just a small concept extracted from the much larger reality.

We have seen that if God *ever* knows something, then, of necessity, he *always* knew that thing, even before the foundation of the world. God is both perfect and outside of time, and he is not gaining knowledge as time progresses. In fact, time itself is his creation. When the Bible says that "Jesus knew their thoughts," Jesus "knew what was in man," or "Jesus knew from the beginning who they were that believed not and who should betray him" (Matthew 12:25; John 2:25; Luke 6:8; John 6:64 KJV), we must realize that he possessed this knowledge before the beginning of time. Further, the whole of biblical prophecy demands that God continually sees and knows the future in infinitely intricate detail, including even the choices that any given human will make on any given day. While the so-called open theists would dispute this assertion, much of the mainstream of Christianity today would have no quibble with the dogma that God knows the future in intricate detail.

The disagreement within the mainstream of today's church would likely come in a discussion of whether God is sovereign over each of these details and whether his will (his purpose) is accomplished in every choice we make and in every circumstance of our lives. Many would assert, unfortunately, that while God certainly foreknows all things, he willingly chooses not to control all things in the future. They suggest that he instead allows human free will to determine the future or perhaps allows humans to choose among alternate routes to a predetermined destination. While this assertion is perhaps more satisfying to human egotism and pride, upon further examination it nevertheless fails to resolve the underlying issues.

This failure is based on two key points. First, if God is indeed God and can actually foreknow the future in intricate detail and with complete accuracy, then he must therefore choose to allow what he foresees. Anything in the future that God foresees could never be characterized as "against his will," or, plainly, he would not allow it to happen—given that he has unlimited power and ability at his disposal to do and allow exactly what he wills and pleases (Psalm 115:3; 135:6; Daniel 4:35). As Jonathan Edwards pointed out, if God knows all events from the beginning of time, then he must either approve or disapprove of them; he must either be willing they should be or not willing that they should be. For God to will that they should be is to decree them, according to Edwards.[2] On the other hand, if it were not God's will for any event that he foresees to happen (even if it is his will to choose to allow an event to happen that is contrary to his stated commands), then he most certainly would change the course of history and make history happen according to his will.

As we have seen from the multitude of Scripture passages cited heretofore, history is most certainly unfolding according to our Father's perfect purpose and his perfect will. To suggest otherwise is to make humans sovereign and would require one to believe the unacceptable notion that God is forced to adapt his flawed plan to human choices he somehow failed to correctly anticipate. Furthermore, if God does not control and author the future, then by definition he would be powerless to change a foreknown event. The true God of the Bible has the unlimited power to simply speak his desires and will into existence, so if God were to foresee and foreknow events that are *not* in his will (at the highest level, including what he wills to permit) and they happen nonetheless, then he is not God at all! Fortunately, we can have the confidence that our God *is* truly God, and that our Father's will *is* always done.

The second problem with denying God's complete sovereignty and instead asserting that human choices and destinies are outside of God's purview—that God merely foreknows but does not exert his control—is that in the end the two views come to one and the same thing. The previously mentioned commentator Albert Barnes, speaking of Acts 2:23, pointed out that divine foreknowledge requires two things: omniscience and that the event itself be fixed and certain. He added the following comment:

> To foresee a contingent event, that is, to foresee that an event will take place when it may or may not take place, is an absurdity. Foreknowledge, therefore, implies that for some reason the event will certainly take place.[3]

For those that seek to incorrectly limit God by suggesting that he only foreknows the future (but is not sovereign over it), the mere existence of this admitted foreknowledge necessitates the existence of a future that is fixed and settled. As Barnes pointed out, even God could not make accurate predictions about an unsettled future, nor could we have any reasonable confidence in the ultimately perfect resolution of an unsettled future that is to be determined by humans rather than decreed by God.

One may well know the ending of a book one has not yet read without being sovereign over the ending of the book, but this is only possible because someone else has already written (created) the settled ending of the book. In other words, the ending is knowable because the ending exists for it to be known as a result of the author's efforts. If we accept that God knows the future and the ending (as demonstrated in Daniel or Revelation), we must then answer the question of who wrote (created) the book and the ending in order for them to be knowable. The only possible answers are God, humans, satanic forces, or nothing at all. There can be no other options.

If the answer is that nothing at all has determined the future and the ending, then our existence is mere chance and we have no hope—our existence is indeed random. Needless to say, the Bible eliminates this first possibility. We do not face a random future. In the beginning of John's vision of the future that is written in the book of Revelation, John was told, "Come up here, and I will show you what *must take place* after this" (Revelation 4:1). God has already determined what must take place, and this comforting fact precludes any possibility that our future is randomly determined.

Alternatively, to suggest the future or the ending is authored by the powers of darkness is of course outright blasphemy and sacrilege, so this second possibility is also eliminated. If we instead assert that humans freely and autonomously author their future and the end of the age, such a proposition would also make the future uncertain and therefore unknowable by God. Moreover, this is also completely untenable since the humans in question were not around to create either the future or the end of the age *before* they came to pass. For example, long before any of the humans associated with Christ's birth, life, and death were ever born, God had demonstrated his intimate knowledge of all of the details of Christ's future time on earth, including all of the choices and actions of the many human wills involved. These humans were not yet in existence to contribute their supposedly unknowable, unpredictable, autonomous free will to God's preexistent, perfect knowledge and eternal purpose. Likewise, long before any of the humans that will be associated with the events that will occur at the end of the age were born (or will be born), God has demonstrated his intimate knowledge of exactly how the age must end and how these events must unfold, inclusive of the innumerable associated human choices and actions.

Since random chance, satanic forces, and human free will are all eliminated as potential authors of the future and the ending of the age, it remains that only God can be the author. This is not surprising since that is exactly what the Bible teaches us. God knows the end of the book because he wrote the book! As such, if we are willing to go as far as to admit that God knows the future, it is therefore contradictory to suggest that the future is not fixed and knowable; furthermore, we must accept that it is our God who has authored this fixed and knowable future. This should thrill us! Our Father knows the future, and he alone is sovereign over the future. Because our loving Father wrote the book, we can have complete confidence in the perfect ending.

As was mentioned earlier, it would seem that virtually all Christians believe that God is omniscient, and we have also firmly established that he knows the future. Therefore, it follows that he knows what decisions each of us will make at any point in the future. This truth can be extended, and we must also acknowledge that God knows the exact day and moment when each of us will die, God knows exactly what each of us will eat for dinner on the second Tuesday of next November, God knows exactly what words each of us will speak to the first person we meet tomorrow, God knows who that person to whom we will speak will be, God knows where and when that person would be born so that they would even exist for us to be able to speak to them, and God also knows exactly how many times we will sneeze in October three years from now. Further, God has known *all* of these things from the very beginning of time! God has always known everything that is ever knowable. If it is knowable, it is therefore settled and certain; to assert otherwise is an untenable contradiction.

The modernist open theism doctrine would hold that God does not know the future, and the future is unknowable and variable because it has not happened yet. This doctrine is in direct contradiction to such passages as 1 Peter 1:1–2, which states plainly that God "foreknew" those who were elected for obedience and belief, or Ezekiel 38:10–11, where God declared directly what humans will think in the future and what they will choose to do. The New Living Translation paraphrase of Isaiah 46:10 also would seem to be quite troublesome for an open theist: "Only I can tell you the future before it even happens. Everything I plan will come to pass, for I do whatever I wish." Apparently, while the Bible states clearly that God knows the words we will speak before we speak them (Psalm 139:4), the open theists somehow believe that God cannot know our choices before we make them. Presumably, unless they reject Psalm 139:4, they must believe that the words we speak are not results of choices we make about what to speak. This sort of doctrine should strike us as absolute human-centered foolishness!

These may seem harsh words, but it is quite clear upon even a cursory examination of the Bible that God knew and accurately predicted countless things before they happened, and he knows and has predicted many other things that are yet to come. This divine knowledge has always encompassed the smallest details, including the choices that humans would make at any point in the future. For instance, we would do well to recall that God gave Jeroboam the ten northern tribes in advance based on the choice Rehoboam would make years in the future, and God also knew in advance the choices, actions, and words of the multiple men that would meet Saul after Saul was anointed.

As another example, consider that God showed Joseph in two separate dreams that his eleven brothers and his father would all eventually bow down to him of their own free will as the inevitable result of free choices made by the eleven brothers and the many other human wills involved in the narrative (Genesis 37:1–11). These dreams from God were many years before any of the events actually happened. Both Joseph's brothers and his father rebuked him when he shared these dreams from the Lord, but the future nevertheless came about exactly as God predicted (Genesis 42:6, 8). Furthermore, Scripture tells us that the human choices that God predicted and anticipated in the dreams were actually choices that he would bring about to accomplish his own good purpose (Genesis 45:5–8; Psalm 105:16–17).

Likewise, God chose and anointed David as king over all of Israel years before the people of either Judah or the other tribes of Israel actually made him their king by their own free wills (1 Samuel 16:1–13; 2 Chronicles 6:5–6; 2 Samuel 2:4; 2 Samuel 5:1–4). This initial choice by God which preceded the choices of humans is hugely significant, and it is devastating to the notions of the open theists. If God merely knew the people of Judah and later Israel would choose David to be their king, then the open theists are wrong because God can accurately foreknow human choices. On the other hand, if God actually worked sovereignly to make David king of Israel, then the open theists are even more wrong because God controls human destinies through human free choice. As it happens, the latter is actually scripturally correct. The people of Israel freely chose David to be their king "according to the word of the Lord" (1 Chronicles 11:3).

The open theists nevertheless cite such passages as Genesis 3:9, where God called to Adam, "Where are you?" They also point to Genesis 22:12, where God told Abraham, "Now I know that you fear God" after Abraham had demonstrated that he was willing to obey God and sacrifice Isaac. They would claim such passages are scriptural evidence that God does not know all things at all times and that he cannot fully know the future. I believe it to be an insulting characterization of our almighty, omnipresent, omniscient God to suggest that he did not already know Adam's location as he called out to him, and it is equally shameful to claim that God had no idea whether Abraham would obey as God told him to sacrifice Isaac in order to provide us a beautiful foreshadowing picture of Jesus' substitutionary atonement. These notions are so despicable as to hardly merit serious consideration—and yet this theology is making considerable inroads into mainstream Christianity today. I suspect this is possible only because we have already watered down the sovereignty of God and elevated the supposed sovereignty of humanity and human free will to the extent that this logical extension of that existing erosion of truth fails to trigger the alarm that it justly deserves. Rather than being instantly recognized as outright heresy bordering on blasphemy, open theism is given serious consideration because the church is already well down the road of ripping sovereignty from God and handing it to humans who are only too delighted to accept such "empowering" doctrines. The real truth is that if God is capable of knowing even one thing in the future (and the Bible is full of passages that exhibit God's knowledge of specific future events *and* human "free" choices), then the future is quite obviously completely knowable by God.

We must never surrender this high view of our God! Stephen Charnock was an English clergyman and a Cambridge scholar who wrote a breathtaking, classic masterpiece on the attributes of our awesome God—an incredible discourse spanning nearly 800 pages. Charnock powerfully denounced those who would even consider limiting God's perfect knowledge of the future: "But what if the foreknowledge of God and the liberty of the will cannot be fully reconciled by man? Shall we therefore deny a perfection in God to support a liberty in ourselves? Shall we rather fasten ignorance upon God, and accuse him of blindness, to maintain our liberty?"[4]

With these compelling words in mind, we should give serious contemplation to our exalted Father's demonstrated capabilities before we hastily embrace doctrines that appeal to our built-in desire for human aggrandizement but in the process strip God of divine abilities he has plainly manifested. Before we suggest that God cannot know human choices before they occur, we should consider that Jesus told his disciples in detail that he would be mocked, scourged, spit upon, and killed, and he told them about this long before evil men ever chose to do these things to him (Mark 10:34). We also read in John 6:5 that Jesus asked Philip, "Where are we to buy bread, so that these people may eat?" We must realize that this question is not any different than God calling to Adam, "Where are you?" (Genesis 3:9). In both cases, God the Father and God the Son knew the answer before the question was ever posed to the human. In the case of Jesus' question to Philip in John 6 before he miraculously fed five thousand people, verse 6 gives us the direct biblical affirmation of what should be an obvious fact about our omniscient Savior: "He said this to test him, for he himself knew what he would do." Indeed, Jesus repeatedly demonstrated his ability to foresee the future (including human choices) during his ministry, yet these shameless modernist theologians do not hesitate to deny that he has the very same power today!

In another exhibition of complete, detailed foreknowledge of human choices destined to occur even further in the future, God predicted in 1 Kings 13:2 through a prophet identified only as "the man of God" that a son would be born to the house of David hundreds of years in the future. God even named this future ruler of Judah by name, predicting the existence of Josiah long before even Josiah's parents were ever born. Furthermore, God demonstrated his complete sovereignty by sharing in advance his knowledge of this future king's choices and actions, proclaiming that the yet-unborn Josiah would one day burn human bones on the abhorrent altar that Jeroboam had constructed. These prophesies were eventually fulfilled, of course, and Josiah's actions can be found in 2 Kings 23:15–18.

God knew the choices and actions of Josiah's parents before they ever existed, God knew that he was going to create a human soul in the womb of Jedidah that would be named Josiah upon its birth, and God also knew the choices and actions of Josiah before Josiah ever existed. It should be equally obvious that our incredible God did not just foresee these choices and actions, but he actually brought them to pass (Isaiah 46:10; Ezekiel

39:8). In any case, the certainty of the foreseen events taking place was guaranteed by God's inerrant, complete knowledge of the future. There was absolutely no possibility that a king of Judah named Josiah would not be born at God's predetermined time, and there was no contingency that this predicted king would carry out anything other than the actions that God had proclaimed in this passage. The future was fixed and certain according to God's knowledge and his words through this "man of God" we see in 1 Kings 13. This is our God! He pronounces, "My glory I give to no other," and he proclaims, "See, the former things have taken place, and new things I declare; before they spring into being I announce them to you" (Isaiah 42:8–9). We must never strip our Father of the glory that is due him by asserting that his knowledge and control of the future is limited in any way.

Nevertheless, the open theists also cite such passages as Exodus 32:14, Genesis 6:6, Jeremiah 18:7–11, or Jonah 3:10 in which God is said to "relent" or change his declared course of action, claiming that these verses prove that God changes his mind in response to human actions. The irreverent silliness of this latter statement notwithstanding, we should consider that these human actions that are said to change God's mind must have been either fully anticipated by God or not anticipated by God—there can be no other possibilities. It should be obvious that if human actions and choices are fully foreknown and anticipated by God, then it is completely irrational and implausible to suggest that God changes his mind or his will in any way because the events he anticipated all along actually come to pass; that would be a complete absurdity. Therefore, the only way that the open theists' assertion could be even remotely plausible would be to assert that God is not capable of anticipating human choices and human actions, and that is indeed the near-blasphemous charge the open theists lay upon our omniscient Father. The critical realization to be made is that if we are to believe that God actually changes his mind and his plan in response to human actions or choices, these actions and choices must necessarily be actions and choices that he neither foresees nor anticipates. As if that were not bad enough, God's sovereignty over these future actions and choices is equally precluded by the open theism doctrine.

This realization should settle the matter and end the discussion, but unfortunately it does not, as many join with the open theists and continue to believe that God does indeed change his mind in response to human actions and choices. The open theists thereby trade an infinite, ascendant

God for a finite, manmade idol only resembling the true God—this in order to aggrandize human free will. This is a foolish exchange, and the price is much higher than we can possibly imagine. It is therefore no wonder we see such little faith and such great worry in our churches today; it is this incorrect belief that destroys the perceived reliability of our Father.

The inseparable connection between our God's unlimited sovereignty over the future and his complete reliability is not merely a new theory for our consideration. Rather, in Isaiah 46:8 God declared, "Remember this and *stand firm.*" What was God telling us that we should remember in order to be able to stand firm? The immediately following verses provide us the foundation upon which we may indeed stand firm: he is the only true God (v. 9); he has decreed the end (the future) since the beginning (v. 10); he has declared the future since ancient times (v. 11); his purpose will certainly be accomplished (vv. 10–11), and his counsel for the future is not subject to change (vv. 10–11). Praise our magnificent Father! If we are to stand firm, we must always remember these great truths and never surrender them at the altar of human free will.

We see repeatedly in Scripture that God correctly foreknows and anticipates the future, including human choices and actions, and we have already considered many such examples in this writing. If, therefore, we know that God can sometimes foresee and anticipate human choices and actions, but we are forced to also believe that sometimes he *cannot* foresee and anticipate human choices and actions (a necessary supposition if he is believed to change his mind in response to unanticipated choices), then we have absolutely no way to rely on his omniscience or on his promises. If God promises us one thing based on an incomplete knowledge of the future, then we must accept that at any time that promise may have to be withdrawn because of changes in circumstances that God could not anticipate.

In other words, if we believe God can only foresee and anticipate the future some of the time, then we can never be sure whether our current circumstance is included in God's knowledge and purpose or not, and we have thereby inadvertently created an unreliable, nonsovereign God of our own design, much to our detriment. Worse yet, we may well pay lip service to his sovereignty and his reliability and yet, deep in our hearts, struggle with the conflict created by our concealed belief in his unreliability born of his inability to totally foresee and anticipate the future. In so doing, we never realize the great damage we have caused to our faith and to our relationship with our Father who wants us to trust him completely with our entire heart and soul.

If we are willing to discard our doctrinal prejudices, it really is not difficult to totally resolve these matters. Taking Exodus 32 as an example, God told Moses in verse 10 that he was going to destroy the entire Israelite nation in response to their egregious sin of making a golden calf and that he would make a great nation from Moses instead. In verses 11 to 13, Moses interceded beautifully for the Israelite people, and in verse 14, we are told that God relented from his threatened destruction of his people. It would seem that God changed his mind from verse 10 to verse 14 in response to Moses' eminently commendable prayer, apparently proving the open theists' point outright. However, such thinking is quite shortsighted.

We should first realize that God is greater than humans, and his ways are higher than our ways (Isaiah 55:9); it is as a gracious act of accommodating love that God interacts with humans on a human level in terms to which humans can relate, including the chronological cause-and-effect nature of time itself. In this passage, from a human chronological perspective, the people's sin preceded God's threat, and this led to Moses' prayer, which preceded God's relenting. This account is therefore clearly anthropomorphic—a big term that refers to the ascribing of human characteristics to God—in this case for the benefit of our own limited human understanding. This concept might be best explained by considering God's words to Moses only shortly after this event. In Numbers 10, God told Moses to make a pair of silver trumpets and directed that these trumpets should be sounded before going into battle and when offerings were made at the tabernacle. We read that these trumpets, when blown, would cause the Lord to "remember" his people as they went into battle (v. 9). Similarly, as the people made their offerings, the trumpets were said to "remind the Lord your God of his covenant with you" (v. 10 NLT) or be "a reminder of you before your God" (ESV, NASB). Can there be any reasonable suggestion that an omniscient, perfect God might have forgotten something he knew previously? Can we believe for a moment that our eternally faithful God could ever need reminding of his own people or his own covenant? No, the language used is anthropomorphic, and the trumpets were clearly for humankind's benefit, in actuality to remind them that the Lord was remembering them.

Likewise, in the case of the golden calf, there was in actuality no portion of this series of events that took God by surprise. God, who operates outside of time, knew that the Israelites would rebel with the idolatrous golden calf while he was giving Moses the law; in fact, he knew this before he took them out of Egypt. He knew that he would threaten to destroy them. He knew that Moses would offer intercessory prayer. He knew that he would hear that prayer and reverse his previously stated intention. In short, it all went according to plan! According to Ephesians 1:11 (NLT), we could expect nothing less: "He makes everything work out according to his plan."

We cannot fully know why God purposed for these events to unfold as they did. We can, however, see that in so doing he brought much glory to himself by demonstrating that while these chosen people justly deserved death, he sovereignly chose to show them mercy instead. Of course, this very theme is repeated often throughout history, and it is a marvelous picture of how God shows mercy to each of us as his chosen when what we deserve as a matter of divine justice is death. We see additionally that Moses's intercessory prayer is a wonderful illustration of how the Holy Spirit intercedes for us before our Father in heaven (Romans 8:26). Moreover, there can be no doubt that God's purpose and the reasons for his actions ran far deeper than these two simple observations.

To suggest that this series of events concerning the golden calf did not unfold according to God's purpose is to make God less than God, as we have seen. We can be sure that God is not fickle and prone to changing his mind as a fit of anger subsides (2 Timothy 2:13; Numbers 23:19; 1 Samuel 15:29; Psalm 89:34). Indeed, it would be blasphemy to suggest such a thing. He does not change his mind, and in fact that is *exactly* why the people were *not* consumed (Malachi 3:6). He did not change his mind and "un-choose" the people because of their great sin and then "re-choose" them because of Moses' great prayer. In fact, he had chosen them with full knowledge that this sin would eventually take place. Likewise, we can be equally sure that Moses did not suggest a better idea to an all-knowing, all-wise God, an idea that had somehow not previously occurred to God! Instead, once again, we see that all things happened according to God's knowledge and purpose. God was not taken by surprise; he did as he pleased, just as Psalm 135:6 demands.

If these conclusions should seem to be mere speculation, we should very briefly consider the ramifications if God had actually purposed to wipe out the Israelites and make a great nation of Moses instead. In short, Moses was a Levite, and any nation composed exclusively of his offspring would obviously be an entirely Levite nation. The largest problem with this is that the incarnate Jesus was to be from the tribe of Judah, not Levi, as had already been prophetically spoken by Israel (Jacob) in Genesis 49:8–10. All the details of the plan of redemption had been set in place before the foundation of the world (1 Peter 1:20; Revelation 13:8; 2 Timothy 1:9). God's purpose for redemption in Christ is specifically labeled as an "eternal purpose" in Ephesians 3:9–11, which means it necessarily existed before the foundation of the world and the creation of mankind. God could not have exterminated the tribe of Judah without invalidating his own perfect purpose and his own unchanging word. It is no coincidence that this was the thrust of Moses' prayer.

Furthermore, we can know that God had ordained that the twelve tribes survive because we see that the twelve gates of the New Jerusalem described in Revelation 21:12 are named after the twelve tribes of Israel, and we see twelve thousand individuals from each of the twelve tribes of Israel (less Dan) sealed unto God in Revelation 7. While the tribes in the latter case may be either literal or figurative, the fact remains that it would not be likely that God would be sealing individuals from all twelve tribes if he had exterminated eleven of them before they ever reached the Promised Land. Jesus also referenced the integral nature of the twelve tribes to God's eternal plan when he told his disciples in Matthew 19:28 that they would eventually sit on twelve thrones and judge the twelve tribes of Israel.

When all is considered, it becomes apparent that the account of the golden calf actually proves the exact opposite of the open theists' argument since it demands a God who will reliably accomplish his purpose for his chosen people according to his perfect, all-inclusive, eternal plan, completely undeterred by human free will choices. He is mighty enough that his purpose will never be thwarted by the rebellion of sinful humans. What folly that the open theists would brazenly suggest that the same God who could know and predict hundreds of years in advance that Judas would betray Jesus for thirty pieces of silver (Zechariah 11:12–13; Psalm 41:9) could not possibly know or anticipate even forty days in advance that the Israelites would rebel in idolatry with a golden calf, and instead our omniscient God was taken by surprise by their sinful actions!

It is true that the Bible does not state directly that God knew the Israelites would rebel with the golden calf. Nevertheless, Scripture does teach us unequivocally that God possesses this ability, so it is foolish for the open theists to suggest that God did not know of this sinful human choice in advance or that these events did not unfold according to God's eternal purpose. Should any doubt this, the Bible *does* give us a direct confirmation of God's ability to foresee sinful human choices in advance, this only a little over forty years later in the history of the Israelites. God had preserved the Israelites in the desert for forty years (Deuteronomy 29:5), and they now stood ready to enter the Promised Land. In Deuteronomy 28 through 30, we read three entire chapters dedicated to enumerating God's perpetual blessings should the Israelites obey his covenant and the inevitable curses should the Israelites be disobedient. It seems that both options were available to the Israelites, and it is true that they would no doubt make choices that would be either obedient or disobedient.

However, this extended discourse on blessings for obedience and curses for disobedience notwithstanding, God made it clear that he already knew (unerringly, of course) that the Israelites would not choose obedience. God told Moses in Deuteronomy 31:16–17 that "this people will rise and whore after the foreign gods among them in the land they are entering, and they will forsake me and break my covenant that I have made with them. Then my anger will be kindled against them in that day, and I will forsake them and hide my face from them, and they will be devoured." Again, in verse 20, God said, "They will turn to other gods and serve them, and despise me and break my covenant." In verse 29, Moses said to the people, "I know that after my death you will surely act corruptly and turn aside from the way that I have commanded you."

Just as God knew the Israelites would build a golden calf while he was giving Moses the law, God also knew the Israelites would forsake the covenant after he gave them the Promised Land. If God is truly God, then we must believe that his eternal purpose cannot be deterred or changed by such fully anticipated disobedience. In fact, Jesus' death was necessary because God knew the Israelites *would not* keep the old covenant. Moreover, God knew the Israelites *could not* keep the old covenant (Acts 13:39; Romans 7; 3:20; 8:3, 7–8), and Jesus' death was therefore planned before the foundation of the world (1 Peter 1:20; Matthew 25:34). Said another way, notwithstanding the protracted promises for obedience and curses for disobedience that God outlined in Deuteronomy 28 to 30, there never was even the faintest possibility that the Jews would still be obediently sacrificing bulls, obeying the old covenant to the letter, and living in God's promised, trustworthy blessings for such obedience in the year 10 BC, much less the year 2000 AD. Instead, it all went according to God's eternal plan—a realization that should make Gentile believers today overflow with gratitude, just as Paul outlined in Romans 11. We should glory and worship in the fact that God's knowledge is completely inclusive of all future human choices, sinful or not, and God's purpose will nevertheless always be fulfilled.

God's knowledge is indeed limitless. Not only does he know the entirety of the actual future, his knowledge also extends to the contingent future—to the alternate future that could have only happened if he had allowed the actual future to unfold differently. This is illustrated concisely in 1 Samuel 23:10–14, where God answered David's inquiry regarding what his enemies would do in the future. God stated specifically what various humans would decide of their own free will in the future, as well as what their actions would be in the future *if* David were to remain in Keilah. This account makes it clear that God can foresee not only the actual future actions and choices of humans but also the contingent choices that he knows will *not* happen (in this case because he also knew David would not stay in Keilah). Furthermore, we also see in verse 14 that Saul's freely chosen, tenacious, and protracted efforts to kill David were not successful simply because "God did not give him into his hand." Saul's free will, not surprisingly, was not able to accomplish that which was adverse to God's will and that which was contrary to God's knowledge and established purpose that David was God's anointed servant to succeed Saul as king in the future. This passage may be small, but it is far from inconsequential in that it provides us with a remarkable glimpse into our amazing, omniscient God's infinite power and infinite abilities.

As another example, pulled from what seem to be countless biblical examples, God predicted the downfall of Egypt in Ezekiel 29. God pronounced that he would use Nebuchadnezzar to "desolate" Egypt, and Egypt would be uninhabited for forty years. At the end of forty years, God said, he would gather the Egyptians back from where he had scattered them and restore them to their land. However, God also said that he would make the restored nation a "lowly" nation, a nation that will "never again exalt itself" over other nations or rule over the nations. Nebuchadnezzar most certainly, at some point, made a "free" choice to invade and plunder Egypt, probably not knowing at all that his choice was the will of God and that he was being used as the instrument of God in accomplishing God's purpose. God not only specifically stated what would happen both at the beginning and the end of the forty-year period, but he also announced what would be the fate of Egypt for the remainder of history. Egypt will "never again" be an exalted, ruling nation (v. 15). There are no contingencies available to the people of Egypt by which that will ever happen. Therefore, from this passage alone, we know that God can and does foreknow human choices (as well as that he is sovereign over those choices), and these choices are indeed knowable. The passage also shows that God can and does foreknow the results of those choices, and even very specific timings (e.g., forty years) are both foreknown to him and under his control. God is indeed "sovereign over the kingdoms of men" (Daniel 4:32 NIV).

God is also sovereign over the realm of heaven, and he has prepared a specific place for each of its eventual inhabitants. In Matthew 20:20–23 (and also Mark 10:35–40), James and John asked Jesus to grant to them the right to sit on thrones to the left and the right of Jesus in heaven. In no uncertain terms, Jesus replied, "To sit at my right hand and at my left is not mine to grant, but it is for those for whom it has been prepared by my Father." Clearly, Jesus was not saying that he would have no role or participation in the judgments and rewards in heaven since we know from many other passages that he will certainly be central to these matters (Acts 10:42; 2 Corinthians 5:10; John 5:22–30; Matthew 25:31–46). Jesus' point was that our Father's eternal purpose and decrees have already determined who will sit in these positions. There are not contingencies available by which these seats might be awarded to other persons (or beings) since God's purpose is fixed forever (Psalm 119:89), and he is not going to change his mind. Stated another way, Jesus was saying that the future had already been sovereignly fixed by his beloved Father.

It is commonly and accurately said that "there will be no empty mansions in heaven." Jesus indeed said he would go and prepare a place for us (John 14:2–3), and Matthew 25:34 speaks of the place prepared for believers from the creation of the world. There could be no rational suggestion that Jesus is preparing places in heaven for people that he knows will never show up! God declares emphatically that his word (his purpose, his decree, his works) will not return to him empty, but it will perfectly accomplish its intended purpose (Isaiah 55:11). As such, we should know that our preeminent God's preparations could never be futile, wasted efforts, nor could our Father ever prepare a place in error or in vain. If a mansion is prepared for a person, then God will make certain he or she is there to inhabit it.

Jesus himself said in verse 3 of John 14 that if he prepared a place, he would also come back and get the person for whom he had prepared the place; these words directly preclude the possibility of a place being prepared for one who is not eventually going to be brought to heaven, and they further demand Jesus' full and complete knowledge and control of the future. Were there empty mansions or empty thrones in heaven, these would be a perpetual, sorrowful memorial to either God's inability to fill these places or his inability to foresee that these people were not coming. Either of these is obviously sacrilege. Furthermore, how could there be unmitigated joy not marred by sorrow in heaven if such constant reminders of the loved ones whose places are perpetually empty were always before us? No, the places prepared in heaven will all be filled in accordance with God's perfect, unerring knowledge of the future and his determined will to accomplish his eternal purpose. God knows who will inhabit heaven, and he has always known who will inhabit heaven. We should either rise to our feet or fall on our faces and offer unbounded gratitude mixed with immense praise to our glorious, loving, powerful Father because he guarantees that our future is heading our way!

Having established beyond all doubt that the future is knowable and is indeed known fully by our great God, we must make some very interesting, compelling observations that come from this realization. As was mentioned earlier, the culmination of the matter is that the two views on whether God is wholly sovereign over the future or merely inerrantly knowledgeable about the future end up coming to one and the same thing, at least in terms of the future being fixed and certain. For example, if it is knowable what clothes we will choose to wear to church next week, then it must follow that there is no chance that we will, in the end, choose to wear anything else but what God already knows we will choose to wear. God cannot ever know wrong! God's knowledge is indeed perfect—a reality assumed by Elihu to be a simple, common fact in Job 37:16.

Concerning a matter of much greater importance than our clothing choices, if we believe that God knows exactly when and how each of us will die, then is there any chance or possibility at all that we can take any action or make any "free" choice that will result in us dying at any other time or in any other manner than the time at which God already knows we will die? If God already knows it, he is never wrong. This fact renders the question, at least in this context, of whether God controls the future or merely foreknows the future (without controlling it) completely moot. The established fact that God knows our eventual destiny (including the smallest details and including every choice that we will freely make) inescapably means that this destiny is already set and that the future will most certainly come to pass exactly as God already knows it to be. Further, God's perfect will is to *allow* the future as he already foreknows it because his perfect purpose will always be accomplished. On the other hand, if our destiny were subject to change based on our own choices or actions, or anybody else's choices or actions, then God could never know the future because it would be unknowable until it happened and the open theists would be correct. Or, stated another way, if God has total knowledge of the future (and the Bible is clear that he does), then the future is already set according to his will and is not subject to change.

Martin Luther expounded on this truth in his response to Erasmus, writing these powerful words regarding the connection between God's perfect will and God's foreknowledge of the future:

> You openly declare that the immutable will of God is to be known, but you forbid the knowledge of his immutable prescience [foreknowledge]. Do you believe that he foreknows against his will, or that he wills in ignorance? If then, he foreknows, willing, his will is eternal and immovable, because his nature is so: and, if he wills, foreknowing, his knowledge is eternal and immovable, because his nature is so.
>
> From which it follows unalterably, that all things which we do, although they may appear to us to be done mutably and contingently, and even may be done thus contingently by us, are yet, in reality, done necessarily and immutably, with respect to the will of God. For the will of God is effective and cannot be hindered; because the very power of God is natural to him, and his wisdom is such that he cannot be deceived. And as his will cannot be hindered, the work itself cannot be hindered from being done in the place, at the time, in the measure, and by whom he foresees and wills.[5]

The compelling truth of these words eliminates any possibility of the validity of the oft-repeated analogy to a video game. In this analogy, it is asserted by some that God does not know what path we will take; rather, he only knows where we will end up. We cannot artificially limit God's power and foreknowledge in such a manner by contending that God does not know in advance which path we will choose to follow or exactly where we will be and what we will be doing at any precise moment in the future. To do so is to remove our basis for completely trusting in our Father, in his purpose, and in his love for us. We are left instead with the simple, wondrous fact that, just like Rehoboam, we will always freely choose our destiny, and this free choice will be the destiny that God both knew and willed before the foundation of the world.

This reasoning, as well as its inescapable conclusion, is not merely an extended exercise in logical thinking; rather, it is an issue with major implications in the formation of a proper concept of God. Psalm 139:16 is abundantly clear when it states, "In your book were written, every one of them, the days that were formed for me, when as yet there was none of them." This Scripture is much too powerful to ignore, but that is exactly what many do! The meaning is clear: every single one of our days—yes, all of them—are written in God's book and "formed for us" before we are ever born and before the very first day ever happens. "No man has the power to retain the spirit, or power over the day of death" (Ecclesiastes 8:8). How then do we as humans think we can usurp God's sovereign role and claim that it is we and our choices that are writing the story of our lives when God says that the story was written before we were ever born? If the days were "formed for us" by another and written in God's book before we were born, then *who* did the forming and the writing? It seems clear that since we were not even around to make the choices and do the writing, it is a foolish attempt to wrongfully ascend to the throne belonging to God alone when we claim that we are the authors and controllers of our own destinies.

Interestingly enough, while Psalm 139:16 teaches us that the days that are formed for us are all written before we are ever born, other scriptural passages might lead to the opposite conclusion. For example, Deuteronomy 5:16 teaches us that we should honor our parents so that our days may be long on the earth, and this is referred to as "the first commandment with a promise" in Ephesians 6:2. Proverbs 3:2 and 3:16 also instruct us that choosing to walk in God's commands and God's wisdom will add years to our lives. This superficial inconsistency notwithstanding, we can be sure that Scripture does not contradict itself, so the source of any contradiction is to be found within our own finite, human understanding. As we should expect, the fact is that *all* of the passages are true. God teaches that certain things will contribute to long life, and he teaches that the lengths of our lives were determined long before we were born. This apparent contradiction disappears completely when we realize the basic fact that God decrees the means as well as the ends.[6] Quite simply, if God decrees that a person will live seventy-three years and twenty-six days, then we can know that he will also decree the means by which that eventuality will certainly occur, including details such as whether that person will honor his or her parents. This must be true if our God is truly God. As Luther wrote, what appears to be contingent to us, and may even be done contingently by us, is necessity to God.

If this is difficult for us to accept, we must realize that to believe otherwise is to assert that God's will can be thwarted and that God's purpose is not trustworthy because it is quite possible, if not highly probable, that someone could hinder or confound it at any moment. We can rejoice that this could never be the case; God's decrees are trustworthy! (Psalm 93:5). No purpose of God's can be thwarted! (Job 42:2). Instead, it is the glorious realization that God decrees the means as well as the ends, including the smallest of details, which allows us to be totally confident in our Father's loving purpose for us and remain contentedly assured that this purpose will certainly be accomplished.

This fact certainly was not lost on the apostle Paul, who wrote that God "set me [Paul] apart before I was born" (Galatians 1:15–16). In fact, the Lord himself told Ananias that Paul had been chosen by God for God's purpose (Acts 9:16; 22:14). Paul related in Acts 22:10 that God had "appointed" this purpose for him, and he walked confidently in what he called an "eternal" purpose for his life (Ephesians 3:7–13; Galatians 1:1; Romans 1:1–2). Many years before, Isaiah likewise asserted that God had called him from within his mother's womb to be God's servant and that God had a very specific purpose for him—to bring back Jacob and to be a light for the nations (Isaiah 49:1–6). In a similar fashion, the Lord told Jeremiah directly that he had elected and set apart Jeremiah for *his* own purpose before Jeremiah was ever born (Jeremiah 1:5). It is in no way unique to John the Baptist, Paul, Isaiah, and Jeremiah that God had chosen them and written their purpose before they were ever born. We are no different; each of us was also chosen by God, and God had a specific purpose for choosing us—a fact that should fill us with unfathomable, unending delight when we come to grasp its great significance.

Paul told us in 1 Corinthians 8:6 that we exist because of God, and, more importantly, we exist *for* God. We can be confident that God chose us, much as he chose John the Baptist, Paul, Isaiah, and Jeremiah, because 2 Thessalonians 2:13 (NASB), 2 Timothy 1:9, and Ephesians 1:4 make it clear that each believer was "chosen…from the beginning for salvation" by God the Father for his own purpose. Additionally, Romans 8:29 (NLT) states that "God knew his people in advance and he chose them," and we are further assured of our Father's purpose for us when we read in Ephesians 2:10 that we believers are God's workmanship, created to do good works that were prepared "beforehand" for each of us that we might "walk in them." Moreover, according to Ephesians 3:10–11, this purpose is an "eternal purpose," to which we can all proclaim, "I cry out to God Most High, to God who fulfills his purpose for me!" (Psalm 57:2).

Charles Spurgeon rejoiced in this glorious truth, and he preached that we should be encouraged and live confidently because "things are not left to chance: no blind fate rules the world." He continued, "God hath purposes, and those purposes are fulfilled." Spurgeon aptly described the ramifications of this wonderful truth with this beautiful metaphor: "The blessed truth of providence is one of the softest pillows upon which the Christian can lay his head, and one of the strongest staffs upon which he may lean in his pilgrimage along this rough road."[7] There is indeed great comfort for the taking in this realization that it is our loving Father who holds our future and that the details of our lives are left neither to chance nor to human whims. As Paul, we should "lay hold of that for which also I was laid hold of by Christ Jesus" (Philippians 3:12 NASB). These are magnificent fundamentals to be embraced and cherished, not threatening doctrines to be resisted, and we would do well to appropriate these truths as both our abiding comfort and our unshakable hope.

CHAPTER 6

OUR LOVING FATHER GOD, OR THE GREAT PUPPETEER?

I have loved you with an everlasting love; therefore I have continued my faithfulness to you.

– JEREMIAH 31:3

When the human will feels that its throne is threatened by a superior being, defensive measures inevitably follow. This defense often takes the form of challenges or accusations designed to call into question the integrity, wisdom, and goodness of its own Creator. Perhaps subconsciously, it is felt that the throne can be retained if it is asserted strongly enough that God's true nature or his sovereign actions unfairly demean human freedom. It is thereby justified that another God may be substituted who supposedly dutifully "respects human free will." For example, it might be argued by some that if our days have already been written for us (as was examined in the previous chapter, Psalm 139:14–16), and we can be certain that God will fulfill his purpose for us, the very purpose for which he created us (Psalm 57:2), then we are little more than robots under God's direction. Or, some might argue that if the host of Scriptures that were considered in the previous chapter concerning the infinite reaches of God's knowledge and the immutability of God's purpose are reliably true and actually mean what they say, then we are merely puppets that have no truly meaningful existence.

However, challenges such as these reflect a profound lack of understanding of God's great love for us as his chosen people, the amazing bounty of his mercy and grace he lavishes upon us, and the incredible gift of *will* that is given to humans but not to puppets or robots. In fact, the mere suggestion that God's supremacy over his own creation could make us puppets or robots is indeed a remarkable accusation and a quite brazen one at that. Consider that our Father, of his own divine free will and because of his great love for his chosen people whom he "appointed to eternal life" (Acts 13:48; 2 Timothy 1:9), seeks us out and draws us to himself (Ezekiel 34:11, 15–16; Isaiah 65:1; Hosea 2:14, 6; John 6:44), chooses to redeem us by paying our ransom price (Titus 2:14; Galatians 3:13–14), delivers us from the domain of darkness (Colossians 1:13), sets us free from the slavery and death of sin (Ephesians 2:5; Romans 6:17–18; Colossians 2:13) that makes it impossible for us to choose him (Romans 8:7; 1 Corinthians 1:18; 2 Corinthians 4:3–6; Colossians 1:21; Jeremiah 13:23), gives us a heart of flesh that will seek him, believe, and choose right (Ezekiel 11:19–20; Ezekiel 36:22–28; Jeremiah 32:39–40; 1 Thessalonians 1:4–5), and gives us by his grace the gift of saving faith that we could not muster ourselves (Ephesians 2:8–9; Romans 3:10–11) by himself calling into being the faith that did not exist (Romans 4:17), thereby giving us the power to become Sons of God (John 1:12), to possess life, and to live it more abundantly (John 10:10), and then, somehow, amazingly, we have the nerve to shrug our shoulders and suggest that all of this makes us "just robots"? God have mercy on us!

Since when did setting someone free from slavery and bondage become an encroachment upon that person's freedom and will? By so doing, is that person robbed of the freedom and ability to choose, or rather empowered with freedom and ability to choose? Augustine said, "Freedom of the will is not obliterated by grace, but is established, because grace heals the will, and thereby righteousness is freely loved."[1] How did we ever come to consider raising someone from the dead a violation of that person's freedom to remain dead? Jesus did not wait for Lazarus to choose to come forth and be raised from the dead; rather, he called him forth by name when Lazarus was not able to choose to do so himself. Could a dead Lazarus choose to believe Jesus would raise him, or was he actually dead? Are we any different than Lazarus or the dead bones that God called to life in Ezekiel 37? Paul stated in Ephesians 2:1–7 that we too were dead in sin, carrying out only the sinful desires of the body, our wills controlled by the "prince of the power of the air," and our nature being that of "children of wrath" just "like the rest of mankind" until, "even while we were dead," God "made us alive together with Christ," this "because of the great love" that he has for us.

We need to fully realize and grasp that this quickening, resurrecting "great love" to which Paul referred is not a general, nonspecific love for those that happen to be lucky enough to "find him," but rather an individual, supreme, effectual love for each of his chosen that has existed since before the foundation of the world (Ephesians 1:4–5). By raising our will from the dead, God does not violate our free will at all, nor does he create a robot; rather, he enables and causes us to exercise our will to freely choose him. When God sovereignly turns a heart of stone that is not seeking him into a heart of flesh that will seek him (Ezekiel 36:25-27) or "puts the fear of me [God] into their hearts, that they *may not* turn from me" (Jeremiah 32:40), he is not creating robots; rather, he is creating a people of which he proudly says, "They will by my people, and I will be their God" (Hebrews 8:10; Jeremiah 32:38). Indeed, our loving Father declares, "I will give them a heart to know that I am the Lord" (Jeremiah 24:7). Praise his holy name!

It is widely accepted (correctly so, I believe) that God's actions in bringing the Israelites out of bondage in Egypt are also a picture of our own salvation, an analogy of God's work and actions in our own hearts. As such, we can learn from God's account of his motives and actions in saving the Israelites, which he gave as a first-person narrative in Ezekiel 20. In this chapter, we learn that while the Israelites were certainly in inescapable bondage from which they could not just choose to leave, they were nevertheless not righteous, innocent people trapped in slavery; they were actually idolaters engaged in practices that were detestable to God. In verses 5 and 6, we see that God *chose* the Israelites while they were still in this bondage and sin, and he promised to bring them into the Promised Land. Their response to that gracious calling (v. 7) and promise was to "rebel" (v. 8) and to continue in their idol worship and detestable practices (v. 8).

If these people were puppets, they were certainly exceedingly rebellious puppets. Rather than pour out on them the wrath and destruction that he declared their rebellion and idolatry justly deserved (v. 8), God instead sovereignly acted to save a chosen people (v. 10, v. 5) who were not seeking him, serving him, or willing to listen to him (v. 8; Exodus 6:9). According to verse 9, this salvation was for the sake of his own glory and his own name. He saved those whom he chose when they had not done a single thing to deserve it and, in fact, deserved the opposite. To this rebellious, idolatrous people trapped in bondage, God's marvelous, affectionate response was "I will *take* you to be my people, and I *will* be your God, and you shall know that I am the Lord your God, who has brought you out from under the burdens of the Egyptians" (Exodus 6:7). We know that this is exactly what God did, despite the initial resistance and refusal of the Israelites' wills (Exodus 6:9).

God sovereignly changed their hearts and their wills, and he accomplished his purpose for their lives. This is a beautiful picture of grace and how our God saves! Interestingly enough, no one reads the account of God bringing the Israelites out of Egypt and suggests that God made puppets of the Israelites by exerting his mighty power through his sovereignly chosen means and thereby delivering them from their bondage. The Israelites were not puppets or robots in any way; rather, they were objects of God's mercy and the beneficiaries of his eternal, sovereign purpose in order to bring glory to his name.

Puppets do not make choices; humans make choices. Robots only follow preprogrammed instructions, and they do not have a will, whereas humans have a will. There are some who teach that humans have no will of their own and that God is the author of the evil and sin that inevitably proceeds from sinners, but these extreme positions are correctly rejected even by the vast majority of those who hold a high view of God's sovereignty. God certainly does hold humans accountable for their choices; this fact cannot be denied by any honest study or interpretation of Scripture. The Bible is full of passages that clearly teach that humans are responsible for their choices and for their sins. In fact, the Bible practically screams of human responsibility. Furthermore, James 1:13–18 demands that we never assert that God is the author of sin. We must accept the scriptural fact that while our sinful nature (1 John 1:8) makes it impossible for us to be righteous (Romans 8:7; 3:10; Proverbs 5:22), we are nevertheless still guilty of our own unrighteousness (James 1:14–15).

Our responsibility might be partially illustrated by a man who borrowed a million dollars for extravagant self-indulgence but is unable to even begin to pay his debt. Nonetheless, he is still responsible for what he owes; the fact that he is unable to pay it back makes him no less morally responsible. Likewise, the self-indulgent sin with which we are all born has created a debt we are completely unable to service. That inability, however, creates neither a valid excuse nor a rightful claim for mercy or forgiveness. Jeremiah 13, for example, is filled with God's warnings and exhortations to his people that they would be punished (held responsible) for their wicked ways, while at the same time pointing out that their sinful nature made it impossible for them to do good (v. 23). The hopelessness of our seeking God on our own does not exonerate us in any way; rather, it demonstrates our complete, desperate need for a rescue of grace. If it seems unjust that we should be held guilty for what we cannot avoid on our own, it may be worth simply noting that if the inability to do good makes one less responsible before God (as some teach), then it would have to follow that the more depraved one became, the less responsible one would be—which is a clear absurdity.

In Ezekiel 14:1–11, we find an intriguing case that is a powerful example of how God holds humans accountable for their own evil, even when that evil is directly said to be under God's sovereign control. Regarding this control, Adam Clarke said of this very passage, "For so absolute and universal is the government of God, that the smallest occurrence cannot take place without his will or permission."[2] In these verses, we see God confronting the situation of men who were ostensibly seeking him for answers. In reality, however, these men did not actually desire answers, and they were continuing to regard their idols in their hearts. In reply, God said that he would answer these men's insincere inquiries according to the multitude of their idols, perhaps giving them the delusion that their sinful hearts wanted to hear rather than a real response (vv. 4–5, 7–8). Moreover, in verse 9, God pronounced that if a prophet should give them an answer, it would be a deception because "I, the Lord, have deceived that prophet." Nevertheless, that prophet would be held accountable for his sin (i.e., perish), as would the people he misled (vv. 9, 10). It is therefore inescapable that God holds men accountable for their sin—the evil choices that they make with their fallen wills—even when he is using and steering that sin for his own sovereign purposes.

Our sinful nature notwithstanding, God tells us that we must be holy as he is holy (1 Peter 1:15–16; Leviticus 11:45), and as a perfect, holy being, the one whose very actions define justice, he can demand no less. And yet, we know that we are not capable of being holy as he is holy. Only by his grace can we face him as violators of this demand, and this grace can be neither earned nor deserved. Through this grace, he gives us his own righteousness in place of our flawed righteousness (Romans 4:4–6; 5:17–19; Zechariah 3:1–5; 2 Corinthians 5:21; 1:30). In other words, the crushing load of human responsibility creates the debilitating burden of guilt for which God's sovereign grace is the sole remedy, through his mercy shown toward his chosen.

To our finite minds, there seems to be an inherent tension in the concept that fallen people who do not even have the natural ability to choose good or live righteously are nevertheless held responsible for their sin by a God who is totally sovereign over everything, including that sin. This paradox of the unity of God's sovereignty and human responsibility has provided the substance for countless books, articles, and debates over the years. Christians, it seems, often have a tendency to "choose a side" in this regard or, at very least, to neglect one side or the other of the scriptural teachings. However, I believe the truth is that there really is no contradiction at all, just as C. S. Lewis, who offered these insightful words:

> Heaven will solve our problems, but not, I think, by showing us subtle reconciliations between all our apparently contradictory notions. The notions will all be knocked from under our feet. We shall see that there never was any problem.[3]

It is undeniably observable that humans have the innate ability to do things that are not according to God's commands, sinful things for which God will hold them accountable. That fact needs little elaboration here; even the "Jesus is our buddy, make a decision for Christ" teachers of today do not seem to miss that. What they do seem to miss are the host of Scriptures that teach that humans are neither desirous nor capable of righteousness or of seeking God correctly unless and until God's Spirit sovereignly removes the blindness and bondage of their hearts and their wills, just as he did for Lydia in Acts 16:14, the Gentiles in Acts 13:48, and the brothers in 1 Thessalonians 1:4–5 (Romans 8:5–9; 2 Corinthians 4:3–6; 3:5; Romans 3; Genesis 6:5; 8:21; Psalm 10:4; 14:2–3; 53:2-3; 1 Corinthians 1 and 2; John 6:44, 63–65; 8:42–47; 15:18; 1:13; Colossians 1:21; Jeremiah 13:23; Matthew 13:11–15; 15:13; Ephesians 2:1–5; Deuteronomy 29:4). Until that point in time, Scripture is clear that the heart of man is *"fully set* to do evil" (Ecclesiastes 8:11; Jeremiah 17:9) as a result of the sinful nature with which all humans enter this world, and it *will not* seek God (Psalm 10:4; Romans 3:10–11).

It should be clear that we are here describing a free will that is hopelessly in bondage to a sinful nature and not a puppet that is manipulated by God. Indeed, until the operation of God's grace, the heart of a person with a fallen free will is hopelessly "held fast in the cords of his sin" (Proverbs 5:22). Such a heart will always choose evil because it loves darkness rather than light (John 3:19). In this regard, Jonathon Edwards correctly held that while the human will is free to do as it pleases, it is not able to determine and control what it pleases.[4] In other words, while we obviously choose and act according to our desires, our desires are contaminated by our sinful nature, and without God's grace we are incapable of desiring better desires.

Jesus also taught of the inability of the human will to choose to do right or believe in him. In John 5:40, Jesus said to the Jews, "You refuse to come to me that you may have life," which is an apt description of the hopeless condition of all human hearts until God's grace changes their will. Likewise, Jesus spoke of how the people of Jerusalem "would not" come to him and be gathered under his wings as a "hen gathers her brood," commenting that the people were instead the ones that "kill the prophets and stone those who are sent" to them (Matthew 23:37; Luke 13:34). Jesus showed us with this teaching that the fallen, blinded will of these people was in such bondage that they would never seek him of their own free will, even when the truth was right in front of them. Indeed, Paul taught, "The natural person does *not* accept the things of the Spirit of God, for they are folly to him, and he is *not* able to understand them because they are spiritually discerned" (1 Corinthians 2:14).

David stated unequivocally in Psalm 14:2–3 that God looks down and fails to find even a single human that "seeks after God" or has turned aside from his or her own corruptness—"not even one." However, it is also undeniably observable that some humans come to God while others do not. Since these passages make it irrefutably clear that *no* human heart or free will seeks God on its own, the difference between those that find him and those that do not must in fact be *external* to the individuals, and this external difference is exactly the role that God's grace fills! Until grace is mercifully applied, God observes, "Every inclination of man's heart is evil" (Genesis 8:21 NIV).

This fallen condition is not something we catch, much like we would contract a virus, since Psalm 51:5 adds that we are all sinners from the very moment of conception. Paul taught us in Romans 7:18 that there is no good at all to be found in this sinful nature with which we are all born, not even a little. Rather, the human heart is "desperately wicked" and "deceitful above all things," according to Jeremiah 17:9 (KJV). Romans 8:7–8 also makes it clear that the sinful heart, with which we are *all* born, is not only "hostile to God," but it also "cannot" choose to submit to God, nor is it even capable of "pleasing" God.

In an extraordinarily presumptuous upending of this Scripture, many churches read Paul's plain words here that the carnal mind is enmity against God and *cannot* choose God, and they then proceed to believe and teach the exact opposite! They teach instead that the human will *can* choose God on its own, and all humans are capable of so doing if they so choose. In effect, they are teaching that the group of people and the condition of the heart that Paul is describing in this passage do not actually exist. The biblical truth is that the hopeless condition of the human heart that cannot choose God is very real, and all humans are in this group unless and until God's grace changes their hearts.

The vital issue to be grasped at this point is that it is not possible to correctly appreciate and understand the magnificence of the loving cure (and its true source) until one correctly ascertains the immense depth of the problem. The hideous, helpless condition of the human heart seems to have been well understood by the respected champions of the faith in years past. In a sermon in which he expounded on the complete inability of the fallen heart to seek God, C. H. Spurgeon offered these words:

> Despite all the Doctrines which proud free will has manufactured, there has never been found from Adam's day until now a single instance in which the sinner first sought his God! God must first seek him. The sheep strays of itself, but it never returns to its fold unless sought by the Great Shepherd! It is human to

err, it is Divine to repent. Man can commit iniquity, but even to know that it *is* iniquity so as to feel the guilt of it, is the *gift* of the Grace of God. We have and are nothing but what is vile! Everything which is God-like, everything which aspires towards righteousness and true holiness, comes from the Most High.[5]

Given the penetrating insight of Spurgeon's words and the cumulative weight of the multitude of passages cited, it would seem obvious that this harsh, brutally honest description of the desperate condition of the fallen human heart and will is in no wise some arcane concept derived from an improbable interpretation of an obscure passage of Scripture. Nevertheless, it seems that many Christians and many churches today either inadvertently or deliberately neglect to grasp the enormous importance and crucial ramifications of this concept. If we are to truly understand our Father's incredible love for us, we must first come to completely understand the foundational concept taught by these many verses: We are hopelessly and eternally lost, completely incapable of pleasing God with our choices or actions, and it is our Father's loving grace alone that brings us to redemption—we do not and cannot contribute even a shred of inherent goodness, wisdom, or openness to our Creator. In fact, unless these passages are willingly or unknowingly ignored, the collective power and impact of this formidable assemblage of clear scriptural teaching leaves no room at all for a Pelagian or semi-Pelagian "man is capable of good" kind of teaching. While this Pelagian doctrine was in fact labeled heresy by Augustine and many councils throughout the history of the Church, it is clear that it has now returned in many of today's churches where its human-exalting egocentricity has apparently received quite a warm welcome.

Despite the resurgent prevalence of such teaching, the biblical fact remains that when a sinful heart weighs the Gospel message, the real question is not whether that heart is wise enough, righteous enough, soft enough, or even humble enough to be saved; these all follow. Rather, at the core of the matter, the question is whether God has revealed the truth of the Gospel by a sovereign act of his grace to that otherwise hopelessly blinded heart. When that heart chooses Christ, all the credit must go to God and his great grace. This is perhaps best illustrated in Matthew 16:13–18, where Jesus asked Peter who he believed Jesus to be. Peter's inspired answer was one we pray will be any sinner's reply: "You are the Christ, the Son of the Living God." What a simple, yet magnificent, statement of faith! Jesus' reply to Peter, however, should teach us volumes about grace and the fallen human heart. Jesus declared, "Blessed are you, Simon Bar-Jonah! For flesh and blood has not revealed this to you, but my Father who is in heaven." This is the glorious truth, plainly stated. When a human heart acknowledges Christ in saving faith, it is only because the Father revealed it to that heart. As was also clear from 1 Corinthians 2:14, the Gospel is not discernible by human wisdom or will (i.e., flesh and blood).

When we come to understand that eyes to see, ears to hear, and the revelation of the Gospel that results from the transformation of our wills are themselves gifts of his grace that are propelled by his great love for us (Ephesians 2:4–5), we look back and gratefully acknowledge that it was our Father's love alone that delivered each of us from the certain death that would have otherwise resulted from our enslaved will and corrupt nature (Romans 1:6; 2 Peter 2:19; Galatians 4:3–7). We rejoice that it was our loving Father who made us alive when we were dead! (Ephesians 2:5). We know that it was God who opened our minds to understand the Gospel (Luke 24:45). We join with David in exalting that God chose us and caused us to seek him and choose him: "Blessed is the man you choose, and cause to approach you, that he may dwell in your courts" (Psalm 65:4 NKJV). We understand with Solomon that it is God alone who can "incline our hearts to him" (1 Kings 8:58). In short, our relationship with our loving Father is transformed when we realize that we never could have found enough goodness in our fallen free wills to accept him. We are instead overcome with a profound gratitude born of the humility that inevitably comes from the knowledge that if it were not for God's grace, which was provoked by nothing other than his divine choice and sovereign purpose, our "free" wills were hopelessly lost and inexorably cursed.

The New Testament teaches of this horrible predicament of human hearts as a result of original sin, and it describes this condition as "dead in sin," "slaves of sin," "blinded," "alienated," or "hardened." However, there are some theologies that would assert that God preveniently applies grace to *all* humans indiscriminately in the sense that he thus gives all humans the ability to choose to do good, the capacity to view the Gospel as wisdom and not folly, and apparently the power to thereby willingly remove themselves from the state of being blinded to the Gospel, dead in sin, and slaves of sin. If this view were correct, God could have had no different type of a love and purpose for Abraham, Isaac, and Jacob than that which he had for

Our Loving Father God, or the Great Puppeteer?

Pharaoh or Judas, since the condition of their hearts would be said to be the result of their own free will choices. Likewise, God would have had no different sort of love and purpose for Jacob than for Esau before either was born, Romans 9:11–13 notwithstanding.

According to this view, all are said to be loved equally by God; each person's destiny is assumed to be dependent solely on that person's free will choices, and an omnipotent God's eternal purpose for that individual can supposedly be either realized or frustrated by that person's choices. Worse yet, it is even taught that one individual's eternal destiny may in effect depend on not just his or her own choice, but will also be determined by whether another individual chooses to attempt to lead them to Christ. It is not difficult to see how God's particular, individual love for each believer is thereby devalued immensely by these teachings!

It is, however, easily observable that God does in fact use people to bring the Gospel to other people, and Paul delighted in God's doing so in Romans 10:15: "How beautiful are the feet of those that preach the good news!" We must never make the mistake of suggesting that God's methods for calling his chosen people to himself do not include preaching, teaching, and evangelizing. Nevertheless, if one's opportunity to even hear the Gospel is believed to be dependent on the decision and actions of another fallible human—who we are taught may well act either haphazardly or disobediently to God's will—rather than depending solely on God's sovereign intervention in human affairs to make absolutely certain that those he has chosen will hear the Gospel, then what kind of a weak, ineffectual love have we ascribed to the God of the universe? Can we ever imagine a loving, human father who knows that his beloved daughter is in grave danger and chooses not to act *himself* to save her, but instead, he merely requests an inexperienced teenager to consider making an attempt to assist her—a teenager whom he knows full well to be weak, irresponsible, and forgetful?

It strains credibility to suggest that our infinitely powerful God loves us enough to give his son for us but then allows the whole matter to depend on another human's so-called free will, such that if that person fails, forgets, or is unwilling to share this good news with us, then we will miss out for eternity. A person saved under this belief may well feel lucky and blessed to have "found Jesus," but this is a far cry from the joy of knowing that in reality Jesus found us because God chose us! (John 17:6–9; 15:16; 10:27–29; 5:21; 6:37, 63). It should be easy to see that our Father's love is minimized in the first view, and it is magnified in the latter view. The Father's love displayed in the latter, correct view is a true, effectual love in which we can place our eternal confidence. This is a love that demands our awe and worship! In this love, we can experience the unspeakable joy of feeling incredibly valued by the God of the universe who chose us to be his own. Blessed are the people whom he has chosen as his heritage! (Psalm 33:12). The Christian who knows and understands that God chose him or her long before he or she could choose God understands completely deep within his or her heart that this is a thing to be profoundly cherished, a fact that makes us neither robots nor puppets but rather *individually* loved sons and daughters of the Most High.

On the other hand, the Christians that hold to the former view (supposing that they found Jesus instead of God choosing them) understandably have a difficult time experiencing the true individual, indomitable love that their Father holds for them. According to this view, God's love is merely a generic love for all humans equally that remains ineffectual and powerless until we manage to tap into it by a virtuous choice of our own free will. To overcome the scriptural difficulties with this view, it is explained that when God said, "Jacob I *loved*, but Esau I *hated*," this "in order that God's purpose of election might continue" (Romans 9:10–13), this choice must have been referring to God's loving of one nation and hating of another nation and not a choice of individuals. However, it remains unexplained how this view, which holds that Jacob and Esau in this passage are nations, could be the full, proper, and adequate interpretation of this important passage when the very same doctrinal viewpoint would also adamantly hold that all individuals within each nation are loved and chosen equally by God.

It is quite possible that proponents of this view have not considered the unavoidable conclusion of their beliefs. If this view were correct, the only possible outcome is also a quite bizarre one: a remarkable collection of people whom God loves individually but hates collectively. The passage makes it unarguable that God made a choice of some sort, and the near-absurd result of this fallacious view would therefore have to be that God must *love* one nation composed entirely of people that he loves and chooses while at the very same time *hating* another nation also composed entirely of individuals that he loves equally and chooses equivalently—this choice made before any person or nation was born. It is quite apparent, therefore, that this erroneous view unfortunately largely depersonalizes the individual love and purpose that God has for each of his chosen, making it exceedingly difficult for Christians to truly understand and experience the Father's love where this doctrine is regularly promulgated. In fact, this is particularly fertile soil in which the noxious weed of legalism can emerge and thrive, be it overtly or covertly.

While most, if not all, Christian faiths believe in a prevenient grace (meaning a grace that quite literally "comes before" salvation), they differ in their views as to the universality of the distribution and the extent of the effectiveness of this grace. Christians that hold the view that advances the supposed universalism of prevenient grace may well love God with all of their hearts. Few, however, seem to realize the damage and assault they have perpetuated upon Scripture. If some serious thought is given to the issue, it becomes readily apparent that the doctrine of a prevenient grace supposedly given to *all* humans in order to solve the problem of the human inability to do good or choose God has a particularly thorny problem of its own. The difficulty is that this belief necessarily renders a vast host of Scriptures referring to people in these classes (dead, blinded, perishing, etc.) as being particularly nonsensical since, after all, according to this viewpoint, *there are no humans within the class being described by these passages.* Instead, *all* are said to have been inoculated with this prevenient grace that neutralizes original sin and renders the recipient able to choose God on their own. As a result, we end up with a multitude of New Testament Scriptures that apparently must be speaking about a class or group of humans that it is asserted do not really exist. Since this inescapable result seems neither likely nor possible, the doctrine is thereby shown to be seriously flawed.

To illustrate this point, consider just a few passages from the large group of applicable Scriptures in this category. 1 Peter 2:8, as the first example, describes humans that are "destined" or "appointed" to disobedience of the word; do we believe that these humans exist? In another place, 2 Corinthians 4:3–4, Paul mentioned those to whom the Gospel is veiled, who have been blinded so as not to see the Gospel and are perishing; do we believe these humans exist? Paul declared in Romans 8:7–8 (NIV), "Those controlled by the sinful nature cannot please God," and they cannot submit to God. Do we actually believe there are any humans who are controlled by the sinful nature ("in the flesh") and *cannot* please or submit to God as this passage plainly states? Or, do we believe Paul was making a largely irrelevant comment by describing humans that do not exist when in reality any human can submit to God if they can just be convinced to do so by human effort or reasoning? We dismiss Paul's plain teaching at our own peril. Paul also taught in Romans 9:18 that God "hardens whomever he wills"; do we believe these humans exist? In 1 Corinthians 1:18 and 1:24, Paul told us that the Gospel is "foolishness to those who are perishing" (notice he does *not* instead say that those who judge it to be foolish will perish) and at the *same* time it is powerful to those "whom God has called"; do we believe there are humans in each of these groups that Paul describes?

Jesus himself also spoke of those humans to whom "it is not granted" to know and understand about the kingdom of heaven (Matthew 13:11; Mark 4:11–12); do we believe these humans exist? In another place, Jesus went so far as to praise his Father that it was his "gracious will" that the Gospel is "hidden" from those who might otherwise be considered "wise and understanding" and that it is revealed to those who are like "little children" (Matthew 11:25–30; Luke 10:21–22). These are, of course, two mutually exclusive groups that Jesus was describing—one to whom the Gospel is revealed and one to whom it is hidden. Do we believe there are humans in each of these classes? Reinforcing the point, Jesus added in Matthew 11:27 that no one comes to the Father except those to whom the Son *chooses* to reveal him. If these many repeated descriptions of two distinct, exclusive groups of humans are somehow not convincing enough, we should also consider that Jesus said that *all* his sheep that his Father gave him *will* listen to him, and those who are not his sheep will *not* believe (John 10:16, 14, 26–29; 6:37–39; 8:39–47). Do we believe there are people in each of these groups?

Jesus spoke of the group that will not believe in John 10:26: "But you do not believe because you are not among my sheep." Not a single English translation out of the eighteen that I have checked renders John 10:26 so as to even faintly suggest that individuals are not his sheep because they do not believe; rather, the translations universally make it painfully clear that individuals within this group will not believe *because* they are not Jesus' sheep. These people are not among those that the Father has given to Jesus (John 6:37; 10:16) or the group to whom Jesus chooses to give life (John 5:21) according to the direction and pleasure of his Father (John 5:19-20). Jesus was not speaking of hypothetical, nonexistent people. There are actual people in each of these groups.

In the parable of the sower and the seed that is found in Matthew 13:3-23, Jesus also spoke of four classes of human hearts (see also Mark 4:1–20 and Luke 8:4–15). Of these four groups of human hearts (the soil) about which Jesus taught, one will reject the Gospel outright (the desires of these human hearts are controlled by Satan), two will initially embrace but ultimately reject the Gospel, and only one group of hearts will receive the Gospel with saving faith and perseverance. Do we believe there are actual humans in each of these groups? We should note that when Jesus was asked to explain this parable, he first pointed out that it is not *given* to all humans to know the things of the kingdom of heaven (Luke 8:10; Matthew 13:11). Jesus instead taught that some humans are blessed with eyes that see and ears that hear (Matthew 13:16), but others have eyes that do not see and ears that do not hear (v. 13), just as Isaiah prophesied (vv. 14–15). It is even more revealing that Jesus did *not* teach that the type of soil could be changed by human choice or effort. He did not exhort the crowd to which he was preaching to strive to make their hearts the "good soil." Rather, he was illustrating the workings of the kingdom of heaven—explaining why some people will believe and others will not. Jesus' choice of soil as a metaphor was not accidental; soil is obviously incapable of changing its nature and type by its own doing or effort. Soil can only be changed by the efforts and intervention of a superior entity, such as the caring hand of a skilled farmer. In this case, the lesson is plainly that it is the creator God that ultimately determines the nature of the human heart in regards to the Gospel.

We must therefore reflect carefully on these many teachings and allow their truth to penetrate our hearts, even if the teaching is not what we might expect or desire. If these prodigious scriptural teachings are not total babbling nonsense, and there are actual humans within the very real groups described in these many passages, then we must either conclude that God's prevenient grace is not in fact given to all humans, or we must be willing to rip out entire sections from our Bibles. We need to realize that we rob ourselves of great blessings when we either choose to ignore or attempt to explain away these clear and copious teachings.

There certainly is a level of grace that God shows to all of humanity in that he does not strike each of us dead instantly as we justly deserve (Psalm 103:10; Ezra 9:13). He instead mercifully gives us our very breath, sends sun and rain to bless us all, restrains evil from utterly destroying us, and forbears our wickedness for even a moment (e.g., Matthew 5:43–48;

Luke 6:35–36). This undeserved goodness from our Creator is sometimes referred to as *common grace*. However, this common grace that is extended to all of humankind is quite different than the prevenient grace of God that precedes and enables regeneration for his chosen people. As we have seen, some theorize that this prevenient grace is merely an enabling of the human will that is given indiscriminately to all humans without exception. However, assuming we are not willing to go the route of selectively removing large portions of our Bibles, we must also realize that this flawed theory of prevenient grace does not actually solve or adequately explain the problem of the human inability to seek or to choose God. Even if one grants that humans do receive a prevenient grace such that all humans are purportedly enabled to freely choose or reject God of their own free will, it must be noted that the issue remains just as before. The entire vast host of Scriptures listed previously—if they are not utter nonsense concerning nonexistent people—must be describing all humans in the state in which they exist before being saved by a miraculous work of God's grace alone.

According to the many Scriptures listed previously that describe the impossibility of humans turning to God on their own (such as Romans 3:10–12), humans in the sinful state in which they are conceived and born are still not capable of choosing God—whether one asserts this state includes a prevenient grace or not. Apart from the saving faith described in Ephesians 2:8 as being *given by grace alone* to those particular humans who are "called according to God's purpose," as seen in Romans 8:28–29, Hebrews 9:15, John 6:37, and John 17:6, we will all inevitably perish as a result of our sinful nature and our sinful actions—held fast by the cords of our sin (Proverbs 5:22). If God does not draw a person specifically, then the Bible teaches us that he or she cannot and will not come to him (John 6:44, 65). On the other hand, if God *does* choose a person and give that person individually to Christ, then he or she most certainly will come to him (John 6:37, 39). If God himself does not "plant the tree," it will be rooted up (Matthew 15:13; John 17:2, 6; 10:29; 6:37). Apart from the power of God extended specifically to those whom he calls, the Gospel will of a surety be rejected as unmitigated foolishness—nothing more than a stumbling block (1 Corinthians 1:24; 1:18; 2:14).

Jesus himself made it unmistakably clear in John 8:39–47 that God's choice precedes faith. He said that if God were our Father, then we would believe (v. 42). Today, many teach instead that *if* we believe, *then* God is our Father, but this is exactly opposite to what Jesus taught. Because sinners' wills and desires are controlled by sin, they cannot choose to believe, as Jesus pointed out in verse 44. More importantly, in verse 47, Jesus made this incredibly unambiguous statement: "Whoever is of God hears the words of God. The reason why you do not hear them is that you are not of God." This strong affirmation of both the sovereignty and necessity of God's initial choice is essentially the same thing Jesus also taught in John 10:26, where he said, "But you do not believe because you are not among my sheep." He did *not* say that if we *choose* to hear the words of God, *then* we will be of God—as is commonly preached today. Instead, Jesus made it clear that those who God chose and gave to him are the same ones who *will* believe in him. This fact is a cornerstone of our abiding confidence in our Father's amazing love.

If we are to truly know our Father and understand the incredible nature of his love and purpose for us, we must absorb Jesus' teaching and learn that it is "the Spirit that gives life; the flesh is no help at all" (John 6:63). Like Jonah, we must learn that "salvation belongs to the Lord" (Jonah 2:9; Revelation 7:10) and ascribe to our loving Father the glory that he deserves. When we surrender to Scripture by putting aside our human biases and preconceived notions, the astonishing power of this great truth becomes the source of a flood of comfort and confidence. Furthermore, the fruit of this realization is also a new and foundational understanding of our Father's real love for each of us. His love for each of us is a love upon which we can confidently stand, knowing that it is backed up by his unlimited power and his willingness to use that power for our good (Ephesians 1:19). When God opens our hearts to an understanding of this great truth, the accusation that our loving Father is just a grand puppeteer or a divine robot-maker seems patently absurd, and our hearts will grieve for those who continue to misunderstand our Father's truth in such a manner.

As we grow in our understanding of God's sovereignty, it becomes a central pillar of our confidence that our Father's love and plan for each of us cannot be thwarted by human choices, be they sinful or not. His words do not return to him empty, and his choices will not be unfruitful. Unlike humans, God never fails at anything he sets out to do. When he chooses us as an intricate part of his purpose, he will in no wise fail in so doing. With this transcendent knowledge, we can face seemingly impossible situations with much faith. It is painfully obvious that humans make sinful choices, but we know our God's purpose is accomplished nonetheless. Moreover, we know that God does not merely work in spite of these sinful actions or strive to narrowly overcome them; rather, he actually uses these actions to accomplish his holy, unchanging, universal purpose.

The fact that humans make choices that are not according to God's commands is seen neatly in Isaiah 30:1, where God labels certain Israelites as "stubborn children," saying of them, "Who carry out a plan, *but not mine*, and who make an alliance, *but not of my Spirit*, that they may add sin to sin; who set out to go down to Egypt without asking for my direction." Of course, many more such references could be cited. Augustine also acknowledged the manifest observation that humans are not puppets but rather agents capable of acting contrary to God's commands, and he commented on God's purpose being accomplished nevertheless:

> These are the great works of the Lord, sought out according to all His pleasure, and so wisely sought out, that when the intelligent creation, both angelic and human, sinned, doing not His will but their own, He used the very will of the creature which was working in opposition to the Creator's will as an instrument for carrying out His will, the supremely Good thus turning to good account even what is evil, to the condemnation of those whom in His justice He has predestined to punishment, and to the salvation of those whom in His mercy He has predestined to grace. For, as far as relates to their own consciousness, these creatures did what God wished not to be done: but in view of God's omnipotence, they could in no wise effect their purpose. For in the very fact that they acted in opposition to His will, His will concerning them was fulfilled. And hence it is that "the works of the Lord are great, sought out according to all his pleasure." because in a way unspeakably strange and wonderful, even what is done in opposition to His will does not defeat His will. For it would not be done did He not permit it (and of course His permission is not unwilling, but willing); nor would a Good Being permit evil to be done only that in His omnipotence He can turn evil into good.[6]

It seems clear, then, that such sinful actions do not actually confound God's purpose. Does God have to make a new plan to account for these sins, which some suppose he failed to anticipate? Or, were these actions and his response determined long before they ever take place? We must be quite careful in this regard, such that our beliefs do not debase our Father in any way whatsoever. A. W. Pink made this crucial point eloquently and powerfully in his well-known 1918 book, *The Sovereignty of God*: "To declare that the Creator's original plan has been frustrated by sin, is to dethrone God. To suggest that God was taken by surprise in Eden and that he is now attempting to remedy an unforeseen calamity, is to degrade the Most High to the level of a finite, erring mortal."[7] We must therefore conclude that sin and actions against God's stated commands are definitely included and provided for within God's eternal, perfect purpose.

Romans 11:30–32 provides us a strong indication that disobedience is part of God's purpose. "God has consigned all to disobedience," verse 32 states, "that he may have mercy on all." (Paul was speaking here of the distinction between Jews and Gentiles, and he was obviously not asserting that God will have mercy on *all* human beings such that all humans will be saved, but rather that members of both groups will be shown mercy.) The truly powerful realization here is that disobedience is necessary for mercy to be present; in fact, there can be no mercy and grace without disobedience. We know that God has quite obviously willed that salvation should be by grace alone, not by works—such that no human (Jew or Gentile) could ever deserve, earn, or have any claim on salvation. Therefore, it stands to reason that God's plan (his will) must also include disobedience (evil), because without disobedience there would be no room (or need) for mercy and salvation by grace alone.

Without disobedience, justice alone would demand salvation and glorification for the hypothetical nondisobedient nonsinner, and grace and mercy would not be needed. Further, if there could ever be a perfect person, one that could stand before God as righteous and obedient without the need for mercy, that perfect person would necessarily be encroaching on God's exclusive claim as the only perfect, holy being in the universe of his creation. Paul, therefore, in this often overlooked passage, has provided a large hint in resolving the so-called problem of evil. We see throughout the entire Bible repeatedly that God works for his own glory. *If the particularly magnificent virtues of God's mercy and his grace are to be displayed to the universe for God's eternal glory and praise, then there must be evil in order for these virtues to be manifest.*

Since God "turns" human hearts "wherever he wishes" like "channels of water" (Proverbs 21:1), then would it be wrong to think that even evil (of which God is certainly *not* the author) can be steered by him in order to accomplish his perfect purpose—much like a river bank restrains and steers a channel of water without being the source of the water—while the evil is still evil and punishable as such? Is not the crucifixion of Jesus the ultimate example of this principle? Was there any chance that evil men could have freely chosen *not* to crucify Jesus and thereby thwart God's singular, perfect, predetermined redemption plan?

The smallest of details within the predetermined events of the crucifixion do not seem to be exempt. Was there any chance that a pagan soldier would not freely choose to pierce the side of Jesus with a spear as God had decreed? (Zechariah 12:10). Was it just a coincidence that a group of pagan soldiers freely chose to cast lots for Jesus' garment just as God had ordained hundreds of years before? (Psalm 22:18). If God said previously that Judas would receive thirty pieces of silver for betraying Jesus and that this money would be used to buy a potter's field (Zechariah 11:12–13; Matthew 27:3–10), was there any chance that Judas would freely choose not to betray Jesus or perhaps would have settled for twenty-five, or even thirty-five, pieces of silver? Was there any chance that the chief priests would have freely decided to use the returned silver for anything other than the purchase of a potter's field? For that matter, what about Judas' parents, grandparents, and great-grandparents—could not any tiny change in their circumstances or free choices have resulted in Judas never coming into existence?

Which of these two following scenarios should give us greater confidence in our God: He opportunistically used the actions of evil people who just happened to exist in the right place at the right time, these people just happened to freely make choices into which God was luckily able to slip his purpose, and he was able to predict these details merely by looking into the future. Or, rather, our mighty God orchestrated, steered, and controlled the entire sequence of events, including the smallest detail, so that our redemption would be certain and his purpose would surely be accomplished. I believe the latter is a more accurate description of our loving Father and more worthy of our complete confidence.

As it happens, this latter view is also the scripturally correct view (Acts 4:28, 2:23; Luke 22:22; Matthew 16:21; 17:22–23). Every single person (thousands of free wills), choice (millions of free choices), and event (thousands of interrelated, interdependent, and interwoven but seemingly random events) associated with the crucifixion of Jesus happened, according to Acts, in accordance with God's "definite plan" (2:23). We are told unequivocally by Scripture that the events were "predestined" and "determined" (Acts 4:28; Luke 22:22), and all those individuals involved freely chose exactly what God's "power and will had decided beforehand should happen" (4:28 NIV). Notice that the verse does not say "would happen," but rather "should happen." It happened exactly the way God willed it *should* happen, not the way he merely foresaw it *would* happen! We should not fail to comprehend that Jesus possessed the most free of any free will, and the Bible tells us that he willingly laid down his life because no human had the power to take it from him (John 10:18). In so doing, his perfectly free will unfailingly chose exactly that which the Bible tells us God had predestined. Moreover, these events that were driven by evil human free wills happened exactly *when* God appointed them to happen and not a moment before (John 8:20; 12:23; 17:1). Praise and glory to our God! The huge truth that we must grasp is that while the events could not have happened any other way, the individuals involved were nevertheless obviously neither puppets nor robots; rather, they were acting out of their own wills, and they will be held accountable for their sins. This concept is elaborated masterfully by commentator John Gill in his writing about these two passages in Acts:

> God not only foreknew that it would be, but determined that it should be, who does all things after the counsel of his own will; and this for the salvation of his people, and for the glorifying of his divine perfections: though this fixed resolution, settled purpose, and wise determination of God, did not in the least excuse the sin of Judas in betraying him, or of Pilate in condemning him, or of the Jews in crucifying him; nor did it at all infringe the liberty of their wills in acting, who did what they did, not by force, but voluntarily.[8]

> It was not their intention and design, to fulfill the purposes and decrees of God, but to fulfill their own lusts, and satiate their rage and malice against him; but it was so in the event, according to the wise disposal of providence, that by their gathering together, by their consultations and conspiracies, they brought about what God in his everlasting council had decreed…God's decrees are from eternity; there is nothing comes to pass in time

> but what he has beforetime determined should be done, either by effecting it himself, or doing it by others, or suffering it to be done, as in the case here. Whatever was done to Christ, either by Jews or Gentiles, by Herod or Pontius Pilate, was according to the secret will of God, the covenant he made with Christ, and the council of peace that was between them both: what they wickedly did, God designed for good, and hereby brought about the redemption and salvation of his people: this neither makes God the author of sin, nor excuses the sinful actions of men, or infringes the liberty of their wills in acting.[9]

The redemption of God's chosen people divinely accomplished by the crucifixion of our Savior gives us a remarkably clear picture of how our Father's sovereignty ensures that his purpose for each of us will certainly be accomplished and can never be thwarted by human free will. However, this is not the only strong scriptural illustration of this concept. We are given another strong indication of the reality of God's sovereignty over all, of the certainty of that which God eternally purposes coming to pass, and of God's use of humans as instruments to fulfill his eternal purpose in 2 Kings 19:25–28, where it is evident that even evil human intentions are steered by the Lord. In this passage, God spoke these words through Isaiah regarding the evil king of Assyria: "Have you not heard that I determined it long ago? I planned from days of old what now I bring to pass" (v. 25). The passage goes on to state that both the king's atrocities and his eventual punishment were determined by the Lord before they ever took place. In other words, God's purpose, his plans, and his sovereignty were *not* taken by surprise by the evil actions of the king of Assyria—the sinful king was just an instrument of God's holy and faultless purpose. In fact, in Isaiah 10:1–17, evil Assyria is said to be "the rod of my [God's] anger," and the "staff in their [the Assyrians] hand" is said to be God's wrath and indignation. We are told in verse 6 that God sent Assyria against Israel, even though Assyria did not realize that it was being used by God (v. 7). Can we deny that exactly this sort of thing happens every day?

Furthermore, the Assyrians would be punished because they arrogantly believed they had conquered by their own power and wisdom and failed to realize or acknowledge that they were tools in God's hand (Isaiah 10:12–19). In verse 15, God ridiculed this amazing transposition of human self-determination and divine sovereignty: "Shall the axe boast over him who hews with it, or the saw magnify itself against him who wields it? As if a rod should wield him who lifts it, or as if a staff should lift him who is not wood!" If we were to translate these words into today's vernacular, it might go something like this: "Shall the 'tail' of human free will 'wag the dog' of almighty God's sovereign rule over his creation?"

If we honestly evaluate much of what is taught in today's churches, can we deny that our doctrines actually venerate this exact transposition? Human free will is exalted and revered, and God is deemed to be barred from interfering with this recalcitrant, self-proclaimed potentate. In an audacious grab of power, we have effectively rewritten Psalm 135:6 to now read something like this: "The human free will does whatever pleases it, in heaven and on earth, in the seas and in the deep." We have reinterpreted Daniel 4:35 such that it now proclaims, "The human free will does as it pleases with the powers of heaven and the peoples of the earth. No God can hold back its choices or its actions." God help us! Little do we realize that by creating a God for ourselves that is subservient to human will, we have severely undermined the very source of our confidence and faith. If we believe that our Father's loving purpose for each of us can be effectively hindered or in any way thwarted by the acts of sinful human free wills, then what real confidence remains?

We must instead discern that our God's purpose is accomplished *through* human wills rather than in spite of them. Cyrus the Great became king of Persia in 559 BC, but approximately one hundred and fifty years earlier God had declared through the prophet Isaiah that he would raise up a ruler named Cyrus from the east and the north (Isaiah 44:28; 41:2; 25). This is yet another dramatic example of God declaring exactly what he will do in the future. When the event actually happens—when God does what he said he was going to do—it may well appear to humans to be the result of human free will. In this instance, God did not drop Cyrus from heaven and declare in a thunderous, disembodied voice to the people of Persia that this was their new king; rather, Cyrus succeeded his father to the throne and united the kingdoms of the Medes and the Persians shortly thereafter in what historians would no doubt characterize as a fairly normal course of events. We know, however, that God called this future Cyrus by name before he was ever born. Our sovereign Father described Cyrus as "his anointed" and said he would use him to subdue nations, declaring, "He shall fulfill all my purpose" (Isaiah 45:1; 44:28).

God's sovereign purpose—revealed in passages such as Isaiah 48:14–15 before Cyrus ever came into existence—included the defeat of Babylon and the rebuilding of the temple in Jerusalem. While Cyrus used the name of the Lord in his decree to rebuild Jerusalem (Ezra 1:1–3; 2 Chronicles 36:22), history tells us that his true loyalties were apparently to the Babylonian god Marduk. Isaiah 45:4 confirms that Cyrus remained an unbeliever even while God was causing him to accomplish God's purpose by stirring up his free will (Ezra 1:1). We can learn much from the illuminating words spoken by God to Cyrus in Isaiah 45:5: "I equip you, though you do not know me." If God's sovereign, eternal purpose was accomplished through a pagan king who did not even know that God was the one equipping him, how much more can we know that even today God equips humans, empowers humans, steers humans, and uses humans who all the while do not know him, do not recognize his hand at work (or deny it), and do not give him the glory that is due him? Cyrus was the ruler of a great empire, and as such he was obviously no puppet. Nonetheless, we know God raised him up and used him to fulfill God's divine, eternal purpose.

Many years before the days of Cyrus, an Israelite named Samson convinced his parents to concede to his sinful desire to take a forbidden Philistine wife. This lustful indulgence was obviously a violation of God's commands, but the Bible tells us plainly that it actually "was from the Lord," who was going to use this aborted marriage plan as his sovereignly chosen method of striking the Philistines (Judges 14:1–20). Once again, it is conspicuously demonstrated that God uses sinful human will to accomplish his purpose. Similarly, Romans 9 reveals that God "raised up" Pharaoh (a rebellious, arrogant, evil ruler) to accomplish God's purpose—in order that God's name "might be proclaimed in all the earth." Exodus 14:17–18 adds that God hardened the Egyptian's hearts to their very death in order that God could "get glory." Likewise, we are also told in Romans 9:11–13 that God ordained that Esau would serve Jacob before either child was even born; however, Jacob secured this birthright from Esau by sinful deception of his own father (Genesis 27).

The principle exhibited within these many accounts is far from being unique to a few humans that occur in some of our favorite Bible stories; all humans make choices, choices based on their desires and what seems best to them. According to the host of Scriptures we have examined, God always accomplishes his purpose in those choices. Whether the choices are good or evil does not affect God's sovereignty or the fact that his purpose will assuredly be fulfilled. As we have already seen, Scripture plainly teaches us that no humans are capable of believing or making right choices (Romans 8:7–8; 3:10–11; Titus 3:3; 1 Corinthians 1 and 2; 1 Corinthians 2:14; Genesis 6:5; Jeremiah 17:9; Ephesians 2:1–3; 4:18; Psalm 14:2–3) unless and until God's grace brings enlightenment to those who are called (1 Corinthians 1:24, 18). Human "right" choices, therefore, can only be a result of God's will. If God does not choose to bring enlightenment to a human heart and an evil choice is made, then it must have been God's will to allow this evil choice—a choice he fully knew would happen if he did not change that human's will. Understood properly, this truth could never be an offensive or fearful thing; rather, it gives us the only solid ground for the calm assurance that our God is in complete control!

If we resist this truth and attempt to usurp God's sovereignty in favor of our own imagined human sovereignty, we are treading on perilous ground. Indeed, there is clearly a danger when humans try to take credit for what should be to God's glory. As cited previously, the Assyrians in Isaiah 10:5–19 were to be punished because they did not give God the appropriate credit and glory for their conquests. They instead believed their success or failure to be a result of their own will, their own free choices, and their own efforts. Does this sound familiar? Do we not see this in much of today's teaching and doctrine?

If the Assyrians were around today, and someone had the nerve to espouse that their free will, their choices, and their circumstances were being guided, used, and controlled by God without their realization of that fact (as was the case in Isaiah 10), the majority of Christians today would undoubtedly rise up against such a teaching and deny its truth. These modern Christians would no doubt claim instead that the Assyrians could only be puppets or robots if it were true that God was sovereignly using them without the assent of their free will. As a result of this great error, God's sovereignty and righteous actions would be scorned rather than receiving the praise and glory they rightfully deserve. If we are painfully honest, we must confess the reality that this is an accurate assessment of how such a teaching would actually be received in many places. As such, we need to humbly reexamine our teaching and doctrines under the light of this truth.

Alternatively, we rob God of his proper glory by claiming that his prophecies and actions are based on mere foreknowledge of human actions and choices rather than on his sovereignty, decrees, power, and divine control. Isaiah 48 speaks to this very suggestion. In this chapter, God declared that he would deliver the Israelites from exile in Babylon by the hand of Cyrus, urging them to flee Babylon and return to their land when this happened (vv. 14–16, 20). He stated unmistakably that he was doing this for his own glory and for his namesake because the people themselves were said to serve the Lord in name only (vv. 9–11, 1). In verse 3, God reminded them of his previously fulfilled prophecies by proclaiming, "I declared the former things long ago" (NASB), "they went out from my mouth," and "I announced them." Having done that, God then declared, "Suddenly I did them, and they came to pass."

God was plainly saying that he did not just foretell these things; he actually predestined them, and then he "did them"—actually making them "come to pass." Furthermore, God made a startling statement in verses 4 to 8. He revealed one of the specific reasons that he foretells and predestines history; this reason is so that "obstinate" humans will not take credit for his (God's) own actions (vv. 7, 5) and because he knows they will want to claim that it was in fact their idols (their own creations, beliefs, and actions) that made the events happen. In other words, it becomes idolatry when we usurp God's glory (which he said in verse 11 that he will not give to another) by claiming that events that God foretells, predestines, and actually brings to pass for his own glory are instead brought to pass by our own free will.

As is stated famously in the very first item of the Westminster Catechisms, the chief end of man is to glorify God and enjoy him forever; however, glorifying God instead of itself is exactly what the fallen, sinful human nature does *not* want to do. In Jeremiah 5:24, God expressed his displeasure with humans that fail to give him credit and glory even for the seasonal rains; how much more must we give him credit and glory for the greater workings of his sovereign purpose. He expects us to recognize his sovereignty over everything and give him alone the glory that rightfully belongs to him! "Ascribe to the Lord the glory due his name" is an often repeated phrase in the Old Testament (1 Chronicles 16:29; Psalm 29:2; Psalm 96:8). As such, whatever virtuous works we perform or wisdom, faith, beliefs, abilities, or talents we possess must be properly ascribed to God and his perfect purpose for our lives.

If we insist on elevating human will or human effort above God's will, pridefully taking credit for what in actuality is God's grace at work in our lives, we should realize that we place ourselves in peril by so doing. As is seen in Isaiah 2:17 (NASB), the Lord will deal with all such haughtiness: "The arrogance of man will be brought low, and the pride of man humbled; the Lord alone will be exalted in that day." Herod, for example, learned this concept the difficult way. By a direct act of God, he was eaten to death by worms "because he did not give God the glory" for the praise that humans were lavishing upon him. Herod wrongly thought his great oratorical skills were of his own making, and these skills were employed in a situation he falsely assumed to be of his own doing (Acts 12:21–23).

A powerful case study of this concept and this danger is also seen in the fourth chapter of Daniel, where King Nebuchadnezzar took credit for all that he mistakenly believed that he had done and built as a result of his own free choices, wisdom, power, and sovereignty (v. 30). God held him accountable for this usurpation of the glory that should have properly been God's, and he drove Nebuchadnezzar into the fields like a beast. Furthermore, God told him in advance that Nebuchadnezzar would *not* acknowledge God's sovereignty for seven "periods of time." Only at the end of those appointed seven times would God sovereignly return Nebuchadnezzar's reason to him and enable him to see that God is the true ruler over the affairs of man. Just like any other sinner, Nebuchadnezzar could neither choose nor acknowledge the God of the universe until God first removed his blindness and gave him a restored reason.

After the predetermined period of time had elapsed—after God, by his own choice, sovereignly restored Nebuchadnezzar's reason, majesty, splendor, and government—Nebuchadnezzar was able to realize that it is God who is sovereign, and not himself (vv. 34–36). Nebuchadnezzar was forced to understand that God's will is always done and that God is sovereign over all humans. As a result, he declared this great truth about our God:

> All the inhabitants of the earth are accounted as nothing, and he does according to his will among the host of heaven and among the inhabitants of the earth; and none can stay his hand or say to him, "What have you done?" (Daniel 4:35)

This message is both salient and powerful: God does according to his own will among humans, and we cannot stop him from doing so. A single statement that God revealed to Nebuchadnezzar in his dream is repeated three times (v. 17, v. 25, and v. 32) within this account: "The Most High rules the kingdom of men and gives it to whom he will." Just like Nebuchadnezzar, we put ourselves in grave danger when we attempt to claim that what was God's work was really our own, thereby usurping both God's glory and God's sovereignty. A. W. Tozer offered these comments regarding Nebuchadnezzar's lesson in Daniel 4:

> We need to have restored again the lost idea of sovereignty, not as a doctrine only but as the source of a solemn religious emotion. We need to have taken from our dying hand the shadow scepter with which we fancy we rule the world. We need to feel and know that we are but dust and ashes and that God is the disposer of the destinies of men. How ashamed we Christians should be that a pagan king should teach us to fear the Majesty on high.[10]

Perhaps our resistance to giving up our imagined control of our destinies is to be expected. Since the fallen nature would always rather rule than be ruled, its defense in the matter is to assert that to be ruled or controlled would be equivalent to being a puppet or a robot. And yet, it is only our prideful shortsightedness that allows us to even entertain such a thought. It would certainly be undesirable to be ruled and controlled by an evil tyrant, but, on the other hand, what could possibly be better than to be ruled and controlled by a totally perfect, infinitely powerful, and incredibly loving Father? For that matter, would it be more loving for our great Father to allow us to be condemned by the actions and choices of our enslaved, fallen will or for him to conquer our will and give us a heart that will freely seek him? If the latter is preferable, would our Father's so doing make us his puppets or his cherished sons and daughters? After honest, prayerful consideration, the answers to these questions will be both readily discernible and inherently life altering.

Nebuchadnezzar's life was certainly altered by the experience that God chose to give him, and while the methodology God used may seem harsh or perhaps even bizarre to us, the lesson was in fact for Nebuchadnezzar's own good. God's judgment on Nebuchadnezzar for usurping God's sovereignty by failing to acknowledge that all things are from God, through God, and for God was not a unique or isolated event. Another example can be seen in how God brought severe judgment on Tyre and the king of Tyre (Ezekiel 26, 27) for exactly the same thing—for asserting in pride that he and his wisdom, rather than God's sovereign blessing and timing, were responsible for Tyre's great wealth (Ezekiel 28). We may feel that these lessons do not really apply to us since we are not kings surrounded by riches, but our circumstances, blessings, wisdom, good choices, accomplishments, and salvation must also all be properly credited to our Creator. Furthermore, we must be vigilant that the glory we offer our Father is genuine and flowing from humble hearts. Let us not be guilty of the kind of lip service offered by the exiles in Isaiah 48:1–2 while in our innermost being we retain the false throne of self-determination. Indeed, we need to be very careful not to trifle with God's sovereignty over all things, through all things, and in all things! We too, as God's chosen, may require discipline from God (Hebrews 12:5–7) in order to learn to give God the glory that is properly due him.

If it is a serious error for us to believe that we humans are operating outside of God's sovereign direction and control, it is an equally serious error for us to believe that Satan is operating outside of God's sovereign control. When the Bible teaches us that God is sovereign over all things, this "all things" encompasses God's entire creation and is necessarily inclusive of Satan and his demons. Unfortunately, this is another area in which Christians regularly fail to comprehend the magnificent reach of God's strong right arm. Even Satan is under God's sovereignty, and he is used by God to accomplish God's purpose.

As we have seen, the crucifixion of Jesus by evildoers acting according to Satan's influence and temptation, yet still according to God's predetermined purpose to accomplish his plan of redemption (Acts 4:28; 2:23), is certainly the greatest example of this truth. We also see evil spirits under God's direct rule and command in passages such as Judges 9:23, 1 Samuel 16:14, 1 Samuel 18:10, 1 Kings 22, and perhaps even 2 Thessalonians 2:11. In Colossians 1:16, we see that all in the spirit realm, be they angelic, demonic, or human, consisting of "dominions," "rulers," "principalities," and "authorities," whether visible or invisible, were created through Christ and *for* Christ. While Satan is at times allowed to inflict suffering on God's people (as with God's servant Job), we must always realize that this occurs only by divine permission and that Satan is continually limited and bounded by God.

Zechariah saw Satan standing before the Lord in order to accuse Joshua the high priest, who was clothed in filthy garments that were likely symbolic of the sins of God's chosen in general. The Lord, however, rebuked Satan strongly for accusing his chosen, even when the accusations were likely true (Zechariah 3:1–5; see also Romans 8:33–34). Moreover, Satan continually accuses us before the Lord, according to Revelation 12:10. This might be quite worrisome, to say the least, if we do not also realize that God has sovereignly purposed that the Holy Spirit will be our advocate, interceding for us before our Father according to his will (Romans 8:26–27). Not just the Holy Spirit only, but, according to Hebrews 7:25 and Romans 8:34, Christ too is always interceding for us and speaking to the Father on our behalf (1 John 2:1).

If we consider the image of Satan accusing us from the left while Jesus and the Holy Spirit defend us from the right, it requires little cognitive effort to realize who truly has our Father's ear. Praise, glory, and honor belong to our God alone, who has created all things for his own purposes and will never allow Satan to destroy his chosen ones! This is a liberating and soaring realization, especially for Christians who have spent years worrying inordinately about Satan and Satan's attacks. In fact, it is matters just such as this in which a proper knowledge of our Father is transformed from an intellectual assent into a practical, triumphant walk of faith with our loving Father. It seems that Paul could hardly contain himself as he declared in soaring language that nothing in all of creation, including Satan, his demons, circumstances, rulers, powers, or any other created beings or things will ever be able to separate us from the everlasting love of our Father (Romans 8:38–39). This should undoubtedly be our great glory and our eternal hope. However, if this knowledge is to provide us the comfort, security, and glory that Paul intended it to convey, it must be interpreted within the context of a correct understanding of our Father's love and sovereignty.

We can correctly perceive our Father's love as a powerful, indomitable, inseparable, and protecting love directed to God's chosen people who would be helpless to serve him or love him without it, or we may view it as a somewhat aloof, generic love that is said to be available to all humans but only actually attained by the few who manage to please him. If we believe this to be a generic love for all of humankind by a God who will not interfere with human free will, a love of which we must avail ourselves with our good behavior, wise choices, and self-generated faith, then we can have little or no real confidence in God's willingness or ability to provide the grace to enable us to withstand any attack from Satan. In fact, in many churches it is often taught that "nothing but ourselves" can separate us from the love of God, thereby hugely diluting the magnificent effectiveness of the love of our Father that Paul described in Romans 8:38–39.

The somewhat specious concept that "only we ourselves can separate us from the love of God" is profoundly flawed. This doctrine neglects to account for the fact that the beings that Paul listed (e.g., Satan, demons, powers) and the things they attempt to do (e.g., temptations, trials, circumstances) all have that exact goal of attempting to separate us from our Father. These enemies specifically attempt to get us to act sinfully or even to reject God—to "curse God and die," just as Job's wife advocated after Satan had inflicted intense suffering. In other words, if and when we were to yield to temptation or hardship and choose to separate ourselves from God by our free will or freely chosen actions, then the attacks by these very powers that Paul said could not be successful would have been successful, and Paul's glorious assertion is proven false. Nevertheless, we seem quite happy to have rewritten this verse to fit our new, watered-down theology, and it now reads something like this: "Nothing in all creation can separate you from your Father unless, of course, they do succeed in causing you to separate from your Father." Is there any real comfort in this twisted interpretation?

I rather suspect that this was not Paul's meaning, and we once again undermine our confidence in our Father's love with our poor theology. As a result of our defective doctrine, we unwittingly transform a potent promise into a powerless platitude. Likewise, we also err when we take this passage to mean that we will inevitably be attacked or afflicted by the whims and schemes of Satan and his demons, who are said to be running wild and out of God's control. After we have endured this unmitigated carnage and perhaps even after we die, then, we are told, God will certainly step in and gather us to heaven, and hence we will never be separated from God despite the best efforts of the enemy. Such a view in reality provides us very little confidence that God is sovereign or lovingly involved in every detail of our daily existence. Instead, we should correctly understand that our Father's sovereign love has filtered everything that is thrown at us, and while the forces of darkness may intend us harm, our Father is using every bit of it for our good (Romans 8:28, just 10 verses before).

We may well suffer (John 16:33; 2 Corinthians 4:7; Acts 14:22), but this is not without our Father's permission or attention. In other words, nothing happens that is separated or compartmentalized from his love for us (cf. Romans 8:37). If we truly understand, however, that God has chosen us and loves us, not as puppets or robots but as his very own, then we can thrill with Paul that none of these forces can ever accomplish their goal of forcing us to separate from our loving, protecting Father, much less ever doubt him. Our Father's sovereign, unconquerable, irresistible love will see to that! Oh that we could grasp how rich, how deep, and how immeasurably great is our Father's love for us! (Ephesians 3:18).

If we are to fathom the unlimited extent to which we have reason to depend on this great love, we must comprehend that because our Father is the totally sovereign Creator, Satan, who is God's creation, could obviously not have afflicted Job without God's permission. This fact should be our great comfort, but it is too easily and too often neglected. As a matter of fact, Satan cannot do anything without God's permission. Even the very existence of any of the powers of darkness at any given instant is necessarily dependent on God's willing forbearance—this to continually accomplish his own holy purpose. The fact that Satan cannot act without God's permission is not only a practical and logical necessity if God is actually God, but it is also demonstrated unmistakably in Scripture. Job's plight is perhaps the most well-known example, but we also see Satan asking permission to "sift" Simon Peter "like wheat" in Luke 22:31. Paul also acknowledged that what he called a "messenger of Satan" and a "thorn in the flesh" was *given* him from God, this for God's purpose and Paul's good (2 Corinthians 12:7).

It should be a great joy and reassurance that Satan must seek our Father's permission before being allowed to test Job, Peter, Paul, or any of us. We are promised in 1 Corinthians 10:13 that God not only must allow any such testing or temptation, but he will also limit the extent to which Satan will be allowed to act. Furthermore, we can know that if this permission is granted him by our loving Father, then Satan will yet again unintentionally, unwittingly, and perhaps unknowingly accomplish God's purpose in those very actions. For example, we see in Revelation 2:10 that Satan is allowed to throw some members of the church in Smyrna into prison, but God is using this for his own purpose, which is the testing and eventual rewarding of these believers. Our great confidence is that Satan "does not touch" we who are born of God! (1 John 5:18).

Our Loving Father God, or the Great Puppeteer?

We often read the account of Satan tempting Jesus that is found in the fourth chapter of Matthew, and we too easily picture Satan as merely appearing at an opportune time to attempt to draw Jesus into sin by employing his own devious methods. We should instead realize that Jesus' temptation by Satan was neither an anomalous coincidence nor an unfortunate distraction in God's unfolding redemption purpose. Rather, in Matthew 4:1 we are told that the entire sequence of events to follow in the desert was in fact part of God's purpose and under his sovereign control: "Jesus was led up by the Spirit into the wilderness to be tempted by the devil." God set up the confrontation, and Satan was not in any manner acting outside of God's control. As a glorious result, according to Hebrews 4:15–16, "we do not have a high priest who is unable to sympathize with our weaknesses, but one who in every respect has been tempted as we are, yet without sin," and we are assured that we can therefore approach our Father with confidence and find grace and mercy in our times of need. God's purpose, as always, was fulfilled!

Another example of God's sovereignty over Satan may be found in the two differing accounts of David's sinful choice to take a census seen in 2 Samuel 24:1 and 1 Chronicles 21:1. In the 2 Samuel account, we are told that the Lord incited David to take the census. In 1 Chronicles, we are told that Satan rose up and incited David to take the census. I have seen many attempts at explaining this seeming contradiction, some even going so far as labeling it a mistake in Scripture. However, my supposition is that the most likely possibility is that the Lord chose to use Satan to accomplish the Lord's own purpose, and we are being given a tiny window into the Lord's sovereignty—even over Satan—by the way these passages were recorded. Satan may have done the actual inciting, but the Lord was sovereign over the entire event, and Satan did not act outside of the Lord's power, control, or purpose. Just like at the crucifixion, Satan's actions accomplished God's eternal, predetermined purpose. As for God's purpose in this particular instance, we can know at the very least that the site of God's glorious temple (to be built by Solomon years later) would be secured as a result of this sequence of events; nevertheless we can never know or understand the fullness of God's purpose and wisdom. In any case, we may be certain that God's purpose is altogether greater than Satan's purpose.

If it were left up to Satan's purpose, the Gospel would never be preached and could never spread. Satan's nature must always be to resist and hinder the preaching of the Gospel. We recognize, however, that the Gospel is preached and that it does spread, which demonstrates yet again that it is God's purpose that prevails. In 1 Thessalonians 2:18, we read that Paul was "hindered" by Satan from returning to Thessalonica and continuing to preach the Gospel there. Are we then to believe that Satan actually hindered God's plan? It would be shallow and imprudent for us to believe that this hindrance occurred without God allowing it, but many believers today seem to labor under that very misconception. Our faith must demand that if God wanted Paul in Thessalonica, then there was no possibility that Satan could have hindered God's plan. Commentator John Gill palpably stated this reality:

> He [Satan] can do nothing but by divine permission, nor can he hinder the will of God, and the execution of that, though he often hinders the will of man, or man from doing his will; he hindered the apostle from doing what he willed and purposed, but he did not hinder the will of God, which was that Paul should be employed in other work elsewhere.[11]

While we will never fully comprehend God's infinite, eternal purpose, we can surely know for certain that Satan's existence ultimately serves God's flawless purpose. There is no "clash of the gods" here; rather, if Satan did not serve God's perfect purpose, God would simply speak Satan instantly out of existence. I believe that sometimes we mistakenly adopt a "comic book" type of mind-set, and we picture God and Satan in some sort of cosmic "battle to the finish," which is simply not a biblically supportable position. We may see references to things such as a "war in heaven" (Revelation 12:7) or our "battle" against powers of darkness (Ephesians 6:12), but we must understand and always remember that God has a high and holy purpose for allowing such conflict instead of merely speaking Satan's instant annihilation. As an analogy, we read in Judges 2:23 that God chose not to drive the remaining enemies of the Israelites out of Canaan quickly—even though he had done so previously with other enemies and was well able to continue to do so. We are told in Judges 3:2 that God did this in order to teach war to the generation of Israelites that had not known it before. In other words, God allowed a conflict he could have easily prevented or ended, and he did so for the higher purpose of strengthening, maturing, and testing his chosen people. The only war is the war that God allows!

If we choose to instead believe that God is locked in a struggle with Satan resulting from God's failure to anticipate his own creation going bad, we yet again artificially limit God's power and his sovereignty, and thereby we undermine our own faith. Worse yet, we may even be taught to believe that God possibly may not win the battle with Satan unless we round up enough people on our own to give God a timely helping hand. The truth is that if God chooses to use us to accomplish his purpose, he will call us specifically, enable us, empower us, and guarantee our success (i.e., Isaiah 48:15; 45:2). We must know that Satan's destiny of eternal punishment is already set by God's sovereignty, revealed to us in God's Word, and not subject to change.

His inevitable, inglorious destiny notwithstanding, Satan is certainly very powerful. Satan was a powerful angel, and just one angel killed 185,000 humans in one night with a single stroke (2 Kings 19:35). Clearly, Satan is more powerful than any human unless the human is wielding God's power, and even then the power is God's, not the human's. This powerful liar (John 8:44) and schemer (Ephesians 6:11) is actively seeking to thwart God's purpose and plan. And yet, we know that our almighty God, who is omniscient, is never taken by surprise by any action of Satan. Imagine God turning to Moses in heaven and saying, "Satan sure got me by surprise there, Moses; help me think up a good plan quickly to react to that one." Of course, that proposition is both sacrilege and ridiculous. In fact, God is never forced to react to Satan's actions or his particular choice of a target at any given time; rather, Satan is always playing unwittingly right into God's hand and accomplishing God's purpose all the while he is attempting to thwart it. As we have examined, the crucifixion of Jesus is the quintessential example of this, and Job's saga is another. This fact is yet another source for our unwavering confidence in our sovereign Father; despite Satan's power, our God's purpose will always be accomplished!

It is vital to realize that Satan has as much free will as any human, and he is certainly no puppet or robot. Nevertheless, his destiny is already set; one can read all about it in the book of Revelation. We may read about his demise and be rightly assured that his destiny will unfold exactly as God has decreed it, and I have never known anyone that has any objection to Satan's destiny being thus predetermined. It may seem a ridiculous proposition, but consider what could happen if Satan were to repent of his own accord and come to God sincerely offering his service and devotion. According to some, God is constantly trying his best to save people, albeit failing at it most of the time, and Satan's conversion would certainly seem to be a great evangelistic tool for God. As such, do we imagine that God is constantly trying his best to get Satan to repent? Or, what if God sovereignly moved to change Satan's free will? If this seems a preposterous suggestion, are we willing to make the blasphemous charge that Satan's free will is so powerful that our God cannot change it?

If our response to this question is to the effect that while God most certainly could change Satan's will, he does not choose to change Satan's will, that would assuredly be closer to the truth. However, if that is the case, then the inexorable conclusion must be that it is part of God's perfect purpose for Satan's will to be just exactly as it is. This whole suggestion of the potential for Satan's repentance could rightly be labeled ludicrous, but the reason it seems asinine is that the fact of the matter is that Satan is not going to repent, no matter how many revivals he visits, how much anointed preaching he hears, or how many Christians pray to bind him up. Quite simply, he will never desire to repent, much less choose to do so. His destiny is predetermined and already set by God alone, and nothing is going to change it—yet no one considers him a robot or a puppet. We should realize that fallen human will is no different! Moreover, if Satan will never repent of his own accord, why would we ever suspect that those whose hearts over which he has dominion (2 Corinthians 4:4; Ephesians 2:1-5; Acts 26:18) would ever repent of their own accord?

Finally, if Satan's free will can never thwart God, surprise God, get outside of God's will, or even cause a minor ding in God's perfect purpose and plan, then where would we ever get the idea that a human could thwart God's perfect purpose or exercise free will in a manner that would necessitate any change or even minor adjustment in God's purpose and will, much less leave God scrambling for an alternative plan? What folly! We "imagine a vain thing" (Psalm 2:1 KJV). God does not change (Psalm 102:27; Malachi 3:6; Exodus 3:14; Revelation 1:8; Hebrews 13:8), and he merely laughs in derision at human raging and plotting against his sovereignty (Psalm 2:1–4). The only way one can even conceive such a thing is to make God something less than the sovereign, infinitely powerful, infinitely knowing, outside-of-time, perfect-in-every-way, almighty God that he truly is. To our great loss, we make God in our own image when we attempt to bring him down to this level.

CHAPTER 7

FAIR IS FAIR, OR IS IT?

To question the wisdom of God, to question the justice of God, to question the love of God, to question the purpose of God is a reflection of your feeblemindedness and mine. To say to God, "Well, that doesn't seem to make sense to me" is the height of folly. Whatever you don't understand or have a hard time accepting has nothing to do with God and everything to do with your own limitations.

— JOHN MACARTHUR, FROM A SERMON ON ROMANS 8[1]

When we ponder the fact that God "works out *everything* in conformity with the purpose of his will" (Ephesians 1:11 NIV), there is a crucial question that naturally springs to our minds: if God is sovereign over everything, including human choices, then how can he hold us accountable for those choices? This question is reasonable enough, and Paul fully expected just such a response to his teaching regarding God's sovereignty in Romans 9. After describing how God raised up and used iniquitous Pharaoh in order to accomplish God's own purpose and bring worldwide glory to God's name, Paul affirmed in Romans 9:18 that God "has mercy on whomever he wills, and he hardens whomever he wills." This teaching would not have struck the original recipients of Romans as "fair" any more than it tends to initially strike us as fair today. How could God harden Pharaoh's heart and then hold him responsible for his actions? How could a just God harden any human's heart and then proceed to hold him or her accountable?

Paul anticipated these natural questions in the very next verse: "You will say to me then, 'Why does he still find fault? For who can resist his will?'" Paul obviously understood the nature of the human will quite well, and he correctly expected this natural, offended reaction to his strong teaching concerning God's indomitable purpose and electing choice. He proceeded to reply to these questions in no uncertain terms, and we can read this reply in verses 20 to 24. Paul taught that there is a poignant truth we must learn about the respective roles of the Creator and the created, and accordingly he declared, "Who are you, O man, to answer back to God?" It is no accident that Paul made absolutely no effort to deny that God's will cannot be resisted as he answered these questions; instead, he affirmed that it is God's prerogative to do exactly as he wishes with his creations, including creating some people to be objects of his wrath and others to be objects of his mercy (v. 21).

As we begin to consider the difficult issue of our human perception of God's fairness, justice, and choices—specifically Paul's clear teaching found in Romans 9 regarding these matters—there is an essential point that absolutely must be grasped at the outset regarding this critical, enlightening passage. *Paul obviously taught something that he fully expected to be startling and offensive to the human sense of fairness.* If the doctrine that Paul believed and taught was in fact merely that God shows mercy on the individuals who choose to obey and worship him of their own free will and that God hardens the hearts of those who reject him of their own free will, then the offended, questioning response that Paul anticipated in verse 19 becomes ridiculous and nonsensical. If the doctrine that Paul taught was that human free will is indeed the determining factor, such a teaching would have been as easily received as just and fair by his initial recipients as it is by so many churches today, and no such questioning response could be forthcoming or even reasonably expected.

Paul's anticipated response from his readers ("Why does he still find fault? For who can resist his will?") *only* makes sense if Paul's teaching was most assuredly an affront to their sense of fairness, a candid assertion that God sovereignly chooses whomever he desires to choose in accordance with his own holy purpose. Paul's teaching undoubtedly must have been a doctrine that he knew full well would indeed make the clay pot desire to question the master potter (v. 20). Therefore, it would not be unreasonable to expect that if we have correctly interpreted Paul's teaching, then our natural, human response to Paul's teaching should initially produce similar questions and resistance. If, on the other hand, we have twisted our interpretation of the passage such that no such questions naturally spring to mind, no offense to the flawed human sense of fairness is produced, and we cannot identify with the need for the questions Paul posed, then it is inescapable that we must therefore have developed an erroneous interpretation of this vital passage.

Paul also anticipated questions from his readers in verse 14: "What shall we say then? Is there injustice on God's part?" These questions reflect the response Paul expected from the natural human will in response to his teaching in verses 10 to 13 that God had selected Jacob according to his purpose and rejected Esau. Paul taught that God made this choice *before* either child was born or ever did anything right or wrong. The response Paul anticipated *only* makes sense if he was teaching something that would initially strike his readers as unfair and unjust. If Paul was teaching that God chooses those who choose him (or who will eventually choose him) and punishes those who reject him, this would certainly be perceived as completely just and fair by his readers, and there is absolutely *no* way that such a teaching could ever possibly evoke the response that Paul anticipated in verse 14! Such a response as Paul fully expected could have only come from recipients who were as offended by God's practice of election as are many readers of Romans today. Paul dismissed these objections by declaring that God is by no means unjust since God himself makes it clear that compassion and mercy are dispensed according to his own pleasure and to recipients of his own choosing (v. 15). In verse 16, Paul further offended the human sense of self-determination by adding that this choice is not dependent on human will, but on God's mercy alone. This ninth chapter of Romans is difficult for us, not because it is not clear and straightforward, but only because the teaching is not the way we would write it or the way we might desire it to be.

There are many today who apparently feel the need to rescue our holy, omnipotent, sovereign Father from what they evidently judge to be an embarrassing teaching by Paul, and they endeavor to do so by undertaking to assist God in defending his justice and his fairness. They attempt to explain away these doctrines—which Paul clearly knew were offensive to human pride—by putting forth some rather convoluted explanations of this chapter. In so doing, they attempt to transform what is to them a distasteful message regarding God's sovereign, holy choice into a watered-down nonchoice that is more palatable to human egotism and supposed human self-determination. We read of peculiar theories that involve God choosing groups of people that contain no particular people (in reply to which we should recall Wesley's assertion cited in chapter 4 that a whole with no parts is "mere nonsense and contradiction"). Or, we are given bizarre word pictures that have Jesus doing curious things like driving ships or buses upon which humans must climb aboard in order to validate some sort of ticket—word pictures that have precious little resemblance to anything actually found in this chapter.

Those advancing such notions may well feel that they are defending God's fairness. However, in so doing, they also do great damage (perhaps unknowingly) to the crucial ability of men and women today to know, experience, and relish the true love and purpose that God has for each of his chosen people individually. In essence, they seek to make the objections to Paul's teachings (which he fully anticipated) become totally unnecessary, if not outright irrational, by explaining away God's sovereign choice between Jacob and Esau within this passage as "only applying to nations" and "not to individuals." Some go even further by asserting that God's election here is only concerning physical, temporal blessings and that the eternal salvation of actual individuals was not in Paul's view in Romans 9. Much has been written regarding this question, more than could ever be considered in this limited book. However, because this issue is absolutely pivotal to a correct understanding of our Father's incredible love for each of us as his elect, I will undertake a very brief survey of these far-reaching passages in these opening pages of this chapter.

The assertion that Paul was discussing God's election of nations to the exclusion of his sovereign, loving choice of particular individuals fails for a number of reasons. A careful examination of this section of Romans quickly reveals that Paul was not merely interjecting a somewhat extraneous discussion regarding God's election of one nation to receive temporal blessings while spurning other nations for those same physical blessings—a discussion that just happened to get sandwiched between chapters that are unmistakably dealing with salvation for those whom God chooses. Rather, Paul was presenting a unified view of God's salvation for all his chosen people, both Jews and Gentiles. We know the chapter and verse divisions in Romans were not inserted by Paul but were added by others well over a thousand years later, so we must also consider contiguous chapters such as Romans 8, 10, and 11 in order to correctly evaluate what Paul had in view in Romans 9.

In chapter 8, we see a copious string of wonderful declarations and promises that are universally and joyfully accepted as dealing with individuals and, more specifically, the salvation of individuals. In verses 16 and 17, for example, we see that individuals are "children of God" and therefore "heirs of God." In verses 9 to 11, Paul assured us that the Holy Spirit lives in *all* individuals who are saved. We are taught in verses 26 and 27 the wondrous truth that the Holy Spirit himself intercedes to the Father with unutterable groanings for *all* saved individuals. In 8:28, we are given the comforting assurance that all things work together for good to those individuals who are called according to God's purpose. In the very next verses (vv. 29–30), we see that all individuals who are predestined by God were first foreknown by God, and all these individuals are also called by God. We are shown further that all those individuals that are called are also justified, and all those individuals that are justified will inevitably be glorified; it is these individuals alone to whom the wonderful promise of Romans 8:28 is given.

This glorious sequence that is described in verses 29 and 30 is famously referred to as "The Golden Chain of Salvation." The progression unambiguously described in this passage (beginning with foreknowledge, continuing with predestination, calling, and justification, and ending in glorification) must be referring to either *all* of the elect individuals who are directly stated to be foreknown by God or to only *some* of the individuals who are foreknown by God. A reasonable reading of the text would demand that we infer the "all" that is implied by the context. R. C. Sproul explored the interpretation and ramifications of this beautiful text at length in his excellent work *Chosen by God*.[2] As we interpret the text, attempting to force the word "some" in the place of the implied "all" results in what Dr. Sproul correctly labeled a "theological monstrosity." Such an interpretation would read as follows: "Some of those he foreknew, he also predestined. Some of those he predestined, he also called. Some of those he called, he also glorified. Some of those he justified, he also glorified."

This bizarre view depicts an inconsistent God who notably often fails at what he sets out to do and who does not reliably finish the good work that he begins in his chosen, foreknown people (see Philippians 1:6). Such a flawed interpretation requires the unthinkable possibility that some individuals who God foreknows and predestines are not even called—they do not even hear the Gospel. Moreover, the text when so interpreted would then also demand that only some of those individuals whom God foreknew and predestined *would* be saved are actually justified, and only some of those who are justified are actually glorified. God's foreknowledge and predestination therefore become both meaningless and powerless. It should therefore be readily apparent that such an interpretation not only produces an untenable "theological monstrosity," it more importantly also robs the passage of its precious actual meaning.

The noted author and theologian Dr. John Piper explained that our Father's foreknowledge of those he predestined (v. 29) is an eternal knowing of his own choice—a taking of a possession to himself—as is seen in Amos 3:2, where God said to his chosen people, "You *only* have I *known* of all the families of the earth" (cf. Deuteronomy 14:2).[3] Piper observed that the equivalence of God's choosing and God's eternal knowing is exemplified in our Father's words in Genesis 18:17–19 regarding Abraham, whom, according to Joshua 24:2–3, "God took" for himself by bringing him out of an idolatrous life in Ur. In verse 19 of Genesis 18, God said of Abraham, "For I have *chosen* him." The word translated as *chosen* is actually the Hebrew word for *known* (cf. ESV text note v.19). Indeed, the King James Version translates the same verse as God saying of Abraham, "For I *know* him." As such, we can rejoice that we too are recipients of our Father's loving, eternal choice when we read Paul's direct statement in verse 29 that God predestined those individuals that God foreknew!

As we move deeper into this wonderful chapter in Romans, we learn in 8:33 and 34 that no one can bring a charge against God's elect individuals or condemn them in any manner, because Christ died for them. The elect referred to here are plainly individuals and not nations, of course. Verse 34 also provides the truly awe-inspiring knowledge that Christ, who is raised and at the right hand of the Father, is himself interceding for the elect individuals that his Father has given him (John 10:29; 6:37; 17:24). Paul taught us in 8:37 that saved individuals ("we," God's elect from v. 33) are more than conquerors through him who loved us. In 8:38 and 39, these elect individuals (v. 33) who have been predestined, called, and justified (v. 29) are given the sweet assurance that absolutely nothing, be it life, death, angels, demons, things present or future, or anything else in creation, can separate these chosen people (vv. 28–30) from the love of their Father.

We have no problem appropriating this multitude of incredible promises in chapter 8 as applicable to individuals, and we do so correctly. It would seem impossible to assert that Paul did not have the eternal salvation of individuals in view as he wrote this momentous passage. Reading further in Paul's teaching, however, some suddenly decide that the term "election," which we were happy to apply to individuals in 8:33 (and which most certainly applies to individuals in 11:5 and 11:7), now somehow only applies to nations when it is used to describe two individuals in verse 11 of chapter 9. This remarkable equivocation is apparently based either on an artificial chapter division that Paul never included or on a preexisting conclusion of what might be fair or unfair for God to do or to not do.

We see in verses 1 to 5 of chapter 9 that Paul lamented that not all individual Jews are saved—so much so that he wished he could give up his own salvation to purchase theirs. Should there be any doubt of this, Paul confirmed this by stating directly in 10:1 that his heart's desire and prayer for them was that they would be *saved*. That salvation, and not mere physical or even spiritual blessings for a nation, is in view is also clear because Paul acknowledged in 9:4–5 that the Israelites indeed did possess the physical and spiritual blessings associated with being God's chosen nation, and yet Paul was still sorrowful for what they were lacking—salvation. In 9:8, Paul said plainly that the election by God to be children of the promise is equivalent to being elected "children of God," which again is clearly salvation. Indeed, in verses 6 through 8, Paul said that not all the children of the flesh (the nation of Israel, the physical descendants of Abraham and Jacob) are children of the promise (saved individuals), and this is also firm evidence that he had salvation in view in this context and not just a temporal blessing to a nation.

The blessings to Israel as a nation fill the Old Testament, and Paul itemized some of them in Romans 9:5. However, as he lamented that not all individuals within that nation were saved (9:2–3), he pointed out that God's promises are nevertheless true because the promise was never made to all individuals within the nation of Israel (9:6–7). It is very revealing that Paul did *not* in any manner make the argument that God's promise of temporal blessings to Israel as a nation was true because Israel *did* receive these promised blessings while still rejecting salvation. Such an argument would have to be the position of those today who claim that the election in verse 11 only has to do with national blessings. Instead, Paul taught that God's promise to choose certain individuals to be "children of God" (salvation) is true and trustworthy because it is realized by all to whom it was made; the promise never included all the genetic descendants of Abraham (vv. 6–8). John the Baptist had taught this same truth, declaring that merely claiming to be a descendent of Abraham was of absolutely no value. John affirmed the sovereignty of God in the selection of the heirs to the promise by proclaiming that God could raise up true children of Abraham from nothing but stones, which may well have been a symbolic reference to the stony condition of the natural human heart before it is changed by grace (Luke 3:8; Matthew 3:9).

The concern that God's choice and promise could either fail or be withdrawn would be a natural concern for the recipients of Paul's letter, in that he had just told them of the incredible blessing of becoming heirs with Christ (8:12–17). He had just given an extensive discourse regarding the glorious promises made to those individuals who are first foreknown by God, then predestined without exception, then called without exception, and then justified without exception such that they will inevitably be glorified (8:29–30). Paul had declared that no one could bring a charge against them as God's elect (8:33) and neither could anything in all creation take this from them (8:37–39). These were tremendous promises, guarantees that Gentiles were not accustomed to hearing.

If all these great promises were to be accepted as being eminently trustworthy, then what about the promises to the Jews who were supposedly recipients of God's unfailing election? It was this natural concern that Paul answered in chapters 9 through 11. Paul showed us emphatically that God's promises did not and will not fail—*all* of the children of promise will be saved (9:6–8; 11:26; 8:28–30). "God's purpose of election" will ultimately "continue" (9:11). It is, however, applied to a different pool of individuals than merely the genetic descendants of Abraham or members of the nation of Israel; the promise is instead extended to the true children of the promise (9:8), who are actually those individuals who belong to Christ (Galatians 3:7; 3:29; John 6:37, 44; Romans 4:16) according to God's purpose (9:11–13, 25–26). The calling of God is indeed irrevocable (Romans 11:29).

The incomparable blessing for the Gentiles to be found here is that God's choice of individuals to be children of the promise is neither limited to nor totally inclusive of the direct physical descendants of Abraham, so therefore some Gentiles also share in the blessing of God's sovereign choice (9:24–26). Paul stated this directly in Galatians 3:29 by saying, "If you belong to Christ, then you are Abraham's descendants, heirs according to the promise." Paul showed that while Abraham's physical lineage split several times, it was always God's sovereign choice which of these descendants would be children of the promise (Romans 9:11). First, Isaac was the child of promise, and Ishmael, who was the firstborn child of the flesh, was not included in the promise (Galatians 4:23, 30–31); rather, it was through Isaac that the children of the promise would be named (Romans 9:7). Next, before either individual was even born (thereby eliminating human will, choice, actions, or virtue), the younger Jacob was chosen by God as a child of the promise while the firstborn Esau was rejected and hated (Malachi 1:2–4; Romans 9:10–13). Both Jacob as an individual and his twelve sons as individuals would bear the promise while Esau as an individual and his offspring as individuals would bear the Lord's wrath forever (Malachi 1:2–4).

We must be careful if we lump these individuals into nations since the very reason that Paul said that the word of God has not failed is that not all individuals within the nation of Israel, or all nations who are descendants of Abraham, are chosen children of the promise (Romans 9:6). If God's sovereign election is only about nations and not individuals, then both Jacob and Esau (Isaac's twin sons) would have necessarily been included as children of the promise, and we know that was not the case. Rather, God's selections of Isaac over Ishmael and Jacob over Esau demonstrated early in Abraham's lineage that God's electing purpose concerned individuals and not a national bloodline. While God certainly did choose and bless the nation of Israel—including rebellious and sinful individuals within the nation (see chapters 10 and 11)—the true children of promise who are the children of God are those individuals he chooses. It is a glorious, confidence-inspiring fact that this "true Israel" most certainly includes some Gentile individuals

(Galatians 4:28; Romans 9:8; Galatians 3:7, 29; Ephesians 3:6; Matthew 8:11–12; Romans 11:17).

As chapter 10 begins, we again see that this entire section of Romans is dealing with salvation rather than national blessings, in that Paul again expressed his hope that the Jews who were not saved would be saved (10:1). In verses 8 to 11, Paul pointed out that all those (without exception) who confess with their mouths and believe in their heart that Jesus is God's son who was raised from the dead will be saved—adding in verse 13 that everyone (without exception) who calls on the name of the Lord will be saved. Paul here echoes the celebrated message of John 3:16 (KJV): "For God so loved the world, that he gave his only begotten Son, that whosoever believeth in him should not perish, but have everlasting life." These passages give us the powerful assurance that anyone who calls on the name of the Lord is a true descendent of Abraham, an heir, and a child of the promise (Galatians 3:29; Romans 4:11, 16). Because there are no national or ethnic limitations on the individuals that may call on the name of the Lord and be saved, it is indeed our blessed assurance that God chooses from *all* types and races of people (1 Timothy 2:4; Galatians 3:28). Jesus stated this same great truth in John 12:32, saying, "And I, when I am lifted up from the earth, will draw *all people* to myself." Jesus further taught that "many will come from east and west and recline at table with Abraham, Isaac, and Jacob in the kingdom of heaven, while the sons of the kingdom will be thrown into the outer darkness" (Matthew 8:11–12).

We rejoice, therefore, that our Father is no respecter of persons, and he wills and purposes that individuals from *all* classes, backgrounds, and nations will be recipients of his saving grace (1 Timothy 2:4; Acts 10:34; Romans 2:9–11). However, there is a crucial distinction that is often neglected by many as they study wonderfully glorious passages such as John 3:16 or Romans 10:9–13: who are the "whosoever" that will actually believe in him and not perish? Indeed, who are the "whosoever" that will accept this general invitation, and who will surely reject the invitation? This pivotal question must be considered in the light of Paul's strong assertions in Romans 8:7 and 3:10–12 that any unsaved person cannot and will not believe on the name of the Lord on their own (cf. Psalm 53:2; Jeremiah 13:23; 1 Corinthians 1:18; 1 Peter 2:7–10; Isaiah 64:6–7; Romans 7:18). In the remainder of chapter 10 and the beginning of chapter 11, Paul explained why not all the Jews have called on the Lord and thereby been saved. He taught us that the objects of mercy prepared beforehand without distinction of nationality (9:23–24) are the remnant that God has chosen for himself by grace (not merit) and thereby enabled to call on him (11:4–7), and the rest were "hardened" by God (11:7).

In chapter 11, Paul again made the point that God's promise has not failed, and he said emphatically that God has not rejected his people (v. 1); rather, God has always kept a remnant chosen by his grace (vv. 4, 5), and there remains an elect remnant even at the present time (vv. 5–7). This remnant, which was composed of elect individuals from among the entire nation, obtained salvation (vv. 5, 7), but the remainder of Israel was hardened by a God-given spirit of stupor (vv. 7, 8). Paul taught that this hardening was according to God's purpose to bring salvation to the Gentiles as well (vv. 11–16). However, obviously not all Gentiles will be saved, so when Paul said salvation has come to the Gentiles, he is clearly again writing about individuals—those elect individuals from within all the various Gentile nations.

Paul showed us that the Gentile individuals who believe and call on the name of the Lord (the individuals from 8:28–30 who are foreknown, predestined, called according to his purpose, justified, and glorified) are grafted onto the Jewish tree (v. 17–19) and thereby share in the nourishment from the rootstock that is God's eternal promises to Abraham and his true heirs. The resulting olive tree is composed of all who believe in Christ; these are the true children of the promise and children of God that Paul mentioned (as individuals) in 9:8. The promise in Genesis was that many nations would be blessed though God's choice of Abraham (Galatians 3:8; 18:18; 22:18), but no nations are chosen except Israel (Genesis 12:2). In Romans 11, we see branches grafted into this one nation, but these branches are individuals—not nations. It is inconceivable that Paul was suggesting that other nations were grafted into the Jewish nation, especially given the language of verses 17 to 24.

The clinching point to the matter may be found in Romans 9:21–29. In this portion of the chapter, Paul pointed out that we do not get to question the fact that God, as the master potter, makes some people to be objects (or vessels) of his wrath, which are created for destruction, and he makes others to be objects of his mercy, which are prepared beforehand for glory (vv. 21–23). Even if these three verses were isolated and taken by themselves, it would seem to be impossible to squeeze a meaning of nations into these verses since, for example, it is individuals that will be glorified with eternal life, not nations. Nations will pass away.

If a particularly determined person nevertheless desired to persist to insist that this passage is referring only to God creating nations either for his eventual mercy and glory or for his ensuing wrath and destruction, such a twisted interpretation is entirely precluded by the very next verse. In verse 24, Paul added clarification to what he meant by his reference to the vessels of mercy "prepared beforehand for glory" in verse 23, and that clarification is stunningly clear: "Even us whom he has called, not from the Jews only, but also from the Gentiles." The objects of mercy that God has prepared beforehand for glory are thereby explicitly defined as those individuals that God himself called, both Jews and Gentiles from many different nations! As would be said in the popular vernacular, "Case closed." Paul stated directly that he was talking about God's election of *individuals* from within *many nations* to be objects of God's mercy that God will eventually glorify.

God's election is here broadened in the sense that it includes both Jews and Gentiles and narrowed in the sense that it does not include all genetic Jews. It must therefore inexorably be referring to individuals, not nations. The words "even us whom he has called" in verse 24 are also hugely significant because in chapter 8 (vv. 29–30) we will recall the sequence for individual salvation was outlined; those whom God *calls* are justified, and those whom he justifies are glorified. This calling is not a mere invitation or wooing. Instead, Paul said that those who are called (created to be "objects of mercy," v. 23) will indeed be justified, this by God, and will further be glorified. In verse 11 of chapter 9, we also see that God's "purpose of election" stands not because of works (the choices and actions of human wills) but because of "him who *calls*." Paul addressed this book of Romans to "all those in Rome who are loved by God and *called* to be saints" (Romans 1:7). These individuals were believers, according to Romans 1:8–13, and Paul said these believers had been "*called* to belong to Christ" (v. 6) and were "from among all nations" (v. 5).

This word *calls* in verse 11 of chapter 9 is quite indicative in regard to establishing this sovereign, electing choice of God as being that of individual salvation, because it is the same Greek root word (*kaleó*) as is used in 8:30 regarding individual justification and again in 11:29, where this calling is proclaimed to be irrevocable. In each case, Paul is teaching us that

God calls those individuals that he chooses before they are even born, this according to his own foreknowledge and purpose rather than any merit, virtue, or belief on their part. In 9:23, recall that the elect individuals are prepared for glory *"beforehand."* These facts should move us to a sweet amalgamation of awe and joy since, according to Romans 8:28–30, our God calls those whom he predestines (elects), and he saves those whom he calls.

This would certainly seem to settle the case. As we mentioned at the outset of this chapter, it does not particularly matter whether this strikes us as fair or not. We should instead remember that Paul fully expected his teaching to initially strike us as unfair. Occasionally, the protest is raised about how unfair it would be for a hypothetical individual who wants to be saved to not be among those individuals elected and called by God. This is pure nonsense, of course. *It is not rational to suggest that someone could ever be reasonably upset because they do not have a thing they have no desire to possess.* The nonelect will never genuinely desire to be truly saved—all their desires are self-centered and evil (Genesis 6:5; Romans 1:21; 8:7–8; Jeremiah 17:9; Matthew 13:15; 15:19).

The individual in question should instead praise his or her loving Father for sovereignly applying his grace to his or her heart such that the person is even worried about such an impossibility, and he or she should call upon the name of the Lord to be saved (Romans 10:13). Indeed, all who wish to be indignant about what they perceive as the unfairness of the whole matter would be better served to instead believe in God's Son, give God the full credit and glory for creating in them the concern and the desire to do so, accept and rejoice in God's perfect and holy fairness in the issue, and gratefully join those who rejoice in being among God's chosen people. It would seem to be self-evident that it will be of little use on the judgment day for any sinner to appeal to the supposed unfairness of the holy, perfect, and just God of the universe.

Nevertheless, concerning this supposed unfairness of the holy, perfect God of the universe, even if the choice made by God to which Paul is referring in this ninth chapter of Romans is hypothetically granted as having specifically applied to nations and not to individuals, it is difficult to understand how those who would strive to defend God's fairness (by claiming that God elects everyone) would not have the exact same objection to this interpretation. That God makes an electing choice that is *not all-inclusive* is undeniable in this passage. That this election is based on his sovereign good pleasure and not on human acts or will is also undeniable—the passage says clearly that God made the choice between two individuals before either was born. Human free will was not a factor, only God's choice to have mercy on whom he chose to have mercy. As Martin Luther pointed out, regardless of what one concludes that Jacob and Esau represent in this passage, the eventual outcome was nevertheless clearly of God and not their human free wills.[4] No matter how the matter is viewed, God's sovereign choice resulted in God's preordained outcome.

God's electing choice described in 9:11–13 was not made about nothing; it had to be made about something! For those who have difficulty with the perceived fairness of this choice if it were made about individuals, why would they not also demand the same fairness when it comes to all of God's choices? Should they not demand God treat all nations identically? Or, bringing the matter to the present, would they not have to also maintain that it would be unloving and unfair for God to choose some individuals to receive physical healing while passing over others who also need physical healing? It is undoubtedly God's sovereign prerogative to make such choices (Romans 9:21), and if it is deemed fair for him to choose a sinful nation from among many sinful, rebellious nations (before the nation was even born) and spurn another sinful, rebellious nation for reasons of his own having nothing to do with the righteousness of the yet unborn nation, then how could his sovereign choice of some individuals from among many sinful, rebellious individuals (before the individuals are even born) be deemed any less fair or just? Moreover, we know that God does exactly this with nations (Acts 17:26; Daniel 2:21; Psalm 108:8–9). It seems, therefore, that those involved in attempting to lend God a hand with these supposed blemishes upon his image and glory before the human race are actually of little use to him. In fact, God tells us that he will actually be glorified and make his name known both by sovereignly choosing some men and women for himself (Ephesians 1:11–12; 1:6; Romans 9:22–23; Isaiah 43:7) and by raising up and using evil men and women for his own purposes (Romans 9:17).

Concerning all of God's choices and actions, Paul told us emphatically in 9:20–24 that we do not get to question God's perfect purpose or second-guess our sovereign God: "Who are you, O man, to answer back to God?" This poignant answer may not give us as much satisfaction as we would hope for, but it certainly shows us our correct position as the created before our ascendant Creator. We have seen that Paul explained that clay pots do not get to question the potter and that the master potter has created both objects of his wrath and objects of his mercy—this for his own purpose. Someone once said that we are not robots, we are clay. Paul showed us that God predestines his elect by creating some humans to be objects of his mercy and that God will also hold other humans responsible for their own sinful actions. God creates those humans in the latter group knowing full well that they will be objects of his wrath. While we might prefer an explanation that is more pleasing to our intellects and more in keeping with our self-importance, this may be the best we get unless we are willing to rip large selections right out of our Bibles! Charles Spurgeon made the following comment about Paul's teaching:

> That God predestines, and that man is responsible, are two things that few can see. They are believed to be inconsistent and contradictory; but they are not. It is just the fault of our weak judgment. Two truths cannot be contradictory to each other. If, then, I find taught in one place that everything is fore-ordained, *that is true;* and if I find in another place that man is responsible for all his actions, *that is true;* and it is my folly that leads me to imagine that two truths can ever contradict each other. These two truths, I do not believe, can ever be welded into one upon any human anvil, but one they shall be in eternity: they are two lines that are so nearly parallel, that the mind that shall pursue them farthest, will never discover that they converge; but they do converge, and they will meet somewhere in eternity, close to the throne of God, whence all truth doth spring.[5]

Spurgeon famously said that he did not make any attempt to reconcile these two truths because they were friends who had never been estranged, and they therefore needed no reconciliation. He further wisely pointed out that while it may be difficult to see where they converge, it is easy to see that they do not conflict.[6] It is therefore incumbent upon us to rightly divide the truth, to ignore neither of these great teachings of Scripture. On one side, Pelagianism (which, in my perception, is far from dead in today's churches, especially when watered down to semi-Pelagianism) would hold that God does not exercise sovereignty over almost anything, humans freely choose virtually everything, and, most importantly, they are capable of making righteous choices of their own free will. There are also those on the opposite end of the spectrum that hold that humans have no real will of their own. It seems to me (and Spurgeon too, apparently) that both of these positions are in error and fail to consider the whole of Scripture. The fact is that God does hold humans responsible for their motives, which are a result of their own sinful nature, even when he is said to direct or use their sinful actions for his own holy purpose.

I may speculate that it could be said that God judges the heart rather than the actions (we sometimes think of this principle in terms of wrong things done inadvertently by one with a godly heart), and, since the heart is already innately evil as a result of the fall, God therefore does no injustice by steering and bounding the actions flowing from that heart while still holding the heart responsible. Having ventured to make such a presumptuous conjecture, I hasten to add that I make no claim to understand or comprehend God fully! I only know that my perfect Father is both totally good and totally just, and he answers to no one, much less to me.

It really should be no surprise to us that there are things that God does that we will not fully understand—things that will very likely strike us as unfair—if for no other reason than he is God and we are human. We must know that "no one comprehends the thoughts of God except the Spirit of God," as Paul testified in 1 Corinthians 2:11, and "the foolishness of God is wiser than man's wisdom" (1 Corinthians 1:25). Certainly one of the more difficult things for us humans to understand is this question of how God remains totally and completely sovereign while still holding individuals responsible for their sins. We can either obstinately minimize and mischaracterize our great God by attempting to explain away what is difficult for us to comprehend, or we can accept in faith what we do not fully understand and offer our praise and worship in response to our God's supremacy.

In a previous chapter, we saw this apparent dichotomy illustrated in the account of the census that the Lord "incited" David to take, but he later held David responsible for this sin (2 Samuel 24:1). Another such example was Ezekiel 14:9, where we saw that the Lord would deceive false prophets that gave answers to idolaters seeking advice and then hold the false prophets responsible for doing so. Likewise, God told Moses long before Moses ever approached Pharaoh for the first time that God would harden Pharaoh's heart as a key element of God's purpose to deliver the Israelites from Egypt (Exodus 4:21, and again in 7:3). In the account of the Exodus,

God is directly said to have hardened Pharaoh's heart six times (9:12; 10:1; 10:20; 10:27; 11:10; 14:8) while Pharaoh is said to have hardened his own heart three times (8:15; 8:32; 9:34). God's judgment on Pharaoh was nevertheless both dramatic and final as God induced him to his underwater death (Exodus 14:3–4, 8, 28). It seems to me to be a direct attack on both Scripture and God's sovereignty to attempt to explain away these sorts of passages.

In the case of Pharaoh, for example, the usual attempt to dismiss God's sovereignty is the suggestion that Pharaoh first hardened his own heart. However, this problematic justification just does not withstand an honest, careful examination of the passages in Exodus where God stated directly that he made the hearts of Pharaoh and his officials stubborn in order that God could display his power, carry out his purpose, and receive lasting glory (e.g., 10:1–2). Furthermore, such an interpretation cannot fit with Paul's teaching on the matter of God's sovereign hardening of Pharaoh's heart in Romans 9:16–18, where Paul told us that the hardening of Pharaoh's heart was a vital part of God's original purpose and not at all a reaction to Pharaoh's free will. Moreover, a false truism such as "God will only harden our hearts after we first harden them ourselves" makes no sense at all when one comes to understand that we are *all* born with a sinful heart that will *inevitably* harden itself to God!

As we examined thoroughly in chapter 6, the natural, fallen human heart will *only* reject God as a result of its own free will, and we have seen that Paul told us in Romans 11:5–10 that God will soften a chosen remnant of these hearts by his grace and harden others. This is the type of biblical truth that does not strike many humans as fair or just. However, if God's actions do not seem just to us, we can know that they are indeed just simply because it was God that did them, and thus we are compelled to accept them by faith. This was the thrust of Paul's response in Romans 9:19–21 (NIV): "One of you will say to me: 'Then why does God still blame us? For who is able to resist his will?' But who are you, a human being, to talk back to God?"

The precept that we must accept in faith what we cannot fully understand with our intellect is not unique to Paul and the book of Romans. God stated the same thing in Isaiah 45:8–13 by proclaiming, "Woe unto him that striveth with his Maker" (KJV). Our Father asserted his rights as our creator as being analogous to those of a potter or a parent, and he then ridiculed our temerity to question his fairness by declaring, "Do you question me about my children or give me orders about the work of my hands?" (v. 11, NIV). Job also questioned the fairness of God's dealings, and God gave him much the same response in the form of an extended discourse that we might summarize in modern language quite simply as God saying, "I am sovereign and you are not." God told Job directly that Job had no right to "darken" God's counsel "by words without knowledge" (38:2) and asked Job how it could be that "a faultfinder" should "contend with the Almighty" (40:2).

These verses teach us that we humans will *not* fully know or understand God's purpose, and we have no standing or right to question the fairness or justness of God's actions or methods. He neither seeks nor accepts either our advice or our criticism (Isaiah 40:13–14). Therefore, we must never be faultfinders contending with the Almighty, but we must instead realize and accept that God plainly states that while he will reveal much to us, he nevertheless always reserves his "secret things" for himself (Deuteronomy 29:29; Acts 1:7). This is a fact of which Solomon was very cognizant. He pointed out in Ecclesiastes 8:17 that humans cannot understand or discover the "work of God" and said, "However much man may toil in seeking, *he will not find it out*. Even though a wise man claims to know, he cannot find it out." Solomon also echoed this thought in 11:5, where he explained, "As you do not know the way the spirit comes to the bones in the womb of a woman with child, so you do not know the work of God who makes everything." There is indeed much wisdom in accepting what we know we do not understand about God. "His greatness is unsearchable," exalted David in Psalm 145:3. We do not know how God breathes a soul into an embryo, but we can worship him who we know does exactly that!

When Paul dealt with the issue of God's sovereignty and human responsibility in Romans 9, 10, and 11, he reached the end of that particular section in 11:30–32, and he stated how God's purpose in election (11:28) and salvation is complex and intertwined: "Just as you who were at one time disobedient to God have now received mercy as a result of their [the Jews] disobedience, so they too have now become disobedient in order that they too may now receive mercy as a result of God's mercy to you [Gentiles]. For God has bound all men over to disobedience so that he may have mercy on them all." It seems as if he recognized that what he had just laid out in three previous chapters was more than his readers could understand, so he hastened to provide us with the correct response to this mystery by immediately launching into a praise song of worship to a God whose ways are higher than our ways. Here are verses 33 through 36 of Romans 11, which wrap up Paul's discourse on this subject:

> Oh, the depth of the riches and wisdom and knowledge of God! How unsearchable are his judgments and how inscrutable his ways!
>
> "For who has known the mind of the Lord, or who has been his counselor?"
>
> "Or who has given a gift to him that he might be repaid?"
>
> For from him and through him and to him are all things.
>
> To him be glory forever. Amen.

This should be our response to this mystery! We accept that we cannot understand, and we worship our sovereign God because we know that "all things" are from him, through him, and to him. His ways are inscrutable, and his purpose is deeper than we can even imagine. He could never owe us anything, but he chooses us anyway. Rather than resist this, we accept it and worship it! We choose to *trust* in the Lord and lean not on our own understanding (Proverbs 3:5). We choose to affirm his sovereignty instead of questioning it (v. 36), and we give him the glory for it. Why would we even desire to make a list of the things that we falsely believe are somehow not included in the "all things" that the Bible tells us are from him, through him, and to him?

God does not condemn us for wondering about these matters, but our response must always eventually be that of Paul's, which was one of worshipping what we cannot fully understand rather than questioning the fairness of the almighty God of the universe. God denounced such accusations towards himself in Job 40:8: "Will you even put me in the wrong? Will you condemn me that you may be in the right?" How often have we been guilty of this! Instead, we should always respond with the words of Elihu, who wisely said, "I will ascribe righteousness to my maker" (Job 36:3). We may find a modern paraphrase of Elihu's timeless words in an eloquent, simple comment by John MacArthur as he was interviewed at the 2010 Shepherd's Conference regarding the natural tension that humans feel about Paul's teaching on these issues: "I'm happy to concede that God can resolve things that I can't."

As we learn to trust that our Creator's ways are always right (Revelation 15:3), we will surely come to comprehend that the reason that what our God does is always just and always fair is not at all because God is the "best" being in the universe and can therefore be counted on to always "follow the rules." To assert this would be to judge God by a human standard and a human measure. The truth is, rather, that what our God does is always just and always fair only because God does it! God is subject to no law, standard, or other external measure of goodness. God does not measure his actions against human expectations or laws—God *is* the standard. Whatever he does is right. As such, his perfect purpose cannot be questioned! While some may be offended by this fact, I find this truth very comforting indeed. When our loving Father tells us that "he has our back" as he fulfills his purpose for us (Isaiah 52:12, author's paraphrase), we can relish that all his actions in so doing will be perfectly just, perfectly fair, and for our own good. Moreover, we know his ways will always be both completely effective and completely trustworthy.

In practical terms, this great confidence means we can know that even what may seem horrible to us is well within our Father's control and encompassed within his purpose. As was mentioned in the previous chapter, Romans 11:32 provides at least a hint into God's purpose by telling us that God "has consigned all to disobedience" in order that he can show his mercy to all ("all" being Jews and Gentiles without distinction). Mercy cannot be displayed without sin being present; for without disobedience, mercy would be unneeded. Paul taught similarly in Romans 2 through 5. Our unrighteousness brings out God's righteousness more clearly (3:5), and grace thrives where sin abounds (5:20). Psalm 130:3–4 reminds us that if God kept a record of our disobedience, we would justly perish, but the psalmist proceeds to reveal God's purpose by adding that God forgives so "that you [God] may be feared." If the magnitude of human sinfulness and unrighteousness were not demonstrated and exhibited to us plainly, we as God's chosen people could never truly appreciate and worship the infinite depths of our Father's mercy and redemptive love. This is a life-changing revelation that we may gain from these passages of Scripture! Only by such a realization can we come to understand the extent of depravity into which the human sinful nature will inevitably fall unless checked by God's abundant grace and mercy.

This hugely enlightening clue notwithstanding, the truth remains that we will not entirely know God's purpose or fully understand his "fairness," or lack thereof, as measured by human standards. Nevertheless, there are two things we *can* know for certain about his purpose. First, we can know that as God's purpose is fulfilled, it will always bring him glory (Ephesians 1:6, 14; Isaiah 43:7; 43:20–21; 48:11; 2 Corinthians 4:15). Secondly, we can know God's purpose will always be for the good of his chosen sons and daughters, any appearances to the contrary notwithstanding (Romans 8:28; 5:3–5; 2 Corinthians 4:15; Acts 14:22). We may perhaps think of this in terms of opening a gift from a loved one at Christmas. We do not know what the gift contains; it may well be an incredible gift, or it could be mediocre. Until the gift is opened, we really have no way to discern the nature of the gift except for our knowledge of the love, thoughtfulness, and resources of the one who is giving us the gift. Once the gift is open, however, we can readily see what was in the package all along. In this sense, the gift to us from our heavenly Father is quite similar.

We should nevertheless come to understand and cherish the fact that the gift from our Father is far superior to any gift given us from a member of the human race. Indeed, how much more does our loving Father know how to give us good gifts! (Matthew 7:11). Some gifts we receive from humans may thrill us, and some may well disappoint us—but none are truly beyond what we could imagine. And yet, we are told that our loving Father does more for us than we could ever ask or even imagine (Ephesians 3:20). Therefore, when our Father gives us the singularly amazing gift of choosing us to be included in his eternal purpose and commits the resources of heaven to fulfilling that purpose for us (Psalm 57:2), we have absolutely no reason to wonder if this gift will turn out to be incredible or mediocre. While we may not know what is included in his purpose (his gift to us), we can know assuredly that it will not only be good, but it will also be better than we can possibly imagine because we know well the unmitigated love, unconstrained resources, and unlimited thoughtfulness of the perfect giver! When his loving purpose has unfolded fully and his gift to us is thereby revealed completely, we will only then fully appreciate the magnitude of his perfect gift. We will undoubtedly look back from our position in eternity, and our hearts will be filled with awe, wonder, and eternal thanksgiving at the intricacy of our God's workings and the detailed perfection with which our Father lovingly fulfilled his purpose for each of us—even during those times when we were not capable of understanding what he was doing.

From our human perspective, the adversities that we often endure here on the earth may truly be difficult to recognize as a part of God's purpose. However, if God is truly sovereign, then by definition his purpose for us on the earth must include the existence of evil, suffering, and pain. C. S. Lewis pointed out that God's purpose is observably not to make life on the earth become as life in heaven.[7] God is quite capable of creating a perfect place that seems perfect even to our imperfect human perceptions, and that place is called heaven! However, he sovereignly has set a time and place for heaven, and that time is not now.

After having been stoned and left for dead in Lystra for preaching the Gospel, Paul responded by promptly returning to the city of the assault and declaring that we must enter the kingdom of heaven through many tribulations (Acts 14:22). Our current life on the earth is not intended to be heaven—if that were what God intended, that is exactly what it would be. Rather, God has a purpose for having us here just the way it is. Some have speculated that God's purpose is to grow us, to improve us, and to mature us (as seen in Romans 5:3–5). I suspect that this is at least a significant portion of the truth, but I also surmise that it falls somewhat short of the whole of God's purpose, a purpose we will never totally comprehend since we are finite beings incapable of fathoming God's infinite purpose.

There is a remarkable passage in Hebrews 5:8–9 that speaks of Jesus "in the days of his flesh" (v. 7). "Although he was a son, he learned obedience through what he suffered. And being made perfect, he became the source of eternal salvation to all who obey him." I could never assert that Jesus was ever anything but perfect; nevertheless, this passage states that even Jesus was made perfect through what he suffered! Even better, the passage gives us a hint about the purpose of suffering here, and that purpose is to teach us obedience and make us perfect. Suffering, then, is part of God's purpose (his will) for life on the earth, and heaven will be heaven in God's own time. When it becomes his predetermined, previously appointed time for heaven (Acts 1:7; Matthew 24:36), then we will joyfully experience that blessed perfection given us from his hand!

In the end, Job never knew God's perfect purpose in his adversities— harsh travails that included the death of his children and the loss of both his status and his possessions. The only answer he was given is really the only answer that we are given: God is sovereign over Job's situation, our situations, and myriads of other things and situations that God listed to Job, and we are not capable of that kind of power or that kind of understanding. We can only know that if it is happening to us, then our perfect, loving Father has allowed it, it is within his sovereign will, he loves us supremely, and he will certainly complete his perfect purpose for us. Because that purpose is God's own singular purpose, we know it will be perfect—no matter how horrible it seems to us right now. In fact, Moses regularly talked to God face to face (Exodus 33:11), and he stated directly that God sometimes wills suffering in order "to humble us and test us," something specifically said to be "for our own good" (Deuteronomy 8:16, 2–4 NLT).

Joseph's story in Genesis 37 through 50 may also provide an uncommonly clear perspective into the way in which God works his purpose through human suffering and steers human hearts to accomplish his own will. Joseph's brothers committed an evil act (attempted murder) that culminated in the nearly unthinkable cruelty of selling their own brother into slavery. These reprehensible actions resulting from the free will choices of the older brothers were manifestly sinful. Nevertheless, Scripture is very clear that what Joseph's brothers "meant for evil" was that which "God intended for good to accomplish what is now being done" (Genesis 50:20 NIV). The NASB translates the verse to say God did this "in order to bring about this present result, to preserve many people alive." Here, then, we get something we do not always get—an explanation of God's purpose that was being accomplished in Joseph's sufferings.

I believe that it is a major distortion to suggest (as many have) that God merely "used" the evil actions of Joseph's brothers opportunistically, and somehow he saw a chance to make good come out of their evil. This minimizes God and, again, paints him as a weak, albeit benevolent, being who just happens to be on our side; he is mistakenly pictured as one who is working on our behalf when and where he can rather than as the mighty, sovereign ruler of the universe that he truly is. We should always "ascribe strength to God" rather than any measure of weakness (Psalm 68:4 NASB).

We must neither overlook nor deny that God ordained and purposed these specific events in the life of Joseph in order that *his* divine plan would be accomplished. Can we really believe that the band of Ishmaelite traders that carried Joseph to Egypt just happened to be passing by from Gilead, and they just happened to be going to Egypt that morning (where God had destined Joseph) for no other reason than that they had risen early and freely chosen to do just that? Is not this so-called coincidence direct evidence of God's sovereignty over both human free choices and circumstances? In fact, Genesis 45:5–8 adds that it was God who "sent" Joseph to Egypt ahead of his brothers (see also Psalm 105:17), and the passage specifically states that it was *not* Joseph's brothers who sent him there, the brother's belief that they had done so notwithstanding.

To people who are accustomed to believing that they control their own destiny, this series of events may be perceived to be mere happenstance circumstances, but in reality the events were in no way coincidental, fortuitous developments for our sovereign God. Rather, many years before the Ishmaelite traders were ever born, God had told Abraham directly that Abraham's offspring would be in Egypt for approximately four hundred years (Genesis 15:13). God's purpose and plan, set before the foundation of the world, included bringing Israel out of Egypt, establishing the law at Sinai, and planting the nation of Israel in the Promised Land, where David and eventually Jesus himself would tread and die—all according to God's predetermined purpose (Acts 4:28; 2:23).

We know from Genesis 45 that God sent Joseph into Egypt ahead of his family in order to provide for the famine that would cover the land; however, we often overlook that God himself was also directly responsible for sending the famine, according to Psalm 105:16 and Genesis 41:25–32. This is an excellent example of how our Father makes every little single detail (yes, even the sparrow) *fall into place* for God's impeccable, flawless purpose to be accomplished! God influenced and used human free choice in order to bring about the appropriate circumstances for this to happen. God did not have to wait around for an opportunity to present itself in order to get Joseph into Egypt for his own eternal purpose; instead, he *sent* him there. God did not just make lemonade from the lemons that humans handed him; we can never put God into that tiny box!

Joseph suffered through an attempt on his life by his own brothers, slavery, false accusations of impropriety, and many years in prison in Egypt before being elevated to Pharaoh's second-in-command (Genesis 41:41). This is not the way we would have scripted the story of a young boy who was to end up saving many, including his own family (Genesis 50:20). While we may empathize that "justice won out in the end," we would nevertheless most likely consider Joseph's suffering to be quite unfair and perhaps even consider God quite unloving to have deliberately put Joseph through such suffering in order to accomplish his purpose. In fact, if such events occurred in the life of a believer today, many would erroneously declare such "bad" events to be "attacks of Satan" rather than the wise actions of a loving Father. However, Psalm 105:19 makes it clear that God purposed Joseph's sufferings not only to provide for his people during the famine that God would send, but also to test and mature Joseph personally. What may not seem fair or best to us is thereby declared to be God's perfect, loving purpose.

As such, we must reconsider the expectation of fairness that we often put on our God. It seems that we have come to expect that whatever we believe about God must be perceived as fair to our human way of thinking, and if it does not seem fair, then it must surely be bad doctrine. As a result, instead of correctly accepting in faith what the Bible plainly teaches, we tend to evaluate and judge certain doctrines and beliefs through the lens of what might be best described as a *human fairness filter*. Worse yet, we do not even seem to apply this fairness filter consistently. For example, why (by human standards) would it be fair that every single human ever born is tainted by, held captive by, and effectually punished for Adam and Eve's sin?

Our human justice system does not imprison the children or the grandchildren for the sins of their parents or grandparents; in fact, it does the exact opposite. It attempts to both protect the young ones from these sins as well as to mitigate the result of these sins on the "innocent" children. By human standards, then, if we are consistent, it was not fair for God to allow the curse to spread, to hold responsible and punish the offspring of Adam and Eve for their ancestors' sin. Hundreds of generations have suffered from the results of their original ancestors' sin. Would it not seem fairer for God to give each new baby a fresh start rather than for each and every person to be born completely encumbered with the integral corruption of original sin? Would not this feel more loving of God to our human senses?

This perceived unfairness of original sin was at the heart of Pelagius' views. In fact, he asserted that God did not allow the curse to spread to Adam's offspring, and we are therefore all born *without* a sinful nature. This, to him, seemed to be more characteristic of a just and loving God than the alternative. However, the problem was (and is) that his views ran head-on into Scripture, and this was why Augustine resisted him and his followers so vigorously. The fact is simple; whether it strikes us as fair or not by human standards for each of us to be born with a fallen and sinful nature, for Adam's sin to be our own, the Bible teaches this doctrine clearly. As such, that is the way it is, and it is most certainly just and not unfair in any way—if for no other reason than we know that this is the way God willed it. Pelagius' fairness filter is of little consequence, because it is God's inspired Scripture that carries more weight.

The doctrine of original sin may not strike many of us as particularly unfair by human standards, probably because we have just always accepted it and never given it much real thought. However, there are other doctrines where we seem to apply our human fairness filter with great enthusiasm and conviction. In all such cases, we must be careful that the true fairness filter should be God's and not our own!

This tendency to judge God by a standard of human fairness seems to be exactly what Paul addressed in such verses as Romans 6:15, Romans 7:13, Romans 9:14, and Romans 9:19, and it can also be seen as a central theme in the book of Job. In Romans, we have seen that Paul addressed the human inclination to be shocked and question God's fairness when confronted with the truth that God "has mercy on whom he wills" and "hardens whomever he wills," which Paul told us God does in order that his purpose might stand. The context of this assertion by Paul makes it quite clear that there are actually humans within each of these two classes or groups, and this fact will likely strike us as both arbitrary and capricious when the human fairness filter is applied. Unfortunately, we too often try to explain away these verses instead of accepting what they are plainly teaching about God. Whether we think it fair or not, God does harden some hearts and soften others.

If we are honest about Scripture, not only do we see God sovereignly choosing to change some undeserving, evil human hearts toward their repentance (as we see with Lydia in Acts 16:14, the chosen brothers in 1 Thessalonians 1:4–5, God's chosen in Ezekiel 11, or the people in Jeremiah 32:26–44, particularly vv. 39–40), we also see God sovereignly choosing to harden some undeserving evil human hearts toward their destruction. This is exemplified well in 1 Samuel 2:25, where we see that God hardened the hearts of Eli's wicked, rebellious sons and caused them *not* to listen to their father's chastening. The Bible tells us that this was because "it was the will of the Lord to put them to death."

We can be certain that God could have just as easily softened the hearts of Eli's sons and caused them to repent if he had so willed. In this case, however, he did not choose to soften their hearts, but instead he sovereignly did what he desired to do—put them to death. John Piper pointed out that the Hebrew word for "desire" (*chaphets*) in the passages in Ezekiel (18:23; 18:32; 33:11) where God said that he does not desire the death of the wicked is the same Hebrew word used in this passage in 1 Samuel where we are told "the Lord desired to put them to death" (1 Samuel 2:25 NASB).[8] It is therefore manifestly observable that God's desire (will) may be either repentance or judgment, as he sovereignly decrees to be appropriate for any situation or individual.

The Lord's will, desire, and actions in this narrative may well strike us as harsh, but they were certainly not unjust. We must nevertheless be careful not to dismiss the ramifications of God's stated desire by observing that these evil sons of Eli merely received what they deserved. There can be no doubt that they deserved what they received, but we must not forget that we all deserve judgment and death, and yet God sovereignly chooses to show mercy to whom he will show mercy (Romans 9:15). We are not entitled to complain of God's fairness—if for no other reason than because he is holy and we are not—as is stated in Lamentations 3:39: "Why should any living mortal, or any man, offer complaint in view of his sins?" The Israelites in exile apparently did not think that God was conducting himself fairly in matters concerning whom he would hold responsible for sin and whom would be granted repentance, and they questioned the justness of God's ways in Ezekiel 18:29. In reply, God told them, "O house of Israel, are my ways not just? Is it not your ways that are not just?"

There are hosts of other illustrations, both scriptural and historical, of God showing mercy to one group of humans while showing wrath to another, and many of these cannot be reconciled to our modern notions of "fairness" or "justice." For example, consider our response if a group of modern Christians were to identify all the atheist, wicked, abortion-performing doctors in America—doctors who worship idols in gods of their own making. What if these Christians proceeded to attack and slaughter all of the atheist doctors, including their wives and children, and then appropriated all of their houses, vehicles, and property for the Christian group's own use? We would quite correctly be appalled by such actions committed by a group calling themselves Christians, and we would rightly condemn them. We would proclaim that our God of love and mercy would never be pleased with such harsh, unfair actions.

Yet, this slaughter is exactly what God commanded the Israelites to do to all of the Canaanites and the other inhabitants of the Promised Land—including women and "innocent" children! For some reason, we do not seem to have any problem with the fairness of that command from God, probably because these inhabitants were evil and wicked. We must bear in mind, however, that *all* humans are evil and wicked until God's grace changes them, and we do not have any record of prophets being sent to these people *before* they were destroyed in order to give them an opportunity to repent. The American abortionists who slaughter children that are still in their mothers' wombs, on the other hand, most likely *have* heard the Gospel, so, under the modern "fairness" view, they would be even more deserving of death than the Canaanites. It seems, therefore, that the Canaanites were objects of God's wrath instead of his mercy when they, just like us, deserved death. The difference between the Israelites slaughtering the evil Canaanites along with their families and the modern Christians slaughtering the evil abortionists along with their families would seem to be that God commanded the Israelites to do so and commands modern Christians *not* to do so. After all, he had already prescribed the sixth commandment ("You shall not murder") before giving the command for the Israelites to exterminate the Canaanites. God is not any different today, and both groups of people were (or are) exceedingly sinful. Nevertheless, by his sovereign prerogative, he shows temporary mercy to one group and commanded immediate death for the other group.

When God displays forbearance toward the sin of one sinner, we must understand that he does not in any way create an obligation to deal the same way with another sinner in order to be judged fair by human standards. As a matter of fact, it should be quite obvious that God fulfills his purposes unhindered by any artificial obligation to deal identically with all humans. For example, God himself commanded that a man in the Israelites' camp who was caught cursing and blaspheming God be stoned to death immediately (Leviticus 24:10–16). Since that man's death, countless humans have engaged in cursing and have spoken blasphemous words against God without being killed or stoned to death. In fact, the public stoning of an outspoken atheist is not something we are likely to witness in today's church. Does God owe the man in Leviticus 24 an apology? Or, did the man deserve the punishment he received even though others have not received the same punishment?

Likewise, in Numbers 15:32–36, an Israelite man was caught picking up sticks on the Sabbath. The people inquired of the Lord what should be done to punish the man, and the Lord told Moses that the man should be stoned to death for breaking the Sabbath. The people proceeded to execute the man just as the Lord had ordered. Since that day, innumerable people have broken the Sabbath without the Lord ordering their immediate execution. Does this mean that God was unfair to the Sabbath breaker in Numbers 15? Does God owe this man an apology for not treating him fairly?

Over a thousand years after this incident, God struck both Ananias and his wife, Sapphira, dead for the sin of lying to Peter and to God about the value of the gift they had given to the church (Acts 5:1–11). Since that sad event, countless humans have lied to God and clergy about countless matters, and yet we do not read in the newspapers of God regularly killing such liars on the spot. Does God owe Ananias and Sapphira an apology because other humans have not been struck dead for the same sin, or did this couple deserve the punishment that they received from the hand of a just God? The truth of these situations is a basic one; God does not answer to our human standard of fairness, and he exclusively reserves his sovereign freedom and right to show mercy on whom he will show mercy or to be gracious only to those whom he chooses to be gracious (Exodus 33:19; Romans 9:15).

Our God is immutable, and the sovereign choices that we have examined thus far in this chapter that seem to show favor or mercy to some individuals and demonstrate wrath to others are not by any means a new or different mode of action for him. In Zechariah 13:7–9, God declared that he will cause two-thirds of the people of the land to be cut off and perish. He announced that he will choose to view the remaining one-third favorably, and he will refine these people and thereby cause them to call upon his name so that he can answer them and claim them as his own people. This divine choice of fates between the two-thirds and the one-third may not seem fair to human perception, but it is stated directly to be an act of God's hand (v. 7) following the good shepherd being struck, which is speaking prophetically of Christ's crucifixion (Mark 14:27; Matthew 26:31; Zechariah 12:10; John 19:37). In his selection of the one-third, we once again see God choosing a remnant for himself by grace.

Another representation of what we humans might consider arbitrary fairness is found in Jeremiah 24, where two different groups of Jewish people are likened to two different baskets of figs. It is important to note that one group is not righteous while the other is evil. Instead, there is a specific reason that both groups are either exiles in Babylon or Egypt or a mere remnant remaining in Jerusalem, and that reason is that God had brought calamity to Jerusalem and driven them out of their homeland because of their evil ways and their wickedness (v. 4). One group of exiles was chosen by God to receive his mercy, and the other group of people was chosen to receive his wrath. God expressed his choice between these two groups of sinful people by simply stating that he would "regard as good" the first group, even though they clearly were not good (v. 5).

To the first group, God himself had inflicted the Babylonian captivity as a divine discipline to those he loved in order to bring about his holy, redemptive purpose. He promised this first group: "I will set my eyes on them for good, and I will bring them back to this land. I will build them up, and not tear them down" (v. 6). Even better, God promised in verse 7 to *give* them a heart to seek him! As a result of this sovereign choice by God to give them the gift of a new heart according to his grace, they would "return to me [God] with their whole heart," and God would be their God and they would be his people (v. 7). Surely, this group was sovereignly selected by God to be objects of his mercy and grace. This theme of God's keeping of a remnant for himself is consistently seen from Genesis to Revelation. Even today, God sovereignly selects a remnant for himself—a remnant chosen by grace alone (Romans 11:5).

On the other hand, the second group of Jewish people was just as clearly selected by God to be objects of his wrath. It would seem that God had rendered them much like he had those individuals mentioned in Isaiah 44:18–20 or Isaiah 6:10: "He has shut their eyes, so they cannot see, and their hearts, so that they cannot understand." In verses 9–10, instead of giving them a new heart as he did the first group, God declared that he would act and "make them a horror to all the kingdoms of the earth" and that he would send sword, famine, and pestilence upon them until they were utterly destroyed. This may not strike us humans as fair, but it certainly is both God's right and God's nature to show mercy to whom he will and to show wrath to whom he will. There is no question of injustice, as the second group was certainly deserving of whatever punishment God chose to give them. However, it should not escape our realization that the first group of exiles that received mercy was also guilty and justly deserving of his wrath.

Interestingly enough, we read in Psalm 136:10 that we should give thanks to "him who struck down the firstborn of Egypt, for his steadfast love endures forever." The King James Version translates the latter portion of the passage as "his mercy endureth for ever." In the same verse, as odd as it may seem, Scripture is linking God's act of killing all the Egyptian firstborn children and animals with his everlasting mercy and love. Here we see God showing great mercy to one group of sinful people (the Israelites, his chosen), who we are told were idolaters in Ezekiel 20:8–9 (also Joshua 24:14, Leviticus 17:7). However, in so doing he also brought terrible tragedy on another group of sinful people (who were not his chosen). The Egyptians who lost their firstborn on that first Passover could hardly rejoice in God's "mercy" or "steadfast love." Rather, it is only God's chosen who have grounds to rejoice in his enduring mercy and love. When we consider the Exodus from this perspective, God's actions may very well not please our human fairness filter, but once again the historical facts demonstrate God's prerogative and willingness to show mercy to whom he chooses and wrath to whom he pleases—simultaneously in this instance.

When we bring this concept from the historical to the practical, we must grapple with the truth that God knows the future, including every choice we will ever make, before we are either born or conceived. Further, God creates each of us by a divine act in our mother's womb (Psalm 119:73; 139:13; Isaiah 44:24). Therefore, whether it strikes us as fair or not, we can know that God creates some people knowing full well that the person he is creating at that very instant will eventually end up in hell. Given that divine, infallible knowledge of their inevitable destruction and punishment, our perfect God proceeds to create that individual anyway. This is a dramatic and startling realization! If we allow this inescapable truth to soak deep into our hearts and minds, then many of the other "tougher" doctrines or more difficult teachings of Scripture fall right into place as both logical and inevitable extensions of this simple, yet incredibly powerful, realization. Proverbs 16:4 states outright that God makes all things for his own purposes, even the wicked for the day of destruction, and we are told in 1 Peter 2:8 and Romans 9:22 that these people are destined for disobedience and wrath.

Likewise, other individuals are created by God who will certainly end up in heaven, an incontrovertible fact that God knows with perfect foreknowledge even while he is engaged in the very act of creating them (Romans 8:29–30; Ephesians 1:4–5, 11–14; 1 Peter 1:1–3). The ramifications of this unambiguous observation can only be resolved by willingly accepting that God creates some individuals to be objects of his wrath and others to be objects of his mercy, just exactly as Paul taught in Romans 9. We do not get to question God's right as the master potter to create and use as he wishes! (Isaiah 45:9). Paul reminded us in Romans 9:14 that God is in no way unjust in so doing. Whether it seems fair to us is not the issue—God's ways *are* indeed just, and his work *is* perfect, as is declared in the song of Moses in Deuteronomy 32:4. We as contemporary believers can rejoice with the believers of Thessalonica that "God has not destined us for wrath, but for obtaining salvation through our Lord Jesus Christ" (1 Thessalonians 5:9). This is shouting ground; it is a truth for which we should praise and glorify our Father and his inscrutable, infinite wisdom rather than a doctrine to be resisted in our limited human understanding. Our Father declares, "For who is like Me, and who will summon Me into court?" (Jeremiah 50:44 NASB), and our response should always be inexpressible joy that is filled with glory! (1 Peter 1:8).

We stumble when we instead begin to expect God to conduct himself according to our own standards of fairness. When we do this, we are in effect asserting that our wisdom is superior to God's eternal purpose. For example, why would it be fair for God to choose only Abram and not any of the other people or nations on the earth at the time? Why not choose more? Why not choose all? Abram, it would seem, grew up an idolater until God chose him (Joshua 24:2), so he certainly did not deserve God's favor. There were plenty of other people that *could* have been chosen to receive God's mercy, but Scripture tells us explicitly that they were instead rejected (Joshua 24:2; Deuteronomy 7:6–8). We must realize that God chose Abraham by grace according to God's eternal purpose, not as a result of any merit found in Abraham—just as he does each of his chosen people. If this should seem unfair, we must be careful to realize that it is the very fact of this undeserved choice by God in accordance with his own purpose that frees each of us as his chosen from the insurmountable predicament of futilely striving to ever be righteous enough to earn God's favor. The blessed result is that we now actually rejoice that our Father is not fair by human standards of justice!

In the same way, as was examined at length earlier in this chapter, why would it be fair for God to "love" Jacob and "hate" Esau—and that before either was born? (Romans 9:13; Malachi 1:2–4). Should not God have loved them both equally? Why was it fair for Esau to be "rejected" by God and given "no chance to repent" even when he "sought it with tears"? (Hebrews 12:16–17). As we considered before, even some of the most exotic, convoluted explanations of Romans 9 that try to dodge the fact that God made a sovereign choice between Jacob and Esau do not seem to address the basic fairness of the simple, undeniable fact that one child was, at the very least, shown outright favoritism by God (for *his* own holy purposes), and this choice was made by God before either child was born, before either had done anything at all either virtuous or evil.

Or, was it fair for God to sovereignly choose to prevent Paul from going into either Asia or Bithynia as we see Paul initially desired in Acts 16:6–14? Instead, God sent him to Greece where Lydia would be saved, despite the fact that there were quite obviously many people that needed to hear Paul's preaching in both Asia and Bithynia. We cannot deny that God guided Paul to where God wanted him, and one group of lost people were deprived of Paul's preaching while another received it. Fair or not, a choice of this kind is not atypical for God. Jesus himself said that it has been given to some people to know "the secret of the kingdom of God," but for others he spoke in parables specifically in order that they would "see but not perceive" and "hear but not understand," so they would *not* "turn and be forgiven" (Mark 4:11–12; Luke 8:10). Moses also said to the people of Israel as they were assembled in Moab ready to enter the Promised Land, "To this day the Lord has *not given* you a heart to understand or eyes to see or ears to hear" (Deuteronomy 29:4).

The great Bible translator William Tyndale addressed this basic question of why God would make a choice to open one person's eyes and not another's. Tyndale was obviously intimately familiar with the whole of both the Old and the New Testament as a result of his translation work; in fact, the Tyndale Bible was probably the largest source used for the King James Version of the Bible. Tyndale's eloquent response to this enigmatic question was to point out that Paul taught us we cannot know all of God's reasons, but we can nevertheless know that God is honored by his sovereign choices and that his mercy is thereby displayed. Tyndale harshly condemned those who were not satisfied to allow God to have his own reasons and who instead sought to explain away God's choice as a reaction to human choice:

> They have searched to come to the bottom of his bottomless wisdom, and because they cannot attain to that secret, and be too proud to let it alone, and to grant themselves ignorant, with the apostle, that knew no other than God's glory in the elect, they go and set up free-will with the heathen philosophers, and say, that a man's free-will is the cause why God chooseth one and not another, contrary to all the Scripture.[9]

Even if one chose to disagree with Tyndale and deny the reality of God's sovereign choice because it is misguidedly preferred to attempt to make human free will more important and more determinative than God's free will, it would still be undeniable that some humans receive much more compelling (or simply easier) paths to salvation than others. Those that contend that "God will only woo us," even if their position be true, are forced to admit at the very least that God "woos" some people in a much stronger manner than he "woos" others. From a flawed human perspective, this too cannot be fair because not everyone gets the same opportunity, and some do not receive any opportunity at all.

Paul, for example, received a divine visitation on the Damascus road while his free will was consumed with nothing other than zeal to kill believers in the early church. He was not seeking or choosing Christ—he was persecuting him! God could have struck Paul dead for failing to give Christ the glory just as instantly and decisively as he struck Herod dead for failing to give God the appropriate glory (Acts 12:23). Instead, while Herod perished with no opportunity for repentance, Paul was chosen before he was born to be saved and used by God for God's eternal purpose (Galatians 1:12–16). The Bible tells us Paul was saved by the "effectual working of God's power" (Ephesians 3:7 KJV) as God "carried out" his "eternal purpose" (Ephesians 3:11 NASB).

How many unbelievers, or even outright atheists, would certainly choose to believe if they too were stopped in their tracks by a supernatural, blinding light and the deafening voice of the resurrected Jesus calling them by name? Would not they too repent if they received such a dramatic, undeniable call to repentance and salvation as that which Paul received? Yet, they receive no such powerful, effectual experience. If one is to assert that it is not God's will that any human should perish in sin, it must also be admitted that it is not God's will that all humans should have a Damascus road experience; it becomes, therefore, both contradictory and incongruous to maintain that "God does all he can" to save every human when he clearly does not do so—whether that seems fair to us or not.

As a single illustration of the fact that not all humans receive equality of opportunity for salvation, consider that Jesus said in Luke 10:13 that the people of Tyre and Sidon would have repented "long ago" if the miracles he did in Bethsaida had been done there instead. They were not, however, and those people perished (Ezekiel 26, 27, 28). God easily could have sent a prophet to do the miracles for those people in Tyre and Sidon, people that Jesus clearly said would certainly have repented if given the same opportunity, but God sovereignly chose not to do so. It is also quite possible that Jesus' words were referring to the Tyre and Sidon of his time on earth, in which case the point is the very same; Jesus did not perform the miracles there that he had in Bethsaida, even though the people in Tyre would have certainly repented had he done so.

Notwithstanding the certainty that these people would have repented if given the opportunity, in God's sovereignty they perished and were *not* given the opportunity—a fact that may not strike us as fair at all. If one attempts to mitigate and lessen this truth by contending that the people of Tyre and Sidon were given *some* opportunity to repent, just not the opportunity that Jesus said would have certainly made them repent, does not that only make the problem worse? A person asserting such a position is necessarily also asserting that God sometimes does not do everything within his power to save some people! Such an assertion is expressly affirming that if God had done more, the people would have been saved—but God nevertheless did not choose to do more. Jesus himself taught that God's sovereign choice and wisdom is such that some people are given a greater exposure to the Gospel than others, and some people that would surely repent if they were exposed to the Gospel are not given the opportunity. Most importantly, Jesus' words are a specific, candid avowal that God does not choose to do all that is within his power to save some people, while on the other hand Romans 8:28–30 teaches us that God will do all that is necessary to save those people whom he has chosen (cf. John 6:37).

As unfair as it may initially seem to us, Jesus' comments about Tyre and Sidon show us that God in his sovereign wisdom, prerogative, and pleasure does not always send prophets or preachers to groups that he knows would repent if he did so. This is illustrated irrefutably in the third chapter of Ezekiel as well. Here, God told Ezekiel that he was sending him to the Jews, who God stated that he knew in advance would *not* listen to Ezekiel. He was not sending Ezekiel to other nations, who God said he knew *would* surely listen and hearken to Ezekiel! In verse 6, God told Ezekiel that "surely," not maybe, "if I sent you to such [the other nations], they would listen to you." In verse 7, however, God told Ezekiel that the house of Israel, where God was actually sending Ezekiel, "will not be willing to listen to you."

From the perspective of human wisdom, was it fair or even wise to waste Ezekiel's time, talent, and efforts on people that God knew would not listen when he could have instead sent Ezekiel to different people that he knew certainly would listen? Here again, rather than find fault with God's fairness and "darken my [God's] counsel with words without knowledge" (Job 38:2 NIV), we must instead yield to God's sovereign choice and wisdom as he gives some people an opportunity while passing others by. We have seen that God passed by Abram's contemporaries in Genesis, the individuals in Joshua 11:20 to whom he chose not to extend mercy, the people from Tyre and Sidon in Matthew 11, the individuals of the other nations in Ezekiel 3, the people in Asia and Bithynia in Acts 16, and many other individuals that he did not choose for obedience (1 Peter 2:8–9; 1:1–3; Romans 9:22; Luke 8:10; Matthew 13:11; John 10:26; 6:65, 37; 1 Corinthians 1:18, 23–24; 2 Corinthians 4:3; 2 Thessalonians 2:13; Acts 13:48; Ephesians 1:4; 1 Thessalonians 5:9; 1:4; 2 Timothy 2:10; Titus 1:1–3). It is incumbent upon us to realize that God's eternal purpose was accomplished in his so doing.

Matthew Henry, commenting on the Matthew 11:20–24 passage about Tyre and Sidon, made these perceptive observations:

> Some places enjoy the means of grace in greater plenty, power, and purity, than other places. God is a free agent, and acts so in all his disposals.
>
> Tyre and Sidon would not have been so bad as Chorazin and Bethsaida. If they had had the same word preached, and the same

> miracles wrought among them, they would have repented, and that long ago, as Nineveh did, in sackcloth and ashes. Christ, who knows the hearts of all, knew that if he had gone and lived among them, and preached among them, he should have done more good there than where he was; yet he continued where he was for some time, to encourage his ministers to do so, though they see not the success they desire.
>
> Our repentance is slow and delayed, but theirs would have been speedy; they would have repented long ago. Ours has been slight and superficial; theirs would have been deep and serious, in sackcloth and ashes. Yet we must observe, with an awful adoration of the divine sovereignty, that the Tyrians and Sidonians will justly perish in their sin, though, if they had had the means of grace, they would have repented; for God is a debtor to no man.[10]

Indeed, how many people have lived and died in remote areas of the world and never heard of Jesus, the only path to eternal life? To human perception, is this fair? Or, is it fair for God to make it easier or more compelling for some than for others to hear the Gospel and to come to believe in him? Some people are raised in Christian homes and are so saturated with the Gospel from a young age that they cannot even remember a time when they did not believe. Other people are raised in outright evil environments where they are taught to be scornful of religion and are thereby hardened at a very young age. Is this fair? Some espousing autonomous free will have suggested that *all* humans receive "at least one chance" at salvation during their lifetime. This assertion is difficult to support either biblically or experientially for several reasons, but, even if this flawed statement is granted, is it not still unfair that some humans receive hundreds of "chances" to be saved while others receive only the one?

There are those that profess that even people that never hear about Jesus will be saved, citing Romans 1 and 2 as a basis for that assertion. Apparently those that hold to such a view see an exception to Jesus' own words that *he* is the *only* way and that no human can come to the Father but by him (John 14:6). Aside from the difficulty that it would therefore be cruel to evangelize such people (and thereby bring condemnation and guilt) if they could be saved apart from Christ, Romans 1 and 2 in actuality only seem to suggest that these people know enough to be guilty and condemned even if they never hear the Gospel. If Paul said they are "without excuse" (1:20), that does not carry with it any implication of salvation or the possibility thereof. Is it fair, then, that some humans (such as those on the island or country untouched by Christian evangelists or missionaries) will live and die, *never* hear the Gospel, and go to hell as a result?

Along this same line of thinking, we should also ponder our belief that the Bible teaches that salvation is by grace and by grace alone. Grace is what makes the difference between one who is saved and one who is not (1 Corinthians 15:10; 4:7; Galatians 2:21). Since salvation is by grace alone, humans, by definition, do not merit or deserve salvation in any way. There is nothing at all that humans can do to earn or contribute to their salvation, but we certainly do plenty to *not* deserve it! In fact, the fair and just thing would be for us to all receive the death and judgment we deserve, but grace means that God does not deal with us according to our sins or iniquities (Psalm 103:10). Grace means that salvation is a merciful, free gift to someone who does not deserve it (and has no claim upon it) in order that God's purpose will be accomplished for that person, a gift given to him or her before the person was even alive to receive it. This is clearly stated in 2 Timothy 1:9:

> He has saved us and called us to a holy life—not because of anything we have done, but because of his own purpose and grace. *This grace was given to us in Christ Jesus before the beginning of time.*

Titus 3:5 states essentially the same thing:

> He saved us, not because of works done by us in righteousness, but according to his own mercy.

Grace is also *not* a response to human will or decision:

> So then it depends not on human will or exertion, but on God, who has mercy. (Romans 9:16)

> But to all who did receive him, who believed in his name, he gave the right to become children of God, who were born, not of blood nor of the will of the flesh nor of the will of man, but of God. (John 1:12–13)

As such, a sinner has *no* legal claim, defense, or argument before God in terms of deserving salvation because God must be "fair," for if he did possess *any* such claim, then his salvation would not be by grace alone. Fairness is neither a claim nor a defense; fairness is not relevant! As the Reformers proclaimed, *sola gratia*, meaning salvation is "by grace alone." Perhaps I have lived in sheltered circles, but I do not think I have ever met a Christian that professed to believe differently than this about salvation. If a person did believe differently, they would be flying head-on into the whole message of the New Testament. Romans 11:6 would be a prime example of such a roadblock: "But if it is by grace, it is no longer on the basis of works; otherwise, grace is no longer grace."

It seems that we too often fail to consider the implications of our beliefs, however, and we end up with contradictory beliefs without even realizing that we have done so. In this case, we must contemplate the deep-reaching implications of the truth that salvation is by grace alone. Grace is God extending mercy toward undeserving humans. If we sinners got the justice that we deserved in place of the mercy we do not deserve, we all would be condemned to hell. *If we really understood this harsh fact, we would realize how utterly silly it is for us to clamor that God must be fair by our own standards.* We believe that a sinner has *no* legal claim before God in terms of deserving salvation for any reason at all; if so, then the sinner's salvation would not be by grace, but it would instead be something to which he or she was entitled. If God *must* extend grace or mercy in order to be just or fair (as measured by some standard external to himself), then grace ceases to be grace and becomes justice.

This is the very mistake that is made by so many individuals in today's churches! The fact that God chooses to save one undeserving human (by grace alone) can never create an obligation that God must also save another undeserving human in order to be "fair." If so, then the second sinner's salvation would be because of fairness and justness and not because of grace—it would be something that God owes to that person. If God's saving of the first sinner creates a fairness obligation to the second, then the second sinner has a claim for his or her salvation. The unavoidable truth is that if we say we believe that salvation is by grace alone, we can never assert that God has some obligation out of fairness to extend mercy and grace to all humans. We know that *no* sinner can ever have a claim on salvation for any reason at all, or salvation is not by grace.

Furthermore, the second sinner just mentioned cannot appear before God on the day of judgment and claim that God was not fair by appealing to the fact that Jesus appeared personally before Paul as a blinding light and a voice from heaven while he or she got no such dramatic, compelling chance at salvation. Such an excuse would hold absolutely no water, of course. We must reject, therefore, any doctrine that would hold that God is obligated to save even a single sinner out of fairness, much less every sinner, as much as we may find that comfortable to believe. Nor is God obligated to offer so-called equality of opportunity to all sinners, or even to a single sinner. We desire to paint our God as a God of love and mercy, and we do so rightly because he is indeed exactly that. But, we proceed to go too far by creating a supposed obligation that God must extend mercy to all human beings instead of "to whomever he wills" (Romans 9:18). If such an obligation existed, then mercy is not mercy any longer—it has instead become justice. Grace that is obligated is not grace at all!

God forgives sins for his own sake, not out of obligation (Isaiah 43:25), and he does so as a gift—this of his own will (James 1:17–18). The scriptural facts are that God shows mercy to whom he wills and hardens whom he wills, there are indeed real humans in each of these classes, and this is not unfair or unjust in any way. As such, we must examine the logical end of our doctrines. If we hold that God does not harden whom he will and have mercy on whom he will because that would not be fair to all (we assert instead that he must offer mercy to all), then we have artificially created an obligation for him to save in order to be just and fair, and thereby we have also completely destroyed the doctrine of salvation by grace alone. This unavoidable conclusion notwithstanding, too many seem to desire to allow these two beliefs to coexist.

Once again, it is incumbent upon us to set aside our preexisting notions of fairness and allow God's Word to teach us about our Father. We can then proceed to worship, love, and obey the holy, perfect God that is revealed therein, rather than a God of our own making. As we shall see, the God of the Bible is a Rock upon which we can build our confidence. We do well to learn that reveling in our Father's great, unfaltering love for his chosen is far superior to the struggle we bring on ourselves by believing in a weak, ineffectual, and "fair" God of own making.

CHAPTER 8

HEAVENLY ROBOTS

I know Christ is all in all. Man is nothing: he hath a free will to go to hell, but none to go to heaven, till God worketh in him to will and to do his good pleasure.

— GEORGE WHITEFIELD[1]

If there should remain any question concerning the flawed allegation that fallen human beings could be more like robots or puppets than creatures with an actual will, then perhaps just a bit more examination is in order. It seems that this "puppeteer" accusation is leveled against our almighty Father in response to any implication that humans are not completely free to make any choice at any time in any way—without considering whether such a choice is in actuality influenced by a sinful nature, a spirit-filled nature, or God's sovereignty. If such a totally free, autonomous choice existed in reality, by definition it would have to be made independently from any desire, circumstance, need, pain, prejudice, or predilection that is either internal or external to the individual doing the choosing. The notion of such an uncaused choice, one not driven by an individual's desires, seems to me to be altogether illusory and fallacious—a near absurdity.

Nevertheless, if it is rightly suggested that the freedom of the will is in actuality limited, bounded, or in bondage in any way (e.g., a sinful person cannot make righteous choices as seen in Genesis 6:5, 8:21, Psalm 53:2–3, 1 Corinthians 2:14, and Romans 8:7), the response by many is to contend that humans could then be no more than the equivalent of a robot or a puppet. If it is correctly pointed out that the human heart will never freely choose to seek God unless and until God first sovereignly chooses to give each of his chosen people a heart to seek him, desire him, and love him, this truth is also resisted as a supposed violation of the human free will. In its place, the erroneous assertion is made that the free ability to choose evil or good is a necessary ingredient for any love or relationship to be genuine and meaningful. Without such supposed freedom of choice, the relationship is labeled "robotic." It is usually further asserted that God wants people to love him out of their own "free choice," not because they are programmed or compelled to do so.

This reasoning is too shallow. We can gain some revealing insight into the profound flaws of this point of view if we reflect on our eternal dwelling place. In heaven, God will have removed any vestige of our sinful nature and totally fulfilled his Ezekiel 36 prophecy by giving each of us a new heart and a new spirit that will seek him and obey him. In glory, our hearts will *always* seek after God, *always* make the righteous choice, and from our spirits will *always* flow good instead of evil, since evil will be no more. We will not have the ability (or even the faintest desire) to do evil. There will be no more pain and no more suffering, nor will we "mess up" and cause someone else hurt or pain. We will all live and exist according to God's commands. Our destiny will be determined and set—we will live with our God and for our God forever! We will be eternally experiencing what was so often alluded to throughout the Old Testament, which has been the purpose of God's heart all along: "I will walk among you and will be your God, and you shall be my people" (Leviticus 26:12).

This idyllic existence is the Christian's supreme hope and goal. However, if in heaven our destiny is determined and unchangeable, and we have neither the ability nor the desire to choose evil, does that make us robots? If so, then count me in for being a robot! What could be better? We should all agree that this state of perfection is anything but robotic. However, if we are not robots in heaven where we possess no freedom to reject God and our destiny is already determined and fixed, how could we ever say that we are robots here on earth, even if one accepted a doctrine of total hyperpredestination?

In glory, without the ability or the desire to sin, we will never reject God. Likewise, sinners on the earth are without the ability or the desire to be righteous or accept God. This condition can never change unless and until the application of God's grace opens their eyes to see and their ears to hear. Before that time, they do and they choose exactly what they desire, and their innate sinful nature makes it certain that this desire will always be to reject God. They are no more robots here on the earth than we will be robots in heaven!

As a useful analogy of robots and puppets, imagine a totally evil dictator who rules a kingdom here on the earth. This hypothetical ruler is not only totally evil, but he also possesses unlimited resources and total power. If he needs an army of ruthless henchmen, he has as many as he may require. If he needs a spy, he has constant access to any information about anybody or anything. If a foreign power was foolish enough to challenge him, his powerful, invincible army would crush this threat without any substantial struggle. This evil dictator has purged his administration and headquarters of all who are not totally loyal to him, so he has no threat from within his government. His rule is an iron fist, and his power is unchallenged.

We should next consider the subjects of this dictator. They are taxed and forced into hard labor to serve the pleasure of the dictator. They are not allowed to leave the country. They can neither marry any person who is not approved by the dictator nor socialize with unauthorized persons. Any subversive actions or critical conversations are certain to be discovered or overheard, and any such crimes are just as certain to be punished by both torture and eventual execution. In fact, nothing less than total allegiance and obedience from these subjects is tolerated. This description could be continued, but the picture should be complete enough for our purposes.

If we may disregard the imperfections of the analogy, the pertinent question is this: Are the subjects of this dictator robots? Are they free agents, humans who are free to choose to act in any way they like? It should be apparent that these subjects are neither robots nor puppets at all. They are indeed free to choose; however, the iron fist over them is so complete that they always *choose* to do what the dictator demands because to do otherwise is certain death. In other words, their choices, while free in a certain sense, are driven by a weighing of possible outcomes, and they invariably choose what seems best to them, which is also the evil dictator's will. In effect, their will is in bondage to the dictator's will. The subjects could still choose death in this example, of course, but this is only available as an alternative choice because the dictator's power and influence in the analogy is not truly without limit. Moreover, in actuality the bondage of the human will to sin is so insidious that enslaved humans are not even aware of their complete bondage, quite unlike the situation with the dictator in the analogy. Not only can they not choose otherwise than evil, they have absolutely no desire to do so because they cannot and will not see their bondage. Truly, they are dead in their sins (Colossians 2:13).

It would be quite possible to pick apart the details and weaknesses of this analogy, but the choosing of what seems best is consistent with Jonathon Edward's famous 1845 treatise on the freedom of the will.[2] What if, however, the ruler were not a totally evil dictator but instead a holy, totally good, totally perfect, and totally loving God? Would it not be worthy of admiration and outright worship to know that his perfect, holy, and loving purposes will always be freely chosen by all of the subjects of his kingdom because these purposes always seem best to them? Proverbs 21:1 states this truth: God "turns" human hearts "wherever he will." When God lovingly gives his people a heart that will seek him, this is a miraculous transformation of the human will by his boundless grace (Jeremiah 24:7; 1 Corinthians 5:17; Ezekiel 36:26; Ephesians 4:24), not the creation of a robot. In no way is the ability of the human will to choose evil the necessary ingredient or determining factor for a love relationship between God and humanity; rather, what is actually required is the divine transformation of the sinful will into a will that will seek after God. In short, it is grace that is the determinative factor! It is God's willingness to freely choose a sinful, despicable human to be in a love relationship with himself that is the mandatory component that brings about such a miraculous relationship between God and his people.

It may be enlightening to give some consideration to the possible ramifications if it is hypothetically granted that so-called unlimited human free will is necessary for a nonrobotic love relationship with God. In this case, totally autonomous freedom of choice would still in no way require that God create those human beings that he knows in advance will never choose him freely, and there could be nothing to stop God from *only* creating those humans who he has always known will choose him completely of their own free will. God possesses perfect foreknowledge, and he creates every human soul individually by a divine act (Psalm 139:13; Jeremiah 1:5; Isaiah 44:24). Nothing could prevent God, therefore, from simply *not* creating those humans who he foresees with perfect foreknowledge will not accept him of their own free will.

This compelling fact should help us perceive that even if the erroneous belief that humans with a fallen will can freely choose God on their own is true, it only creates more questions than it solves. If God *only* created the humans who will eventually freely choose him of their own free will, the fact that all humans in existence would invariably choose him freely would in no way demand or even imply that they are thereby robots or puppets, even though absolutely no rebels would exist. In fact, because everyone living would freely choose God and opt to do good, it would be much easier for humans to always freely choose God and to opt to do good since everyone around them would be doing the same. It could be speciously argued that this would be the best world that God could create. No charge of unjustness or unfairness could ever be laid on God because there would be no humans in hell; by his own divine free will, God decided not to create those humans. It would seem, superficially at least, that this would be the most loving thing he could do (or not do), because he would thereby be sparing souls from eternal punishment. Moreover, if it were true that it is not God's will that any human should perish in the sense that many advocate, then exactly what has been suggested here would necessarily be his will. Were it not, he assuredly would not create humans that he knows even as he is creating them will most certainly perish.

If this seems a ridiculous proposition, we should realize that it is indeed very much a presumptuous and foolish exercise when we begin deciding how we as humans believe God should have done things or, worse yet, how he could have done things otherwise to make them turn out more to our liking. The cogent fact is that our Father is perfect in every way, and *everything* that he does is perfect. God will never decide to do something the second-best way! It would be absurd to suggest that God could ever say, "Well, my perfect wisdom and power tell me it would be best and perfect to do this thing in a given manner, but I just believe I will do it in an inferior way anyway."

While this thought may perhaps strike some as mere irreverent rambling, this very serious concept was displayed eternally and beautifully for us in Jesus' prayer in Gethsemane. Facing death, Jesus prayed to his beloved Father: "If it be possible, let this cup pass from me" (Matthew 26:39). Jesus is God's beloved, perfect, sinless Son, and we can know that God would have certainly granted Jesus' request instantly if there had existed any alternate, superior method of accomplishing humanity's redemption. Jesus' redeeming death, however, was the perfect, eternal plan of our Father, so it was not to be changed—even by a prayer from Jesus himself! There was no better way, as God had already determined the perfect way. Paul explained in Acts 17:3 that Christ's suffering was indeed "necessary." We can know, therefore, that whenever God does something, it is the perfect thing to do—whether we understand his reasons or not. Instead, we can have the great assurance that the mere fact that our God willed something inescapably means it is indeed perfect; for God to do otherwise would be for him to act contrary to his very nature. Were a single action, plan, or purpose of God not perfect, he would necessarily cease to be God. When we couple this knowledge with the transcendent truths that our Father is sovereign over all and that his purpose is inclusive of everything, we will inevitably find that our worries flee and our faith soars.

As a result of this very powerful realization, we can likewise know that when God creates a human who he knows in advance with perfect foreknowledge will reject him, die in sin, and eternally perish, God nevertheless wills to do so because that is the perfect thing to be done. Likewise, when God creates other humans whom he knows with perfect foreknowledge he will save by a merciful act of his grace, this is also the perfect thing to be done. Therefore, we can know that it is God's perfect will for the universe to be exactly as it is at this moment, and we can know that it is God's perfect will for some to be saved and some to be lost. All of this can be no other way. God creates perfectly, and if God is God, then this is the only way his creation can unfold.

If this seems offensive, we must realize that the alternative is the blasphemous suggestion that the universe has somehow spun out of God's control, and he is now frantically attempting to do his best to regain the upper hand. Such a frustrated, inept, ineffectual, struggling, and seemingly perpetually disappointed God is not the God of the Bible. Our God is in total control, and the fact that God creates some that choose him (by his grace) and some that will never choose him does not make his creations puppets or robots any more than they would be robots if he only created those that would choose him. This state of affairs may or may not strike any of us as the way we might design things ourselves, but that is of no matter. Because this is the way our supreme God designed things, we can know that it is the only perfect design, and obviously it must also be the very best way.

More to the point at hand, we can know that it is God's perfect will and design for every human will to be born in sin, enslaved and unable to choose good until God's grace supplies the remedy. When the time for our dwelling in heaven arrives, it will be God's perfect will for human will to be unable to sin. This too is God's flawless plan. Augustine wrote of God's perfect design for the condition of the human will in his *Enchiridion* and *Admonition and Grace*. He described four states of the human will as pertaining to sin, and these are illustrated in the table below:[3]

Adam; Before the Fall	Able to sin	Able to not sin
Fallen Man	Able to sin	Unable to not sin
Born-Again Man	Able to sin	Able to not sin
Glorified Man	Unable to sin	Able to not sin

Adam's will, according to Augustine, was not in bondage to sin in its unfallen state, and it was able to choose either to sin or to not sin. As a result of the Fall, mankind lost the freedom to be able to choose not to sin. God's grace provides the remedy to those who will believe and restores the freedom of their will to be able to choose not to sin. Only when salvation is fully complete—when God's grace is culminated with our eternal residence in heaven—will we have the freedom of being unable to sin. Speaking of that eventuality, Augustine suggests, "Just as in our present state, our soul is unable to will unhappiness for ourselves, so then it will be forever unable to will iniquity."[4]

Albert Outler, who translated *Enchiridion* into English, expounded on this concept in his footnote to this illuminating writing by Augustine, noting Augustine's wordplay:

> Man's original capacities included both the power not to sin and the power to sin ("posse non peccare et posse peccare"). In Adam's original sin, man lost the posse non peccare (the power not to sin) and retained the posse peccare (the power to sin)—which he continues to exercise. In the fulfillment of grace, man will have the posse peccare taken away and receive the highest of all, the power not to be able to sin, non posse peccare.[5]

Clearly, then, being able to sin is *not* at all a necessary ingredient for an eternal, infinitely wonderful relationship with God. Even though we will not be able to sin, we will certainly not be robots in heaven; we will be the eternal people of our loving Father God. On a more terrestrial note, we have seen that this fact destroys the too common assertion that without our having the unlimited moral ability to either sin or not sin, God could not have a meaningful relationship with us. We have examined many passages that prove just the opposite. In passages such as Ezekiel 36:24–32, Jeremiah 32:30–41, Exodus 6:7–9, and Ezekiel 20:4–12, to mention just a few, God is repeatedly seen to change sinful, rebellious hearts that were neither seeking him nor choosing him—doing so only because of his great love for his chosen and his zeal for the glory of his name. It is thereby biblically demonstrated that, contrary to popular teaching, God can and will bring about a loving, satisfying, intimate relationship with beings who are not choosing him of their own free will, and he does so by changing (healing, freeing) fallen human will and causing it to seek him and choose him.

In Jeremiah 32, for example, the people are specifically said to have "done nothing but evil" in God's sight from their youth (v. 30), and God said, "They have turned to me their back and not their face" (v. 33). These people undeniably deserved God's eternal wrath and punishment, but God instead gave them discipline followed by grace. He made an astoundingly beautiful promise to these sinful people in verses 39 to 41:

> I will give them one heart and one way, that they may fear me forever, for their own good and the good of their children after them. I will make with them an everlasting covenant, that I will not turn away from doing good to them. And I will put the fear of me in their hearts, that they may not turn from me. I will rejoice in doing them good, and I will plant them in this land in faithfulness, with all my heart and all my soul.

What a glorious truth is expressed here! God stated that he would act sovereignly "for their own good and the good of their children after them" (v. 39). It is God that will bring about a love relationship between himself and his chosen people—quite simply because he chooses them of his free will and not at all because they choose him of their free will. As God said in verse 39, this is for our own good, and it is in fact the single most loving thing he could do for us.

Horatius Bonar wisely pointed out that Abraham was a specimen of a sinner saved by grace, a sinner called out of the world by God. God chose Abraham because it was his purpose to do so and not because Abraham was seeking God. It would be foolish to assert that God chose Abraham because God foresaw that Abraham would choose God. In fact, God chose Abraham knowing that Abraham would *never* choose God first. Bonar wrapped up these thoughts with these brilliant words: "And so it is with us. God chooses us, not because he foresees that we would choose him, or that we would believe, but for the very opposite reason. He chooses us just because he foresees that we would neither choose him nor believe at all, of ourselves."[6]

Our Father's matchless grace is likewise displayed clearly in Ezekiel 36. God told how he will bring glory to himself by redeeming his chosen people, and he gave an incredible promise to sovereignly change the hearts of a people that he said had "defiled it [the Promised Land] by their ways and deeds" (v. 16) and had "profaned" God's name "among the nations" (v. 22–23). To these as yet unrepentant people, he said the following:

> I will take you from the nations and gather you from all the countries and bring you into your own land. I will sprinkle clean water on you, and you shall be clean from all your uncleannesses, and from all your idols I will cleanse you. And I will give you a new heart, and a new spirit I will put within you. And I will remove the heart of stone from your flesh and give you a heart of flesh. And I will put my Spirit within you, and cause you to walk in my statutes and be careful to obey my rules.

This magnificent passage teaches us directly that our loving Father gathers us to himself, cleanses us, and puts his Spirit in us to cause us to seek him and to love him—all without waiting on us to first seek him or choose him. Moreover, it is evident in all of the passages examined here that God is demonstrating that if the matter is left up to the enslaved, sinful, rebellious human will, then the love relationship between deity and mortals will never happen. The capacity to choose God freely from a sinful heart is an impossible illusion, an ability we cannot muster of our own will (Romans 3:9–18; 8:7; Psalm 14:2–3). Nevertheless, when God shared with Jeremiah the seemingly impossible things that God was going to do to change the hearts of the sinful people mentioned in chapter 32, he proclaimed of himself, "Behold, I am the Lord, the God of all flesh. Is anything too hard for me?" (Jeremiah 32:26).

We can praise and worship our incredible Father because his beneficent grace poured out according to his everlasting love for his chosen children supplies this vital missing ability. The blessed fruit of his sovereign actions should be our deepest desire: "And they shall be my people, and I will be their God" (Jeremiah 32:38). When God himself moves upon human will and brings about this beautiful, incredible relationship, it is near-blasphemy to accuse him of creating robots by so doing. On the contrary, if it makes us robots for our affectionate Father to individually choose us to be his sons and daughters, to sovereignly give us the ability to choose him and love him in return, and to determine our destiny according to his limitless love facilitated by his infinite power, then the privilege of being our Father's robots should be the most fantastic, wonderful, blessed thing we could ever possibly imagine!

CHAPTER 9

UNCHANGING PERFECTION

Your thoughts concerning God are too human.
— Martin Luther, in a letter to Erasmus[1]

God is God alone, and God alone holds the outcome of the universe in his hands. We, as his creation, are not greater than our Creator (Isaiah 45:9; 64:8; Romans 1:25, 21), and we do not hold the outcome of the universe in our hands! If human will were truly autonomous and unbounded as is suggested by so many today, no less than the eventual destiny of the world would necessarily vacillate wildly based on unpredictable, ostensibly free human choices—choices of which God is said to be incapable of knowing in advance. I do not believe that God has ceded his sovereignty in this regard to humans (Psalm 103:19); rather, the Bible is quite clear that it is God who does as he pleases regarding this world and not humans who do as they please (Daniel 4:35; Psalm 115:3; 135:6). Because it is our perfect, unchanging God who controls the future and not imperfect, changing humans who control the future, the destiny of this world is thereby certain and fixed. Otherwise, as R. K. McGregor Wright pointed out, how could God have certain knowledge about an uncertain future?[2] This crucial point alone demonstrates the shortcomings of the undeserved elevation in stature that the modern church has given to the near idol of "free will."

In Daniel 11, God's angelic messenger to Daniel described what must take place in the future, and in verse 36 he affirmed to Daniel these illuminative words: "What is decreed *will* be done." Indeed, the outcome of the universe is not in question (Revelation 22:6; Revelation 19, 20, and 21; Isaiah 40:7–8; Ecclesiastes 7:13), and that which our Father has decreed from eternity will most certainly be done. The absolute perfection of God's "final product" is not up for debate, subject to alteration, or open to revision in any way by human action, choice, or effort that is unanticipated in God's perfect plan (Isaiah 46:9–10; 45:9–13). In fact, the final outcome could never be characterized as perfect if alternate outcomes or alternate paths were equally acceptable or even possible. Rather, God has already created the perfect tapestry of the whole of his purpose (his will) outside of time, and we will one day admire and worship the role that each of us has in its complete, total, and unified perfection.

The word *tapestry* is a useful, analogous term appropriate for describing God's purpose, in that his single eternal purpose must necessarily be composed of an intricate, interwoven web of a seemingly infinitely large number of tiny events that come together to form the single, unique, and perfect outcome. For instance, what if my great-great-great-great-grandparents had not married because my great-great-great-great-grandfather was run over by a train "by chance" before he could get married? If that had happened, I would not be here today, and my place in God's perfect tapestry would be missing. Because it would be missing a piece, the tapestry could not be perfect any longer. There can be no detail too small to be outside of God's sovereign control if his perfect tapestry is to be completed—and it will be completed!

To coin a phrase of the type for which Yogi Berra became famous, I believe that it is tremendously difficult for us to understand how infinite is God's infiniteness and how perfect is his perfection! We read that his power is unimaginable and his understanding is infinite (Psalm 147:5; Isaiah 40:28), but I believe we nevertheless fail to grasp how God's purpose is both perfect and infinitely inclusive. In so doing, at best we make God smaller than the infinite God that he is, and at worst we create a God of our own making. David encourages us to magnify God, not minimize him! (Psalm 34:3; 69:30). God tells us that he does not change, and because he does not change, we are not consumed (Malachi 3:6). Indeed, the interminable steadfastness of his loving purpose is our great hope.

It is imperative, therefore, that we strive to understand the foundational nature of the fundamental necessity that because God's purpose (his will) is perfect, it cannot be improved or changed. Pause and ponder that postulate for a moment. If God *ever* changed his purpose, the purpose that he said that he *would* certainly accomplish (Numbers 23:19; Isaiah 14:24; 46:10; 55:11), then either the first purpose or the new, changed purpose would have to be better in some way; *they could not both be perfect*. The result runs deeper still, though, because if God *ever* changed his purpose, then he cannot be God at all! A god that discovers a better plan or is forced to change his plan to adapt to an unforeseen development is not a god at all. Further, the very foundational reason for which we can trust God at his word is that he will never change it. If we even dare to consider that our God is not immutable, then we have created a God that is inconsistent and variable, perhaps even capricious, and there can be no real confidence or comfort in such a god.

If we believe God changes his purpose, his will, and his plan, then why would we not believe that he could very well one day issue this shocking declaration: "With great apologies to the inhabitants of the earth, the plan has now been changed, and I have developed a new purpose. The Bible has been withdrawn in its entirety, as has the previous plan of redemption. A new, but still changeable, plan will be provided to you within several hundred years. In the meantime, hope for the best." This ridiculous example demonstrates with absurdity how this bad doctrine can be exposed by carrying it to its logical end. The illustration is asinine only because we know that God does not change his eternal purpose and plan even a tiny bit.

Preposterous as it may be, this illustration is nevertheless not far from the concept that is actually believed by many. It is a common notion that the "Old Testament God" came up with the idea of making a deal with Abraham and later providing the Ten Commandments and the Law in order to save his chosen people, the Israelites—a plan we call the "old covenant." It is then suggested that when it became apparent that this plan was not working very well because the people were not capable of obeying the Law as a result of their fallen, sinful natures, God came up with a new, better idea and sent Jesus to pay the price for humankind's sins. This supposedly new and improved plan is what we call the "new covenant." We must be careful to comprehend the extreme danger of this view. If we believe that the new covenant is God's "better idea" developed after humans fouled up the first plan rather than the glorious eternally-planned culmination of his single, ageless plan, we have made our God into a less than perfect, mutable, and thereby unreliable God.

Jesus himself confirmed that not even the smallest detail will go unfulfilled from the portion of God's perfect plan that we now refer to as the "old covenant" or "the Law" (Matthew 5:18). We can therefore base our faith on the absolute certainty that our Father will not at one time have a purpose that includes loving us but then later develop a better or different plan that does not include us (Malachi 3:6; Psalm 119:89–91; Isaiah 40:8). The surprisingly common notion that God reacts to our actions and changes his plan accordingly has to be carefully examined under the light of God's perfect supremacy, and it ultimately must be rejected. We are not in a friendly chess match with our maker!

This vital concept is much more than just an exercise in critical thinking; Isaiah 31:2 informs us categorically that "he does not call back his words," and we read in Hebrews 6:17 of "the unchangeable character of his purpose." We should note carefully that no exceptions are found in these verses for the possibility that the omniscient God of the universe could be taken by surprise by unanticipated human choices or actions. Additionally, we are given a wonderful assurance in James 1:17 that there is "no variation" at all with our God, not even a "shadow due to change." This point is driven home with the magnificent and powerful declaration found in Psalm 33:11: "The counsel [purpose] of the Lord stands forever, the plans of his heart to all generations."

If an earthly father were to promise to take his child fishing on a given weekend, we know the plans of even the best of fathers could be changed by unforeseen circumstances such that he may be unable to keep that promise. If we are to truly know and trust our loving heavenly Father, then we must understand that there exists no such possibility with our God. There are no unforeseen circumstances or unanticipated complications for our Father—despite much bad teaching to the contrary. Our Father's intentions are pure and holy, his plans for his chosen are for our good, and his ability is as limitless as his love for his chosen. It is we humans who artificially place limits on his power and thereby on his love as well, and in so doing we rob ourselves of the real security to be found in our Father's steadfast love and purpose.

Twenty times in the Psalms David exalts our God as his "Rock." Could David have joyfully written about this Rock if he had served the weak, ineffectual God that is presented in too many of today's churches? How can a God that is said to be constantly adapting to the sovereignty of the human free will be in any way characterized as a "Rock"? We truly should be ashamed. We should instead come to savor the unchangeable character of our God's purpose and rest comfortably in the assurance that he does not call back his words. What comfort, what contentment, what rest, and what joy is ours for the taking if we can come to grasp the depth and the reach of this single fantastic statement: "The plans of the Lord stand firm forever, the purposes of his heart through all generations" (Psalm 33:11 NIV).

As an illustration of this immutability of God's purpose that is both practical and contemporary, consider the case of a test tube baby. We know that each of us was formed by God in our mother's womb (Psalm 139:13; Jeremiah 1:5; Isaiah 44:24). The process may well be biological, but the creation is nonetheless a divine act. Here we see God's sovereignty over human choices on display yet again; if a life is formed in a human womb, it is God who forms it! While this may be a startling realization for some to whom this thought has never before occurred, it is nevertheless an incontrovertible truth with far-reaching implications. God also tells us that our names were written in the Lamb's Book of Life before the foundation of the world and that he chose us before the foundation of the world (Revelation 17:8; Revelation 13:8; Matthew 25:34; Ephesians 1:4; 2:10; 2 Timothy 1:9). This choice was quite obviously made before our Father formed us in the womb, but it was certainly not made before he knew he would create us.

In the case of a test tube baby, however, humans have developed technology to invoke biological processes and thereby fertilize an egg that would not otherwise have been fertilized. Hence, one might erroneously conclude that the free will choices of humans and their advanced technology has resulted in a life being created that God did not intend to create or had not planned on creating when he created the earth and the universe. If we choose to believe that human purpose and choices are not subservient to God's purpose, then we must also believe that it is indeed possible that a life comes into existence that God did not create, intend, or choose. If so, then how would it be possible for that person's name to be in the Book of Life from before the foundation of the world? If not, can test tube babies be saved? If the open theists are correct, and God cannot foreknow human choices and actions until they actually happen, then he could not have foreknown that these babies would even exist, much less write their names in the Book of Life before the foundation of the world.

The question of a test tube baby's salvation is admittedly a fairly ridiculous proposition, a question meant to invoke thought and perception regarding a much more serious question: Did humans foil or thwart God's purpose with their test tube babies? Did God have to come up with a new, improved, "more perfect" purpose to adapt to those pesky humans with their incessant technological advances? Of course not! God was not surprised by this technology. In fact, it could not have been developed apart from his will, as we know that all things are from him and through him (Romans 11:36; Colossians 1:17). Furthermore, this is hardly "high tech" for a God who sovereignly caused an elderly, postmenopausal Sarah to conceive thousands of years before (Genesis 18:11).

God's purpose, which was set in eternity past, included the test tube babies just as much as it did those conceived by normal means, and God is no less their creator and maker than he is those of us who were conceived normally. They too are fearfully and wonderfully made, and they hold a necessary and indispensable place in the immutable tapestry of God's perfect purpose for the entire universe. Human inventions and human choices do not confound God's purpose in any way! If this truth seems a bit self-evident, we should be careful to understand the conclusions that must follow. For example, if it is not possible for humans to invent a technology that creates a life that God's purpose never anticipated or intended, then why would we ever think that we could make a "free will choice" that could somehow confound, detour, or negate God's eternal purpose for the universe and for ourselves?

It is axiomatic that God's word and God's purpose are actually one and the same thing. Even if these were different things—which they are not—one could never contradict the other even for an instant. Any possibility that God's purpose is open to change is eliminated completely by Psalm

119:89, which declares, "Forever, O Lord, thy word is *settled* in heaven." Psalm 33:4 is yet another reminder that God's purpose is "right and his works are done in truth," or, in a word, perfect. Peter repeated Isaiah 40:6–8 in 1 Peter 1:24–25 (NIV), and he taught us that even though humans and the things of humans are transient, changing, and fading, the "word of the Lord stands forever." In these passages, the word *word* is obviously encompassing God's entire purpose as well as his spoken words of action and truth, and it is not referring only to the Bible—although the Bible is certainly both included in and revelatory of God's purpose. Moreover, the purpose spoken by God with his settled word will *always* be accomplished (Isaiah 55:11).

It is essential that we realize and acknowledge that these passages do not invert the relationship between God and humanity by suggesting that the word of the Lord is transient and is constantly adapting to humans' sovereign ("free") choices and actions, as seems to be so popular in recent teaching. In fact, these passages disallow any such possibility; it is God's purpose that is unchanging and he alone who is truly sovereign. It is God who is working out with perfect faithfulness his own plans that were formed long ago (Isaiah 25:1; 46:10; Psalm 40:5). Why, then, do we often hear the exact opposite preached in today's church? We must perceive that when we incorrectly believe God to be changeable and incapable of unerringly anticipating human choices, we inevitably make him weak and undependable in our estimation, even if we are not cognizant that we have so debased him.

Sometimes, however, the assault upon our Father's reliability, wisdom, and preeminence is not directly based on his alleged inability to accurately foresee every detail of the future, but may instead originate from the rather fantastic notion that humans may well have an idea or plan that is better and more desirable than God's eternal, perfect plan. This mind-set has established a solid foothold in today's churches, with the sad result that our concept of God is weakened even further. Perhaps without realizing it, we create a God who is not worthy of our faith, trust, and confidence when we believe that our thoughts and ways may well be superior to his. As a result, we commit the inestimably great error of believing we should strive to have God work in the way we see fit rather than accepting as best the way God sees fit, confident that his is the holy, perfect, and inerrant purpose. This error is all too common in our churches, and it is seen clearly in these astounding words from the book of a popular author:

Prayer affects God more powerfully than His own purposes. God's will, words and purposes are all subject to review when the mighty potencies of prayer come in. How mighty prayer is with God may be seen as he readily sets aside His own fixed and declared purposes in answer to prayer.[3]

This is an astonishing, bewildering assertion—to say the least. We should first recall a few key Scriptures that have been examined previously. We have seen that "the plans of the Lord stand firm forever, the purposes of his heart through all generations" (Psalm 33:11 NIV). Can this be reconciled in any manner to this writer's assertion? God declared, "My counsel shall stand, and I will accomplish all my purpose" (Isaiah 46:10), but we claim to have discovered a way to make the God of the universe set aside his divinely perfect purpose and willingly substitute our own flawed thinking. In so doing, we ignore the writer of Hebrews who asserted that God's purpose was "unchangeable" (Hebrews 6:10). Yet again, it seems that the Bible is being willingly rewritten. In the real Bible, we read the following unmistakable words that are backed by the oath of God himself: "The Lord of hosts has sworn: 'As I have planned, so shall it be, and as I have purposed, so shall it stand'" (Isaiah 14:24). The version rewritten to suit our presumptuous usurpation of God's supremacy would read more like this: "The Lord of hosts has acquiesced: 'As humans have planned, so shall it be, and as humans have purposed, so shall he do it.'"

This brash belief may perhaps make many Christians feel more empowered since they suppose they may wield the power of the Lord Almighty in accordance with their own whims rather than in subjugation to his perfect will, but in reality this belief undermines a Christian's true hope and comfort. *How can we worship as perfect a God whose mind we are striving to change?* With this sort of message being systematically taught—that our Father's purpose is both changeable and subject to our desires in prayer—is it any wonder that we so often fail to live in the security of our Father's loving purpose? In this quotation, the author actually has the temerity to suggest that Christians should view it as a good thing that God's purpose is "subject to review." Who do we think we are? God's will subject to our review? God says, "Who is this that darkens counsel by words without knowledge?" (Job 38:2). Not only do we brazenly think that we may have a better purpose than our God's, we must also thereby labor under the burden created by the assumption that his purpose for us is constantly changing. It would therefore have to be our responsibility to strive to keep our Father constantly updated with good ideas for how to improve his "no longer perfect" purpose for our lives.

Can we really expect God to honor such human arrogance? When this kind of teaching lodges in our hearts, it is no wonder we live lives characterized by striving instead of stillness (cf. Psalm 46:10). Moreover, how can we truly trust in our Father to always work effectually for our good and for his glory when we are taught that we need to earnestly endeavor in prayer to have our human will done in heaven rather than his perfect will done on earth? It should be trivially obvious that when Jesus taught us to pray, he did not in any way suggest we pray that our will be done in heaven; rather, he made it plain that we should pray to our Father, "Your will be done, on earth as it is in heaven" (Matthew 6:10).

However, the problem with this poor teaching runs much deeper. It is rooted in the arrogant belief that there could be even the slightest possibility that the plan suggested by a human in prayer could be a plan superior in any way to God's previously "fixed and declared purpose," such that God would actually "readily set aside" his own perfect plan and adopt a flawed, human plan instead, as was directly suggested by the writer above. What folly! Do we actually suppose that we could come up with a plan or a course of action that has not occurred to our loving Father, that we could provide the Almighty with a better idea? It may well inflate the human sense of self-importance for a person to falsely believe that he or she could ever talk God into doing something that was not originally God's will and purpose, but this reversal of sovereignty—this exchange of thrones—is a usurping fantasy that can in no manner be pleasing to God. Moreover, those who take up this flabbergasting belief are inevitably the very same individuals who adamantly argue that God is a gentleman who respects human free will so much that he will not interfere with the human will. While they say God will not change the human free will, they have absolutely no problem believing that humans can change God's eternal free will. Heaven help us when this fatuousness is exposed in the light of glory!

For example, do we really believe we can pray hard enough, long enough, forcefully enough, or with enough people agreeing together such that we could change who God has determined will sit at his left and his right in heaven when Jesus himself said that even he could not change his Father's fixed and determined purpose? (Mark 10:40). God also makes it plain that we cannot know the day or the hour that he has precisely and eternally set for Christ's return; in fact, Jesus said that even he did not know the date and the hour (Acts 1:7; Mark 13:32). Do we believe that we could get enough people together to pray hard enough or long enough to change God's declared, fixed purpose in this regard? These questions have an obvious answer: "Not in this eternity!" And yet, the writer above states that God is willing to "readily set aside his own fixed and determined purpose" in response to human prayer. If we were to pray without ceasing until Christ returns and interrupts us in the act, we are still not going to get God to change his purpose and give us the date and time of Christ's return. Nonetheless, the same writer also amazingly states, "Prayer can get anything that God has."[4] Does that mean we can have that throne to God's right after all? Does that mean we can pray our way to a special revelation of the exact date and time of Christ's return? Unless we really believe God has given his throne over to humans, it should strike us as utter nonsense to suggest that we could ever use prayer to "get anything that God has."

We should be careful to make yet another critical observation at this point. There well may be those who attempt to defend the notion that God will change his fixed and determined eternal purpose in response to prayer by suggesting that the examples cited in the previous paragraph are not inclusive of the types of circumstances in which God is willing to allow his perfect purpose to be substituted with human purpose. However, we should readily see that this very suggestion is what undoes the ability to trust in our God. If we do not believe that humans can change God's fixed purpose as to who will sit at his right and his left in heaven, as well as other prayers in this category, but we persist in believing that human prayer does indeed change God's fixed and determined purpose in other circumstances in other categories, then how are we to know which prayers fall into which category and thereby pray with confidence? We cannot suggest that humans decide which prayers fall into which category, because that returns us to the very same usurping of our Father's throne. Therefore, if we conclude that God will only *sometimes* change his "fixed and determined purposes" in response to our prayers and *sometimes not*, then how can we ever pray with confidence? Is not the faith born of such utmost confidence the key ingredient in effectual prayer?

If we teach that sometimes we can change God's will by our prayers and sometimes we cannot, there is obviously no confidence to be had in that belief, and no true way to pray in real faith. If instead we say the answer is that we pray in submission to God's will, we have of course come across the correct solution. However, we must notice that we have thereby defeated the entire supposition that God will change his "fixed and determined" will to suit our own. Indeed, by correctly asserting that we should pray in submission to God's will, we are acknowledging that God will not act contrary to his established will in response to human prayer. True confidence in prayer comes only from knowing with certainty that God's purpose will always be accomplished, that his will must necessarily be done because he alone is God.

By teaching that we can get anything we want from God if we pray earnestly enough, hard enough, long enough, and with enough people agreeing, we believe we have created a bounty for ourselves. We may think we have come upon a divine windfall by believing that God can be made to set aside his purpose and do our will instead. In fact, we have unknowingly created an unreliable, untrustworthy God. This may seem counterintuitive, but it is inevitable because if we are brutally honest about our experience in prayer and brutally honest about Scripture, both will clearly teach us that these beguiling assertions cannot possibly be true. When we think we have fulfilled all of the components of the formula for a prayer that will get God to change his purpose and do things our own way (many books are filled with such formulas), and yet God still fails to do as we petitioned him to do in our prayer, we must conclude that either God is unreliable in answering prayer, or we must try all the harder to get him to see the wisdom of our ways and the error of his own, thinking that perhaps we will get it right next time. Either conclusion robs us completely of our ability to rest in quiet trust in a loving relationship with our affectionate and caring Father who we know will always fulfill his perfect purpose for our lives.

If we believe we can change God's will, and yet he does not reliably answer as we ask, we have no true confidence. On the other hand, if it is never certain whether we have been earnest enough, had enough faith, been repetitious enough, or gathered enough prayer partners, then prayer is still not reliable, and it remains impossible to pray with true confidence. If we are taught that God's failure to change his eternal purpose and do things our way is only a result of shortcomings in our own efforts, methods, or faith, we may well respond by striving all the harder, and our inner hearts will become even more convinced of either the unreliability or the aloofness of our God.

As a silly example of a very serious concept, consider the reliability of God in prayer concerning the color of the carpet for the new church building. What if two groups of Christians are both praying to get God to set aside his fixed and determined purpose and to instead bring about the installation of the carpet color of their own choice? Assuming the two carpet colors are quite different, will the stronger Christians prevail in this prayer? Or, perhaps it could be that each group will change God's purpose back and forth in rapid succession as they pray, and quite simply the last group praying will prevail and have its way with God and the new carpet. Can we not realize that neither of these silly groups is going to change God's purpose, and God's fixed and determined purpose will inevitably prevail, just as it always does?

This example is obviously flippant, but the concept is nevertheless crucial. If what the author cited above set forth is correct, and if what is taught all too frequently in many churches is also correct, then God's fixed and determined purpose, his will, can be changed by Christians' prayers. Therefore, it would have to be possible for a Christian to "pray through" about a concern, a circumstance, or even another person and thereby change God's purpose; after all, the author asserted strongly that God would readily set aside his own purpose and adopt the praying Christian's purpose instead. This may all seem well and good because the Christian was seemingly able to pray confidently and effectually. But all is not as it seems. There are at least two problems here, and the first is that the Christian's imperfect will is being done in heaven instead of God's perfect will being done on earth. The second issue is that this praying Christian is not the only praying Christian.

It is likely, if not certain, that other Christians are also praying about the same concern, circumstance, or person. They too, if this notion be correct, have the power to get God to set aside his determined purpose and substitute their own will. So, just when the first praying Christian believes he has the matter all settled in prayer—that God is going to act according to his prayers instead of God's original, eternal purpose—along comes the second praying Christian and talks God into something entirely different. In so doing, the first praying Christian's prayer is negated and obliterated. The first Christian may have thought he could rest comfortably in God's newly settled purpose that was according to his prayer, but before he could even get comfortable, God had changed his purpose yet again. Suddenly, a changeable divine purpose is not the incredible blessing he might have initially suspected.

Of course, the second praying Christian's answer to prayer is now subject to the prayers of a third praying Christian, and who knows but what the first praying Christian may return to prayer, bring along extra prayer partners this time, and get God's purpose changed back to his way of thinking? Hopefully, it now becomes brilliantly obvious why the notion of the writer previously quoted cannot stand in actual practice. Moreover, it should be plainly apparent why such a notion actually destroys confidence in prayer instead of supplying it! A God of our own creation that is no longer immutable is an imperfect, variable, unreliable god. Confidence in prayer comes not from knowing that we can change our Father's purpose, but rather from knowing that his purpose can never be changed!

Prayer is certainly vital, and prayers are certainly answered. But we must also realize that prayer is part of God's purpose. If he can move the hearts of Assyrian warriors to attack foreign countries without their realizing he has done so, he just as easily can move his people to pray. As such, both our prayers and his answers are, and always were, a part of his eternal, unchanging, and perfect purpose. For example, God answered Daniel's prayer regarding the interpretation of Nebuchadnezzar's dream (Daniel 2:18–19). However, God did not change his purpose to do so. Daniel's exile to Babylon along with the other Hebrews was God's purpose. It was God's purpose to send the dream to Nebuchadnezzar to reveal the future. God's purpose to reveal the future to Nebuchadnezzar and later generations through the dream would have been thwarted had not someone been able to interpret the dream, but we know that God's purpose is never thwarted. God had placed Daniel there so that Daniel would pray for an interpretation and receive the interpretation. Not surprisingly, all this is exactly what God made happen. Indeed, when we realize that prayer is about aligning our hearts with his will and that prayer is about changing us instead of changing God, we can pray with complete confidence. We have no false need to ratchet up our external earnestness or emotion if it appears we are not getting the job done. We pray confidently, knowing that we are not attempting to alter God's perfect purpose with our own ideas; rather, we are affirming and accomplishing his perfect purpose with our prayers!

We need not undermine the very foundation of our confidence by striving to get God to change his perfect purpose. When we come to understand the unchanging perfection of God's holy, eternal purpose, we no longer fear what our fellow humans may do to us or may not do for us. We recognize that we would not want to change our loving Father's flawless purpose for our lives even if we could. We know, along with Paul in Romans 8:31–39, that nothing in all creation can separate us from our Father's loving purpose.

Furthermore, we no longer fear what Satan or his demons may do to us. Our Father's purpose, plan, and power are eternal, unchanging, and infinite, and they will most certainly overcome any finite resistance. Just as the human free will is finite, so we can rejoice that Satan and his demons are finite as well, which renders them all completely incapable of even the tiniest amount of rebellion or resistance in excess of that which God's perfect, indomitable purpose allows. God knew exactly what would happen in the future if he were to create Satan, and he nevertheless sovereignly chose to do so for his own purpose. Indeed, the twenty-four elders in heaven worship our God for his awesome wisdom and power in creating *all things* (which would include Satan) and giving all things their very being in order to accomplish his will, and these elders exalt our Father because nothing exists apart from his holy purpose! (Revelation 4:11).

Because of this great fact, we know that our God cannot truly be God and ever be surprised by Satan's actions, nor could he ever have any need at all to react to these actions by changing his own will, purpose, or actions. To do so would mean that God's original, perfect purpose was somehow thwarted by an inferior, finite, created being (Satan, demon, human, or any other), such that God had to come up with a new and better purpose to meet the challenge. Of course, this is sacrilege. Nevertheless, this mind-set still creeps into much, if not most, of our preaching and teaching today. The straightforward fact is that God's plans and purpose are neither deterred nor detoured by either human choices or demonic challenge—they *will* prevail (see Romans 8:38–39, for example). Isaiah 14:26–27 also makes this truism exceedingly clear:

> This is the purpose that is purposed concerning the whole earth, and this is the hand that is stretched out over all the nations. For the Lord of hosts has purposed, and who will annul it? His hand is stretched out, and who will turn it back?

It is important to see that the Lord does not mention in this passage that he might conceivably have to change his purpose or come up with a better, more effective plan if either humans or Satan resist or surprise him. While an earthly general might be surprised by his adversary's actions and be forced to sacrifice some of his own soldiers or resources for the greater good in order to adapt and react to the enemy's change of tactics, God's perfection does not allow for any such possibility. We can take great comfort in that realization! Further, the passage does not allow for any possibility that our Father's purpose encompasses anything or anybody less than the entire earth and all of its peoples.

Ultimately, the blessed truth that "one perfect purpose is all it takes" is why we can proclaim with the psalmist that "God is our Rock!" This unchanging perfection is why our Father is worthy of complete trust and unbounded worship. "Let us offer to God acceptable worship with reverence and awe" because his is a "kingdom that cannot be shaken"! (Hebrews 12:28). What comfort could we possibly have if we knew that God's purposes were constantly changing, knowing that the next change might leave us out in the cold instead of being immutably "chosen before the foundation of the world"? (Ephesians 1:4; 2 Timothy 1:9). As was quoted earlier, Martin Luther contended, "If you hesitate to believe, or are too proud to acknowledge, that God foreknows and wills all things, not contingently but necessarily and immutably, how can we believe, trust, and rely on his promises?" The alternative (and the perfect one at that) is laying hold of the certainty that God will *never* change his word, his will, and his purpose; what he says is what he will do—absolutely, positively, and with no exceptions. As it is said in Psalm 33:9, "For he spoke, and it came to be; he commanded, and it stood firm."

David Clarkson, a scholar, writer, and preacher from the 1600s, wrote succinctly of this very fact: "God's saying, is doing." To this lucid explanation, Clarkson added this enlightened observation: "The root of all certainty is God's will. If he is willing to promise, he is willing to perform. They are the same to him."[5] Paul also exalted in Romans 11:29 that "the gifts and the calling of God are irrevocable." The only solid foundation and reliable basis for our abiding confidence is that our Father's purpose is perfect, and, as such, it cannot and will not change. He is not God if he is not unchangeable! Our foundation is indeed solid because we can know that "the counsel of the Lord will stand forever" (Proverbs 19:21; Psalm 33:11; Hebrews 6:17–18; Isaiah 46:10). Our confidence is unshakeable because our loving Father tells us, "As I have planned it, so shall it be, and as I have purposed, so shall it stand" (Isaiah 14:24).

Finally, we must know there is in actuality only one purpose (counsel, or will) of God. *All* things are included in this singular purpose. As such, the actions of one human that are supposedly contrary to God's purpose cannot possibly snuff out God's purpose for another human. The actions of one nation do not change God's eternal purpose for all the other nations. It is *all* interwoven (recall the tapestry analogy), and there is just one eternal purpose (Ephesians 3:11; Hebrews 6:17), which was established before the foundation of the world (Isaiah 37:26; Isaiah 46:9; Titus 1:2; 1 Peter 1:20; Ephesians 1:4). God does not have one constantly changing purpose for one person and another constantly changing purpose for another. God is One, and his purpose is One; he sovereignly declares that "his purpose will stand" (Isaiah 46:10). We may audaciously trust our ever-attentive and absolutely faithful Father because we have the certitude in our soul that "his way is perfect" (Psalm 18:30) and because we possess the calming assurance that "whatever God does endures forever" (Ecclesiastes 3:14). The unchanging perfection of our Father and his eternal, indomitable purpose should fill us with amazing joy, just as the psalmist declared: "The Lord reigns, let the earth rejoice" (Psalm 97:1). He is our true, perfect Rock!

CHAPTER 10

THE GOD OF OUR CONFIDENCE

We never know so much of heaven in our own souls, nor stand so high upon the mount of communion with God, as when his Spirit, breathing on our heart, makes us lie low at the footstool of sovereign grace, and inspires us with this cry, "O God, be mine the comfort of salvation, but Thine be the entire praise of it."

— Augustus Toplady,
Eighteenth-century clergyman and writer of the hymn
"Rock of Ages"[1]

We have seen that God's perfect, unchanging purpose encompasses all things: our very existence, our surroundings and conditions, our friends, our family, our salvation, and our eternal home. As this truth permeates our beings, we begin to walk in the glorious confidence of knowing that our loving Father's eternal purpose for our good will certainly be accomplished. This is positively a life-changing awareness. Having disposed of the false worry that God may not be willing to interfere with our own free will or the free will of others with whom we interact, we constantly recognize that God's hand is at work in our lives even when we do not understand his purpose at the moment.

It is this glorious realization that enabled Paul and Silas to sing in prison (Acts 16:25). In the same manner, this great truth gives a solid foundation for our faith, and we can truly "give thanks in all circumstances" (1 Thessalonians 5:18). In fact, a firm understanding of our Father's preeminence is the only means by which such a command may become a blessed reality instead of an impossible platitude. It is only this knowledge that can truly empower us to live our lives "giving thanks always and for everything to God the Father in the name of our Lord Jesus Christ" (Ephesians 5:20). We remember the lesson of the sparrows, and we walk in confidence rather than worry. We join David in reveling, "Because he is at my right hand, I shall not be shaken" (Psalm 16:8). Even forgiveness is dramatically easier as we realize that what our offender meant for harm, God meant for our good (Genesis 50:20). Unwavering in our awareness of our Father's constant presence, attention, and love, we too may exultingly proclaim, "Therefore my heart is glad, and my whole being rejoices; my flesh also dwells secure. For you will not abandon my soul" (Psalm 16:9–10).

Conversely, when we fail to fully perceive and apply this truth, we are guilty of neglecting to acknowledge our Father's complete involvement in every detail of our lives and destinies. Worse yet, we may incorrectly ascribe his divine workings to haphazard human effort or choice. As an illustration that is necessarily just a small component of this much larger concept, we can consider the hypothetical situation where a person's aunt Mabel leads that person to Christ. In this divine act, we see God's purpose and will unfold as observed in the lives of two different people at a moment in time when the two lives intersect. If, as we so often hear, the newly saved person is taught to believe such that he gives credit and honor to Aunt Mabel for leading him to Christ (saying, for example, "If it had not been for my aunt Mabel, I would have never found the Lord"), he is, in effect, asserting that he and Aunt Mabel have something—even if we are careful to say that it is a very small something—to boast about in his salvation. He is claiming that it was in fact brought about or helped along by something other than God's purpose or something in addition to God's purpose. He is claiming that Aunt Mabel caused him to "find" the Lord rather than understanding that his loving Father first found him! However, Scripture clearly teaches that we have *nothing at all* to boast about in our salvation except the Cross—we may not take credit for even a miniscule contribution. Such thinking runs cross-grain to a host of New Testament teaching, including Ephesian 2:9, Romans 3:27, Romans 4:2, 1 Corinthians 1:29, 4:7, John 6:63, and others, by boasting or suggesting that a person is in Christ because of anybody or anything else but God's perfect purpose and effectual power (1 Corinthians 1:30; 2 Timothy 1:9; James 1:18; Romans 9:16; 1 Peter 1:3; Hebrews 9:15; John 1:13; 3:27; Titus 3:5).

This misattribution of the credit for salvation, while very serious indeed, may not be the most crucial result of this failure to properly apprehend our Father's sovereignty and loving purpose. None of us should be comfortable in believing that our own salvation, or anybody else's, depended on whether Aunt Mabel or any other human managed to find the time or opportunity to lead us to Christ. This view minimizes and severely diminishes the sovereign love that our Father has for each of us individually, and it artificially limits his power, thus making him smaller and less trustworthy instead of magnifying and glorifying him. We may think that Aunt Mabel could have chosen to witness to anybody, but it was actually God who chose us, gave us to Christ before we even accepted him (John 6:37–39; 17:24; 17:6–9; 10:29), pursued us, and *"caused* us to be born again"—not Aunt Mabel (1 Peter 1:3; 1 Corinthians 1:30; John 15:16; 6:44; Romans 8:29–30; Ephesians 1:4; 1 Peter 5:13, 10). According to Acts 2:47, it is God who adds to the church those individuals who are saved—not Aunt Mabel. It is Jesus who "gives life," and he gives it "to whom he will" (John 5:21). If and when we come to comprehend that we are the direct objects of God's transcendent purpose, this incredible revelation makes all the difference in our relationship with our loving and pursuing Father.

Can we even conceive of a God who is said to "choose us" and "love us greatly" but allows us to go to hell because nobody happened to "freely" chose to share the Gospel with us since God was unable or unwilling to interfere with their free will and thereby cause them to decide to do so? Could we ever really believe in and trust in God's personal love for us as individuals if our redemption and adoption as his sons and daughters were allowed to be dependent on whether some ostensibly "free" human shares the Gospel with us or not? Furthermore, even if they did freely decide to share the Gospel with us, would not that just mean that we "got lucky" and were fortuitously informed of a wonderful opportunity of which we could avail ourselves? This is altogether different from experiencing the incredible wonder of the God of the universe—who is our own loving Father—choosing us in his infinite love and seeing to it that we are absolutely called unto himself by his own power and doing. What confidence could be placed in his love if the former were the case? If the former were indeed the case, would we not have to believe that if more people just "helped God out," then more people would somehow be informed of this "lucky" opportunity of which they too could avail themselves? *Since this kind of teaching has become both pervasive and rampant, is it any wonder we struggle to truly experience the Father's love in today's church?*

If we are ever to understand or truly experience the incredible love that our Father has for us, we must understand the huge difference between the God of the universe choosing us in love, redeeming us, calling us, and bringing us to himself, thereby *"causing* us to be born again" (1 Peter 1:3; 1 Corinthians 1:26–31; 1 Thessalonians 5:24; John 6:37; 6:44; 10:14–16; Matthew 11:27; 2 Thessalonians 2:13) and that of Aunt Mabel serendipitously happening to find the time and opportunity to lead us to the supposed God of the universe who could not reach us by his own doing. We are told that the God of the latter view is benevolent enough to accept us if we somehow manage to find him, ostensibly for Christ's sake, as if we were a stray dog that Christ brought home and begged his Father to keep. It should be quite obvious to us which of these two views of God's love for us and his role in our salvation is correct and trustworthy, but Paul also settled the question clearly in Ephesians 2. In verses 1 through 8, he showed us that it was God himself who made us alive "even when we were dead" expressly "because of the great love with which he loved us," and this specifically is "not your [our] own doing" (v. 8).

God saves us for the purpose of bringing glory to himself, according to Paul in Ephesians 1:5–6, 1:12, Romans 9:23, 2 Thessalonians 1:12, and Romans 1:5. Peter told us in 2 Peter 1:3 that God calls us to his own glory. God also makes it clear that he will not share his glory with another (Isaiah 48:11), so we must indeed be careful to give God the glory that he alone deserves. However, the major truth that we are considering here is not that *all* the glory must go to God instead of Aunt Mabel (which it must), but rather that God's singular, unchanging, immaculate, and inevitable purpose encompasses the entire earth and all of humankind, right down to the smallest detail when one human leads another human to salvation—this for God's own glory. This is the root from which our confidence springs. Jesus himself spoke of the certainty of this particular part of his Father's purpose in John 6:37, where he stated categorically that *"all* that the Father gives me *will* come to me." These powerful words teach us that when Aunt Mabel leads someone to Christ, we must give the glory to God alone (Matthew 11:27; John 6:44) and realize that our loving Father's singular purpose was fulfilled, and it was fulfilled in the exact manner, place, and time as he has eternally known and willed it would be.

Regarding this loving, eternal purpose, I have heard it taught that although God is sovereign over, predestines, and controls circumstances and situations, he nevertheless does not interfere with actual human choices since he is said to be a great respecter of human free will. This reasoning seems specious at best, if not downright irrational. The first problem is a logical inconsistency, in that human choices are clearly influenced by and based upon circumstances and situations, so it would be contradictory to suggest that any being could control circumstances and situations on earth without thereby influencing and interfering with human choices. A second problem with this assertion is even larger than the first. Consider, for example, that Esther's circumstances (the position and opportunity to choose to risk her life by approaching the king uninvited in order to save her people) were occasioned only as a result of Ahasuerus' choices, which were clearly influenced and directed by a sovereign God. It seems very clear, then, that one person's circumstances are the result of other people's choices, and it is therefore impossible to place one outside of God's sovereign control without placing the other outside of God's control as well.

When we attempt to make such an arbitrary distinction between what God controls and what is outside of his control, the resulting "god" is an unscriptural, weak, ineffectual god, and one symptom of believing in such a god would necessarily be to ascribe the credit and glory for one's salvation to a human instead of to God alone, where it rightly belongs. Such a view denies that all things are truly from him and that all things are truly through him (1 Corinthians 8:6). As we saw in the previous chapter, God's purpose is an impeccable, single, eternal, interwoven tapestry that does not exclude any of us. God's purpose for a single human cannot be extracted from the whole, nor can a single human change or alter God's singular purpose by his or her actions or choices. It is God who is sovereign, not humans.

It is my perception that we notably miss this truth in many of today's churches—this to our great loss. While the truth of God's preeminence and sovereignty is seen all around us (Romans 1:20), contained in our Bibles, and found in many of the songs we sing, it seems we nevertheless often remain oblivious to this great reality. A case in point worthy of our reflection is the old hymn "Amazing Grace," a hymn that is perhaps the most loved of all the songs sung in today's churches. Do we, however, really believe what we are singing when we sing this wonderful old hymn? Do we even stop and think about it? Do we give careful consideration to the powerful message of the indomitable supremacy of our Father's grace that the author of this grand old hymn was attempting to convey?

John Newton, the man who wrote this beloved hymn, was a slave trader whom God laid hold of to become a minister of the Gospel. He is quoted as having said, "I read the newspapers to see how God governs the world,"[2] thereby conspicuously demonstrating that he fully understood both God's sovereignty and God's willingness to interfere with and steer human will. Mr. Newton understood well that current events do not happen outside of our preeminent God's control and that ultimately current events reveal the unfolding of the will of God and not the accomplishments of the will of humanity. Mr. Newton further wrote: "There is many a thing that the world calls disappointment, but there is no such word in the dictionary of faith. What to others are disappointments are to believers intimations of the way of God."[3] This comment is a brilliant affirmation of our God's complete preeminence in all things (Romans 11:36).

As an ordained preacher for the Church of England, Mr. Newton understood God's sovereignty very well, and he wrote these strong words regarding a person's salvation by faith alone, a faith that is a gift from God alone and not something that can in any way be mustered by that individual: "Man is an enemy to the justice, sovereignty, and law of God, and to the one method of salvation he has appointed in the Gospel by faith only, by such a faith, as it is no more in his power to contribute to the production of in himself, than he can contribute to raising the dead, or making a world."[4] Near the end of Newton's life, he is said to have told friends: "My memory is nearly gone; but I remember two things: That I am a great sinner, and that Christ is a great Savior."[5] Newton's high view of the sovereign God he loved and worshipped can be plainly seen in these much-beloved words:

> Amazing Grace, how sweet the sound, that saved a wretch like me.

Newton does not say that he found enough good in himself to choose to be saved or to deserve to be saved; rather, it was God's grace alone that saved him while he was still a "wretch." Here again, we see sola gratia!

> I once was lost but now am found, was blind but now I see.

Again, Newton points us to a sovereign God who found us and gave us sight. Blind men do not just become "unlost," nor can they heal their own sight. Newton does not suggest that we were once lost and then we somehow found a way out, nor does he say that we somehow just found God on our own. Instead, Newton asserts correctly that we were found by God, a God who sought after us (Luke 15:4–5; Ezekiel 20:34; 34:16), gave us sight (2 Corinthians 4:4–6; Psalm 146:8), and saved us with his amazing grace! (Titus 3:5; Ephesians 2:4–5).

> T'was Grace that taught my heart to fear.

Newton shows that our hearts cannot turn to God or fear God until God chooses to apply his grace to our hearts. A human heart will never fear God on its own, but only by God's amazing grace will it turn to God. By teaching our hearts to fear, grace creates the desire to choose God.

> And Grace, my fears relieved.

Praise our Lord, his grace alone provides the remedy for our guilt that his grace teaches us to feel. When we understand his indomitable grace, our fears are vanquished and replaced with an unshakeable confidence in our loving Father.

> How precious did that Grace appear
> The hour I first believed.

When his grace is applied, our hearts are no longer veiled; the blindness of our hearts is healed, and we can finally see the truth. Only because of God's triumphant grace, the Gospel now appears precious to us instead of foolishness (1 Corinthians 1:18, 24), and we can now choose to believe!

> Through many dangers, toils and snares
> I have already come;
> 'Tis Grace that brought me safe thus far
> and Grace will lead me home.

Newton acknowledges that it is God and his grace that will accomplish the good work he began in us, and grace will accomplish his purpose in us. Grace will get us home, not our own striving. Newton does not try to usurp God's glory by claiming anything but that God is the author and finisher of our faith.

> The Lord has promised good to me.
> His word my hope secures.
> He will my shield and portion be,
> As long as life endures.

Here again, Newton places his hope in a sovereign God who loves us supremely and has promised good to those whom his amazing grace has saved. We can have a secure hope in his word and know that he is our shield and our portion because his will is perfect, unchanging, and certain to be accomplished. Because his word (his purpose) is secure, our hope is secure!

> Yea, when this flesh and heart shall fail,
> And mortal life shall cease,
> I shall possess within the veil,
> A life of joy and peace.

> When we've been here ten thousand years
> Bright shining as the sun.
> We've no less days to sing God's praise
> Than when we've first begun.

Praise him! Our hope is secure, and we will spend eternity worshipping God's perfection and praising his amazing grace that found us, gave us sight, and saved us!

Given the immaculate and immutable nature of God's purpose, the certainty of the perfect outcome, and the singularity of his purpose, would it not then be biblical and reasonable to put our complete faith in our God's absolute reliability in fulfilling his purpose for each of us, including the very smallest of details? God is able to keep his word, even when it would seem insurmountably difficult for him to do so as judged from our human perspective. At one point Moses questioned God's ability to fulfill his word, and God's reply to him should drive our doubts away even today: "Is the Lord's hand shortened? Now you shall see whether my word will come true for you or not" (Numbers 11:23). Needless to say, the Lord fulfilled his purpose exactly as he had told Moses that he would. When we encounter doubts, we should be reminded that our mighty God's hand has not been shortened, and he remains firmly in control of the big, the small, and everything in between.

It seems that Solomon had a greater confidence in God's sovereignty over the big, the small, and everything in between than we in a modernist society can even begin to comprehend. Solomon stated in Proverbs 16:33 that while we may cast lots seemingly at random in our laps, every outcome of the lots is from the Lord. Solomon was acknowledging that even the way the lots land is controlled by the Lord. In fact, the Lord commanded the Promise Land to be divided up between the tribes according to how the lots landed (Numbers 26:55–56; 33:54; Joshua 14:2), and Jacob's prophecy concerning his sons in Genesis 49 clearly reveals that God had sovereignly determined these specific areas for each tribe hundreds of years before. The disciples and the early church were also quite comfortable with this concept as they chose the replacement disciple for Judas by casting lots (Acts 1:26). Once again, we see the grand concept on display—the tiniest things, even the way lots land when they hit the ground, are controlled by God in order to accomplish *his* larger purpose; in this case, God controlled the choosing of Matthias as the replacement disciple. God is not just involved in some things. God is not just sovereign over a few things. Rather, "the whole disposition thereof is of the Lord" (Proverbs 16:33 KJV). God is sovereign over all things in order to accomplish his grand purpose.

Even if we so desired, we can no more keep God out of the details of our lives than Jonah could run from God (Jonah 1), David could find a place to flee from the Lord's presence (Psalm 139:7–12), or Darius could put Daniel in a place in which God could not protect Daniel from ravenous lions (Daniel 6:16–22). This fact is not hidden from us; Paul made it clear in Ephesians 4:6 that our Father is "over all and through all and in all," and he stated in 1 Corinthians 8:6 that "all things" are from God and through God. The imperative question, then, is this:

> Why would we think, or even desire to believe, that we are not included in our Father's grand, divine purpose—that the details of our lives are the exceptions to the "all things" over which God exercises his loving, unlimited sovereignty?

Was it not the near-perpetual sin of the Israelites after being brought out of Egypt by a humanly impossible work of grace initiated by an incomparably loving God to fail to grasp and embrace that they were part of God's grand purpose? Instead of realizing the foundational truth that Almighty God's sovereign purpose would always be fulfilled and that God was certainly going to finish what he had started in them as an act of love and deliverance for his chosen people, they instead worried, panicked, and rebelled at every difficulty or hardship, be it real or imagined. The mindset thus displayed by the Israelites is painfully analogous to many of our own beliefs and behaviors, and this fact should bring us to our knees before our Father.

The Israelite's actions plainly demonstrate that the alternative to fully embracing God's total sovereignty and the certainty of his purpose is indeed rebellion! Psalm 106:7–10 makes this truth very clear. The Israelites are said to have rebelled right at the Red Sea (v. 7); there they questioned God's purpose and his sovereignty by failing to trust in his purpose to save them. Nevertheless, we again see God move sovereignly for his own purpose to save a people that he had chosen long ago, a people whose hearts were rebelling against him instead of choosing him. In verse 8, we are told that he saved these rebellious people at the Red Sea "for his name's sake," that "he might make known his mighty power." Because God works for his own glory and for the good of his chosen, it should be readily apparent that he often works in our lives in spite of our bad beliefs or misguided doctrine, and his merciful actions obviously do not thereby confirm or validate either our silly, human notions or our carnal rebellion.

The Israelites did, in fact, give God glory and trust him after he parted the Red Sea and saved them—which he did even while they were rebelling! However, the tragedy is that from that point forward it seems that they continued to fail to comprehend the complete reliability and faithfulness of God's sovereign purpose and methods. Every time the way looked rough or difficult to them, rather than trust that God was sovereign and that he would indeed care for them, they chose instead to believe that they were encountering a situation which God did not intend to come upon them or from which he was unwilling or unable to help them escape. This near-perpetual rebellion against God's sovereignty did not just result in a few unnecessary gray hairs for the Israelites; instead, they perished in the wilderness because they failed to embrace and trust the ways of the sovereign God who had chosen them and brought them out of Egypt. Needless to say, it is incumbent on us not to repeat this colossal mistake in our own lives.

"I cry out to God Most High, to God who fulfills his purpose for me." This powerful, magnificent proclamation from Psalm 57:2 was echoed and reinforced by the apostle Paul as he declared, "I am sure of this, that he who began a good work in you *will* bring it to completion at the day of Jesus Christ" (Philippians 1:6). The texts here are quite clear that the good work within each of us who believes was begun by *him* (not us), and it is *he* who will fulfill his loving purpose and bring it to a perfect completion (not us). We should be quite careful not to miss the immense power that is summed up in Hebrews 12:2, which teaches us the marvelous truth that it is our own loving, merciful Savior who is both the *author* and the *finisher* of our faith. We sometimes like to think that we muster up the faith to believe in Jesus—apparently we want to be the author—but Scripture teaches instead that Jesus is the author of our faith, not we ourselves. Faith is of divine origin, "not of ourselves" (Ephesians 2:8 KJV; John 6:44; 1:12–13; Romans 9:16; 1 Peter 1:3; James 1:18), and it is this faith that sets us free to believe (Galatians 3:22–25).

There is no doubt that we each must choose to believe. This very belief, however, is "through grace" (Acts 18:27), and grace is from God; grace is not of human origin (Matthew 16:16–17). If we trace back to where that faith to believe came from, to what or who is the true source of that faith that sets us free from bondage in order to be able to believe, we will surely never find its source in the depravity of our sinful nature; rather, we will inevitably find that we are in Christ "by *His* doing" (1 Corinthians 1:30 NASB), "because of *his* own purpose" (2 Timothy 1:9), "of *his* own will" (James 1:18), as a result of *his* call (Hebrews 9:15; John 6:44; Romans 8:29-30), *not* of our own will (Romans 9:16; John 1:12-13; 6:63-65; 2 Timothy 1:9), and because *he* "caused us to be born again" according to *his* great mercy (1 Peter 1:3), "apprehending us" and "laying hold of us" (Philippians

3:12 KJV, NASB). Thus, the writer of Hebrews can make the glorious declaration that Christ himself is the author of the faith of each of us. It is our loving Father himself who "has rescued us from the domain of darkness and brought us into the kingdom of the Son he loves!" (Colossians 1:13). As the old-timers would say, "That is shouting ground!"

If it is shouting ground that we can know, believe, and experience that God is certainly the true author of our faith, it is equally glorious, if not even more so, that we can have just as much confidence that he is also the finisher. We can rest in the assurance that if it is his desire to author our faith, then it is also his will to finish it (Romans 8:28–30); God finishes what God starts! God is not God if he ever fails to accomplish what he sets out to do. If the matter is given some honest reflection, would we not expect that our omniscient, holy, loving Father could do an infinitely better job of writing the chronicle of our life's journey than that which we could accomplish with our limited, carnal capabilities? I would much rather have God writing the story of my salvation and my destiny than myself!

God chose each of us who believe from the beginning to be saved (2 Thessalonians 2:13; 1 Thessalonians 1:4; Ephesians 1:4; 2 Timothy 1:9; 1 Peter 1:1–2, 20), and we can glory in the fact that he made that choice with a full and complete knowledge of every sin, error, or shortcoming that we will ever commit. Because of this wonderful fact, we can know that he will never be surprised by our failings or become regretful of his choice; therefore, he will never be inclined to abandon his choice and his purpose for each of us. Indeed, J. I. Packer pointed out that our Father's perfect foreknowledge makes his love for each of us "utterly realistic."[6] This is an absolutely brilliant statement! God unerringly saw *all* of our past, present, and future flaws and nevertheless knowingly chose to love us first and act to make us his own. This is a Father we can trust explicitly. This is a Father from whom we have no need to hide anything at all. We can give him no less than our complete worship and undiluted love.

Because we can know that our Father's love for us is utterly realistic, we can be certain that he will indeed be the finisher of that faith in us of which he was originally the author (many translations render "finisher" as the "perfecter" of our faith). He is a personal God who effects his will in us and perfects our faith! "For it is *God* who works in you [us] to will and to act in order to fulfill his good purpose" (Philippians 2:13 NIV). Given the choice, which would we rather have? Would we rather have the outcome (the "finish") be up to God or up to ourselves? This should not be a difficult choice at all. I know that I find it greatly comforting to know that he is my *loving Father,* and he tells me that *he* is the finisher, not me! (Philippians 1:6). He is not as a man that could lie or change his mind (Numbers 23:19; 1 Samuel 15:29; Titus 1:2), nor will he retract his words (Isaiah 31:2).

Since we know that our loving Father does not retract his words, we can have total confidence that he will complete what he says he will complete. Not only is his love for us utterly realistic, his purpose for us is utterly reliable! He tells us that he will never leave us or forsake us (Hebrews 13:5), so we can possess the unflagging assurance that he will not leave the job half-completed. His calling is irrevocable, as are his gifts (Romans 11:29). Because he who calls us is completely faithful, he will surely complete his work (1 Thessalonian 5:24), and he *delights* in unchanging love for his chosen remnant (Micah 7:18; Zechariah 8:6–8). Why would we take issue with this wonderful truth? After all, the promise that "all things work together for good" in Romans 8:28 is offered only to those "who are called according to his purpose." We know God's purpose *will* be fulfilled, and we know it will be good. As such, we can declare along with David, "I cry out to God Most High, to God who fulfills his purpose for me"!

Why would we resist the truth that the God of the universe loves us supremely, has a purpose for us, and has had this perfect, unchanging purpose all along? Should not we rather positively rejoice in the absolute certainty that our own Father will fulfill his wonderful purpose for each of us because he has the great willingness to use his great power to back up his great love? Would not that be about the greatest thing a person could ever hope for? Should not it make our hearts leap with awe and joy to know that the same God who calls even the stars in the heavens by name and causes them to "stand forth together" in response (Isaiah 48:13) also loves his chosen enough to call each of us individually to himself? It is he who "apprehended us" and "laid hold of us" (Philippians 3:12 KJV, NASB). Why would we prefer to serve a god of our own design, a god who we would say is always doing his very best to save people but failing at it most of the time? Ephesians 1:3–11 declares the glorious truth of the real God and gives us a truly solid foundation:

> Blessed be the God and Father of our Lord Jesus Christ, who has blessed us in Christ with every spiritual blessing in the heavenly places, [4] even as he chose us in him before the foundation of the

world, that we should be holy and blameless before him. In love [5] he predestined us for adoption as sons through Jesus Christ, according to the purpose of his will, [6] to the praise of his glorious grace, with which he has blessed us in the Beloved. [7] In him we have redemption through his blood, the forgiveness of our trespasses, according to the riches of his grace, [8] which he lavished upon us, in all wisdom and insight [9] making known to us the mystery of his will, according to his purpose, which he set forth in Christ [10] as a plan for the fullness of time, to unite all things in him, things in heaven and things on earth. [11] In him we have obtained an inheritance, having been predestined according to the purpose of him who works all things according to the counsel of his will.

Verses 4 and 5 are abundantly clear: "In love, he predestined us for adoption as sons through Jesus Christ, according to the purpose of his will." Praise him! To use today's vernacular, this should absolutely "blow us away." *Here we see our Father's love for us tied directly to his purpose for us*, a purpose that he promises he will fulfill! Is this because we worked hard enough to please him, or because we wisely chose him? No, verse 4 instead makes it certain that he chose us before we chose him, and this choice of his took place before the beginning of the world. Verse 6 ("to the praise of his glorious grace...") shows us that we praise his glorious grace alone for his choice. In other words, all the credit and glory is his. Here is a loving choice in which we can truly rest!

There is another vital realization that we must pull from this wondrous passage. We should ponder again the beautiful phrase "In love, he predestined us" (Ephesians 1:4–5), and then we should consider that no rational being would ever love a robot or a puppet enough to sacrifice their only son for it! How much more so if one had the power to simply speak a bigger, better robot into existence anytime one so desired? The amazing realization that a robot would never be loved by God ultimately destroys the accusation that the truth of God's predestining love somehow makes humans into robots and puppets. Based on the simple, amazingly beautiful phrase "In love, he predestined us," one cannot make the accusation that God's sovereignty over all things and all people renders humans as mere robots without altogether insulting and defying the love of our Father.

The God of Our Confidence

On a very brief side note, the dreaded "p-word" in these verses has been the subject of much discussion among God's people. While in truth this word should be cherished as our greatest assurance of our Father's eternal love, it has unfortunately instead become a divisive point of contention for many. There are those who say simply, "I don't believe in predestination," and the matter is thereby considered closed as far as they are concerned. However, not only does this viewpoint needlessly throw away the tremendous blessing of this hallowed reality, it also usurps God's glory and comes dangerously close to triggering the curse in Galatians 1:9 because the Bible declares directly and without equivocation that we are indeed predestined (e.g., Ephesians 1:4–5, 1:11, and Romans 8:28–29). One cannot profess to believe and study the Bible and still honestly reject this fact; the only legitimate question can be what it is that one considers this predestination to encompass.

If the matter is given a bit of research and honest thought, the inexorable, biblical conclusion will unavoidably be that we are taught clearly that God predestines his elect. What remains is that we must then decide how these scriptural terms should be correctly understood. We cannot in good conscience simply ignore these biblical teachings and pretend they are not there, but unfortunately that is exactly what many do. This is the moral equivalent of ripping pages out of the Bible because those pages do not happen to suit one's human, preconceived conception of God's love and fairness. While ignorance may be bliss in some cases, it is not rational to reject the correct biblical view of predestination outright without even offering a reasonably plausible alternative interpretation of these clear passages.

There are two essential questions in this matter: who are the elect that the Bible attests are predestined, and who does this electing? Some have said that all humans are elect and all are predestined for eternal life. From a scriptural perspective, however, this viewpoint borders on absurdity if for no other reason than we are told plainly that the angels will gather the elect to heaven, and this is quite obviously not all-encompassing (Matthew 24:31; Mark 13:27). Paul taught us in Romans 8:30 that God will save (justify and glorify) all those who are predestined, which is also plainly not all-inclusive unless one embraces a doctrine of universal salvation. Likewise, in Matthew 24:22–24, Jesus spoke of the days being shortened for the sake of the elect and of the elect not being deceived as other humans; any reasonable reading of these verses would demand that not all humans are included in the group Jesus referred to as the elect. That not all humans are elect is also unmistakably demonstrated in Acts 13:48, where all those present in Antioch who were appointed for eternal life believed; if all humans are predestined for eternal life (elect), then surely all present would have believed.

We are told in Romans 8:33 that a charge cannot be brought against God's elect, whom he alone justifies, and this again is clearly not speaking of all humans since charges will most certainly be brought against many sinners. In Romans 11:7, Paul taught that the elect humans among other humans obtained salvation, and the rest were hardened—yet again, the elect is a group that is not inclusive of all humans. We also read in 1 Peter 1:1 that Peter said he was writing to the elect individuals scattered among a host of other humans; again, this is not all-inclusive. This same differentiation is also seen in 2 Timothy 2:10, Titus 1:1, 1 Peter 5:13, and 2 John 1:13. Therefore, if we are honest and objective in studying the Bible, we are forced to conclude that the elect are necessarily a selected subset of the total human race.

But who elected the elect? Indeed, who did the choosing? Is it the elect who elect themselves, as some have suggested? This might make for an interesting discussion if the Bible did not spoil the debate by providing the direct answer in Mark 13:20, where Jesus, speaking of the last days, stated, "But for the sake of the elect, *whom he chose*, he shortened the days." There can be no other interpretation of this passage than it was God who did the choosing, and, furthermore, it is also again clear that not all humans are elect. We should also consider once more the marvelous words "In love, he predestined us" and "He [God] chose us in him from the foundation of the world," both from the first chapter of Ephesians. These magnificent declarations make it obvious yet again that it is God alone who does the predestining. Moreover, these powerful affirmations of God's sovereignty were not addressed to the general population of Asia, but were instead written by Paul to the "saints who are in Ephesus" (Ephesians 1:1). In these striking texts, therefore, the "us" who are said to be predestined by God and chosen by God are exclusively believers! This is also plainly seen in 1:13, 1:15, 2:1–5, 2:8, 2:12, 2:19, 2:22, 3:6, 4:1, 4:30, and 6:10.

The incontrovertible fact that it is God who does the choosing is also quite evident in 1 Thessalonians 1:4, John 15:16, 19, Romans 8:33, 1 Peter

5:13, Romans 11:5, 7, 1 Peter 2:9, 5:13, and many other passages. Paul left absolutely no room for equivocation when he declared, "God has chosen you from the beginning for salvation" (2 Thessalonians 2:13 NASB), and "God has not appointed us to wrath but to obtain salvation" (1 Thessalonians 5:9). Paul also wrote specifically to the *believers* in Rome (Romans 1:8–13) and addressed them as "all those in Rome who are loved by God and called to be saints" and "you who are called to belong to Jesus Christ" (Romans 1:7, 6). Assuming that one's heart is open to scriptural truth, once it is realized that the biblical term *the elect* cannot possibly be inclusive of all humans without exception and that it can only be God who does the electing, the remaining scriptural teachings that previously seemed problematic fall right into place. Instead of being passages that we consistently ignore—and perhaps secretly wish really were not in the Bible—they become a glorious source of encouragement and faith!

It is also unmistakable that these elect individuals are given to Jesus by God our Father before they ever believe, as evidenced by Jesus' many plain teachings in John 8:42, 8:47, 6:37, 10:16, 17:6–9, 17:24, and 15:19. For example, Jesus' resplendent prayer for his disciples in John 17 is both exceedingly powerful and immensely enlightening. In verse 6 of this gorgeous prayer, Jesus prayed to his Father, saying, "I have manifested your name to the people whom you gave me out of the world. Yours they were, and you gave them to me." He added in verse 8, "They have received them [Jesus' teachings] and have come to know in truth that I came from you." These verses make it plain that the disciples were given to Jesus before they chose to follow Jesus. In John 15:16–19, Jesus said directly that they did not choose him; rather, it was actually he who had chosen them out of the world.

If we direct our consideration back to John 17, we see in verses 20 and 21 that Jesus also prayed for those future believers who have not yet believed: "I do not ask for these only, but also for those who will believe in me through their word, that they may all be one, just as you, Father, are in me, and I in you, that they also may be in us." It is clear from Jesus' continuing prayer in verse 24 that God had already given him these future believers who had not yet believed: "Father, I desire that they also, *whom you have given me*, may be with me where I am, to see my glory that you have given me because you loved me before the foundation of the world." It is critical to realize that Jesus specifically prayed *only* for "those who will believe," which cannot include all humans unless one advances a doctrine of universal salvation. It would be ridiculous, if not blasphemous, to suggest that Jesus did not know specifically for whom he was praying! Both he and his Father knew exactly which individuals, both living and as yet unborn, were included in that limited group of humans that "will believe" and had been given to him by his Father (v. 24), and it was only for these exact people that Jesus was praying. Moreover, because Jesus is God's Holy Son, we can be completely confident that his prayer will be answered. The people for whom Jesus prayed will certainly be with him eternally in glory, exactly as he prayed in verse 24.

In verse 9, Jesus confirmed the fact that he was not praying for all humans to be saved: "I am not praying for the world but for those whom you have given me, for they are yours." If it could be possible that any doubt remain, we should also note that Jesus said in John 10:16, "I have other sheep [among the Gentiles] that are not of this fold [the Jews]." He referred to these "other sheep" as already belonging to him, before they were even saved, and he said with unerring certainty that the Gentiles within this group *"will* listen to my voice" and will eventually come into his fold. This is no mere twisting of words because Jesus also plainly taught us in John 6:37, 10:26–27, and 17:6–9 that *all* the individuals that the Father *gives* him will eventually come to him, and furthermore, he will eternally save all those that the Father gave him (6:39). A practical application of Jesus' words can be seen clearly in Acts 18:10; God told Paul to stay in Corinth because God had "many in this city who are my people," referring to those individuals in Corinth who already belonged to him but had not yet believed. Paul stayed for another year and a half, and these people that belonged to God believed under Paul's preaching exactly as God had purposed. Once again, then, we see clearly that we are given to Jesus by our Father *before* we come to him.

There are some theologies that deal with passages such as these or Romans 8:28–30 by going so far as to accept that the elect are given to Jesus by his Father before they believe, but they contend that God's electing choice in eternity past is based on his foreknowledge of autonomous human choices in the future. This viewpoint would assert that "we are chosen because we believe" rather than "we believe because we are chosen." However, this flawed doctrine fails because it throws salvation back on human works and human will in spite of the many scriptural teachings to the contrary. It also deliberately disregards the reality of human depravity. This erroneous viewpoint strips sovereignty from God and turns it over to humans, and it also notably fails to adequately resolve the question as to why an omniscient God would create people who he knows will *never* accept him—even as he is engaged in the very act of creating them. Moreover, if it were true that God chose us because he foresaw our future virtue, then his choice would really be no choice at all, nor would it be based on grace alone; rather, it would merely be his response to a foreseen virtuous human act, again contrary to many scriptural teachings. In essence, it is being suggested that humans predestine themselves before they are ever born, which is a logical impossibility—not to mention it creates a salvation based on future works.

Another huge problem with asserting that God chooses in response to a foreknown human choice to believe in him is found within the dependencies of the chain of events enumerated in Romans 8:29–30. We are told there that God predestined all those he foreknew, but we are also told that he calls and justifies all those he predestines. Since we know that not all are justified, we also know from this passage that not all humans receive this effectual call (which is quite different than the general invitation to the Gospel that is extended to all humans but will always be rejected unless and until God's grace is applied). It is not rational, therefore, to suggest that some will not receive this predestined, justifying call because God foresaw in advance that they would reject this call—it is necessarily being said that they will receive the call only if they choose to accept the call. This puts the cart before the horse by making the opportunity to even make a decision dependent on the result of that very same decision, which is a practical absurdity. Taken to its logical conclusion, the result of such teaching can only be a never-ending exercise of circular reasoning.

Furthermore, if "we are chosen because we believe" (or will believe), then a crucial question begging for a scripturally plausible answer must be faced: what is the reason why some humans believe and are thereby chosen by God in advance while some do not believe and are thereby not chosen in advance? The answer inevitably given is simply "free will." In other words, it is actually being maintained that the difference between those who are saved and those who are not is a difference in the respective people's free wills. This dangerous answer should trigger serious alarms for students of the Bible because the unavoidable result of such a contention is that it must be concluded that some humans have a better, more virtuous free will than others. This notion flies in the face of a host of scriptures previously examined, and it is being asserted that some human free wills can in fact do exactly that which Paul told us plainly they cannot do, which is to turn to God of their own free will (Romans 8:7–8). This view requires that we believe that there are some humans who are righteous enough to seek God when the Bible tells us there are no such humans (Romans 3:10–12; Psalm 53:1–3; Psalm 14:1–3; 10:4; Genesis 6:5; Jeremiah 17:9; 13:23). If it is indeed free will that makes the difference, this gives saved humans solid ground for boasting, and it cheapens God's grace while enthroning human will. This fallacy, however alluring, immensely damages our relationship with our loving Father because when the depth of human depravity is discredited or denied, grace is ultimately devalued. As such, this erroneous view must be rejected, its initial appeal to the prideful human sense of self-determination notwithstanding. Unless grace ceases to be grace, the reason for God's choice can never fall on the human side of the equation!

It should be apparent that God chose us because he willed "we *should* be holy," not because he foresaw we *would* be holy (Ephesians 1:4). We must instead recall the compelling observation of Horatius Bonar that was mentioned in chapter 8; the truth is that God chooses us first because he foresees that we will never choose him of our own volition.[7] If he foresaw that we would choose him, he would have had no need or reason to choose us! In other words, if it were indeed true that God looks forward from eternity past, sees who will accept him, and then predestines accordingly, the entire exercise is thereby rendered unneeded and useless at best, and in actuality would be pointless and nonsensical. Why would God need to predestine those whom he sees with certainty will accept him on their own, and what would he accomplish by so doing since these people were already certainly going to accept him? Moreover, if we believe God chose us in eternity past based on what he foresaw we would choose of our own free will *after* he created us, this tremendously dilutes his great love for us. His grace, love, and eternal choice become things we supposedly earned with our virtuous belief, and therefore remain contingent upon our continued virtue—a daunting, confidence-depleting task in the face of Paul's blunt assertion that there is not even one person that is righteous (Romans 3:10).

If this is not reason enough to reject this flawed explanation, it must be noted that this viewpoint also fails to provide the so-called free will that its proponents so desperately seek! As Wayne Grudem ably points out in his well-known *Systematic Theology*, if God knows in eternity past that person A will believe and person B will not believe, and he bases his predestining choice on this knowledge (this is one way that Romans 8:29–30 is explained away by those promoting unfettered, autonomous free will), then these individuals' destinies are inevitably thereby fixed and certain by God's knowledge.[8] According to God's perfect, inerrant foreknowledge, it will be impossible for person A to not believe, and it will be impossible for person B to believe; their lives will not turn out differently, no matter what they do, how many sermons they hear, or how good they attempt to be. It is exactly this inflexible, fixed destiny that so offends the proponents of this viewpoint that God supposedly elects based on a foreknowledge of which humans will choose him of their own free will. In the end, their viewpoint produces the same fixed result they seek to avoid! Furthermore—as was discussed extensively in the earlier chapter "Fair Is Fair, or Is It?"—this erroneous view also renders the two objections anticipated by Paul in Romans 9:14 and 9:19 as both particularly nonsensical and completely unnecessary.

However, this brief detour notwithstanding, the purpose of this book is obviously not to debate the p-word; such a discussion is only necessary in order to establish the reality of this solidly biblical doctrine. The real focus is on the magnificent splendor of the inseparable connection between our Father's love for us and his sovereign purpose for us as evidenced by the fact that he predestined us in love (Ephesians 1:4–5). Because he chose us to be his own in eternity past compelled only by his individual love for each of his chosen, an election of a remnant for himself based on grace alone and not our choices or works (Ephesians 2:4–5; 1:4; Romans 11:5), we can possess an unmatched, wonderful, calm assurance in his unchanging resolve and irresistible power to fulfill that purpose for each of us. Anxiety is vanquished (Philippians 4:6), and in its place is the peace of our own Father that surpasses understanding (Philippians 4:7).

Concerning this assurance of our God's resolve to accomplish his plans for his chosen, there are two passages in Jeremiah 29 that are quite familiar to us because they are quoted often, sometimes out of context. Despite their familiarity, it seems that few realize that the two passages back up against each other and are expressing two sides of the same truth. Verse 11 is often quoted as a promise; here the Lord stated, "For I know the plans I have for you, plans for welfare and not for evil, to give you a future and a hope." Verse 13 is also often repeated, usually as an exhortation for us to work hard at seeking the Lord's will, and here the Lord said, "You will seek me and find me when you seek me with all your heart." The entirety of the passage is really all about God's sovereignty and his sovereign plan to bless his chosen.

Both of these verses were written by Jeremiah in a letter to Jewish exiles in Babylon. The exiles had been carried there by Nebuchadnezzar, who was the Lord's chosen instrument (28:14, and others). The false prophet Hananiah had promised these exiles that they would be restored to Jerusalem within two years (28:1–4), and he had made the people trust this optimistic lie (28:15). Jeremiah's letter, on the other hand, spoke the truth about the situation to these people who were exiled by God through his chosen instrument Nebuchadnezzar. Jeremiah told them that they might as well settle down in Babylon because they were not coming back until seventy years had elapsed (29:5–6). The seventy years was God's sovereign timetable, and the restoration was not going to happen before then. Only after the seventy years would God visit the exiles and bring them back (vv. 10, 11), fulfill the good purpose and plans he had for them (v. 11), and *cause* them to call upon him and to pray to him (v. 12). At that time, the people would seek him and would indeed find him (v. 13) because he would fulfill his purpose to be found by them (v. 14). The beautiful thrust of the passage, then, is the wonderful assurance that God *will* fulfill his good purpose for his chosen people on *his* timetable—including causing them to seek him, just as in Ezekiel 36 or Jeremiah 24.

There are those that would attempt to equate this certainty that God will lovingly fulfill his perfect purpose for his chosen people with a belief in a fatalistic, robotic existence. Nothing could be further from the truth, however. We must never think that God's effectual, sovereign work in our hearts is a passive, internal event that bears no fruit, nor should we hold that because he chose us there will be no resulting response on our part. Jesus united these two truths in John 15, where he said that when we are genuinely converted, our Father is glorified by our bearing fruit (v. 8). He elaborated in verse 16, "You did not choose me, but I chose you and appointed you that you should go and bear fruit and that your fruit should abide." Jesus thereby made it plain that our bearing lasting fruit is part of the very purpose for which we are chosen and appointed. The fruit of God's work of grace in our heart—and our inevitable response to a correct understanding of our Father's love for us as his chosen—will be an intense longing to know him more, a passionate desire to obey his commands, and a humble willingness to serve him faithfully in whatever he may lead us to do.

The glorious, empowering knowledge that God will finish the work he began in us fills our hearts with an intense and compelling desire to reciprocate the love of him who first loved us. Absolutely no room remains for the abuse of his grace by continuing in sin and presuming on his grace for eventual deliverance, as has been termed "greasy grace" by many. This abuse of grace by continued sin is what Paul condemned soundly in Romans 6:15–18, 6:1–2, and 3:8. In fact, John told us that "no one born of God makes a practice of sinning, for God's seed abides in him, and he cannot keep on sinning because he has been born of God" (1 John 3:9). We can thereby know that the truth is not actually in one who claims to know God but does not keep his commandments (1 John 2:4). *In essence, John tells us that we know that we are loved because we obey, and we obey because we know that we are loved.*

Just as there is no room for the sinful abuse of grace in a heart genuinely changed by God's grace, there is likewise no room for fatalism in evangelism. As J. I. Packer aptly points out, the truth of God's absolute sovereignty in no way removes the need or the urgency to evangelize, rather it empowers evangelism by giving it its only real hope of success.[9] We are both humbled and joyful to know that "when God sends us to evangelize, he sends us to act as vital links in the chain of his purpose for the salvation of the elect."[10] When God decrees the end, he also decrees the means,[11] and we rejoice in having a role to play in the unfolding of the magnificent tapestry of God's purpose. Indeed, when our lives bear lasting fruit, that too will be a result of God fulfilling his eternal purpose in us and for us. We become living testimonies that all things are from him, through him, and to him! (Romans 11:36).

I have heard it taught all of my life that "God has a purpose for each of us," but we are usually told that as Christians we must make it our business to earnestly seek, discover, and fulfill that purpose. This is often labeled "finding God's will." While it is certainly true that that there is a synergistic component of our walk with God after our salvation (2 Peter 1; 1 Corinthians 3; James 2; Hebrews 5; Galatians 5; Colossians 3; 2:6; 1 Thessalonians 4:7; 2 Timothy 2, and plenty more), I wonder now if it really is so hard to "find God's will." If a Christian has a heart to seek God, and God has a perfect Father's heart to love and grow all of his chosen children, then how can we get all worked up about how hard it is to "find" God's will and worry so much about "missing" God's will? Can it really be as hard as we make it out to be, or is this a fear born of our dismissal of God's sovereignty?

Does a loving God really hide his will from his children who are seeking him? What if we truly love him but are just not quite earnest enough in our seeking? Do we then have to settle for God's "second best" will, as I have often heard taught? Is this really possible from a loving Father who will always give us good gifts and not stones or snakes (Matthew 7:9-11), a loving Father who we can know will graciously give us all things since he did not spare even his own Son? (Romans 8:32). Does this lifelong, worry-laden quest to avoid "missing God's will" in any way resemble the rest for our souls that Jesus promised? Do we not have this backward? Have we not severely distorted our Father's great love for us?

In Isaiah 42:16, God gave us this auspicious assurance as his chosen people: "And I will lead the blind in a way that they do not know, in paths that they have not known I will guide them. I will turn the darkness before them into light, the rough places into level ground. These are the things I do, and I do not forsake them." This is an astounding promise worthy of our complete confidence! God does not demand that we must somehow find the path that he declares we do *not* know. Instead, God says that we are the blind who are not capable of finding a path or a way that we do not know, but he, our loving Father, will lead us along the unknown way, turning our darkness into light and our rough places into level ground. Furthermore, his leading is not in doubt; he says plainly that this is what he *will* do and that he *will not* forsake us. In Isaiah 49:10 (NIV), we are given this wonderful affirmation: "He who has compassion on them will guide them and lead them." One more time, our loving Father promises to lead us; he does not threaten to give us his second best if we fail to find the correct path because we did not seek to discover his will quite earnestly enough—that would hardly be the mercy and compassion that is promised in this passage.

In the face of these comforting passages, it would be preposterous to suggest that God may not fulfill his purpose for us if we do not spend quite enough time begging him to reveal his will to us. This same message is found in the much-loved twenty-third Psalm. The Lord is our shepherd, and we are his sheep. Sheep do not worry and fret about finding the shepherd's will! Instead, they follow where their good shepherd leads them, trusting him to lead them to the pasture that is best for them. Rather than despair over "finding God's will," we should trust that our loving Father is leading us and understand that where he leads us will be for our eternal good.

In the very same passage in which Jesus said that no one can know the Father except those to whom the Son chooses to reveal him, Jesus went on to say that he offered rest for those who labor and for the heavy laden (Matthew 11:27–30). Jesus said that his yoke is easy and his burden is light, and that in him we will find rest for our souls. If we insist that it is hard work to find God's will and that we could very well miss out on his will if we are not earnest enough or worried enough in our seeking, have we not contradicted Jesus' words? Have we not thereby created a heavy burden and a never-ending pursuit of the promised rest that remains elusive? How can we ever truly rest if we are constantly worried that we could easily miss God's will, and as a result his purpose for us might not be fulfilled? Paul taught us that God himself will certainly glorify those whom he has called (Romans 8:30), but rather than rest in this wonderful assurance, we inexplicably seem determined to throw this responsibility on the shoulders of we who cannot bear it.

If we actually believe that it is the earnestness or emotionalism of our seeking that is the determining factor in whether God will fulfill his eternal purpose for each of us, we would do well to correct this notion by recalling how God brilliantly displayed his own unfailing zeal to fulfill his purpose for his chosen in his dealings with Jacob. We know that Jacob was chosen by God before he was born, a choice that was according to God's electing purpose (Romans 9:10–13). And yet, in Genesis 28 we find Jacob as a liar, deceiver, and thief fleeing to a foreign country in fear for his life because of threats made by his own brother (27:41–43), whom he had twice cheated. According to much modern theology, we would have to believe that although God had chosen Jacob and had a "will for his life," Jacob had rebelled of his own free will and strayed from God's will. God would have therefore been forced to wait (as would be said to be appropriate for a gentleman) for Jacob to have a change of heart in order for the unfolding events to come back in line with God's desires. Perhaps God could hope that Jacob would hear some good preaching in Haran and thereby have a change of heart. However, instead of adhering to the silly constraints of such human notions, God continued to work sovereignly to accomplish his purpose through the scoundrel Jacob. Jacob was not seeking God; he was fleeing for his life under the pretext of traveling to a foreign country to seek a wife (Genesis 35:1), but God would not wait on Jacob's free will.

One night during the journey, when this deceitful scoundrel laid his head down on a rock for a pillow, God appeared to him in a dream (Genesis 28:10–22). God's words were stunningly powerful for Jacob then and decidedly revealing for us today. Our Father told the unrepentant Jacob, "I am the Lord, the God of Abraham your father and the God of Isaac. The land on which you lie I will give to you and to your offspring" (v. 13). God continued, "Your offspring shall be like the dust of the earth, and you shall spread abroad to the west and to the east and to the north and to the south, and in you and your offspring shall all the families of the earth be blessed" (v. 14). Amazingly, this "fleeing felon" received a huge helping of grace instead of the large dose of judgment that he deserved!

Here we distinctly see the real God of the Bible—a God who is doing as he pleases (Psalm 135:6, 115:3) and never subordinating his desires to human will or human actions (Daniel 4:35). In so doing, his great love for his chosen people is also clearly displayed, along with his unyielding zeal to accomplish his eternal purpose. God's next words to Jacob are worthy of no less than outright worship, and they are life changing in their impact when we come to realize that God wants us to appropriate these words as his never-ending promise to each of his chosen. Through the power of his irresistible word, our Father extended his loving purpose to Jacob and vowed that he, the incomparable and infinite God of the universe, would see that it was absolutely accomplished! Here, then, is what our loving Father next told Jacob: "Behold, I am with you and will keep you wherever you go, and will bring you back to this land. For I will not leave you until I have done what I have promised you." Praise our awesome God!

These are incredible words, words that contradict much of the teaching we hear in today's church. God was promising Jacob that God had destined Jacob's future and that Jacob could walk confidently in the knowledge that the God of the universe would fulfill his purpose for Jacob. God told Jacob that he would not leave him until God finished what God had authored! Interestingly enough, Jacob did not resent this fact that was revealed to him—that God had destined his future and done so according to God's own purpose. Instead, Jacob responded by making a vow to God, saying that if God was going to do this great thing for him, then "the Lord shall be my God" (vv. 20–22). In God's perfect time, God had sovereignly changed Jacob's will and given him an eternal promise. As the rest of the book of Genesis unfolds, we learn that Jacob certainly had much more maturing to do, but God nevertheless kept his promises to Jacob with unfailing love and faithfully brought Jacob to the maturity that he had planned for him all along. What a magnificent work of grace God performed for Jacob! This is our Father, the God of our confidence!

The astoundingly beautiful fact of the matter is that God extends this same grace and same certainty to each of his chosen people. God's powerful words to Jacob and his unwavering fulfillment of his holy purpose should fill us with unshakable confidence and abiding joy. We are coheirs to these great words (Galatians 3:7–8, 29) and an integral part of God's settled, abiding purpose. We read in Psalm 138:8 that "The Lord will fulfill his purpose for me; your steadfast love, O Lord, endures forever." What a fantastic statement! Yet again, we see the Father's steadfast love tied to the certainty of the fulfillment of his purpose. This should be an incredible source of strength and encouragement for our lives. Instead, in a remarkable exhibition of human presumption, we seem to be quite happy to turn this verse upside down. The verse, if stated to match what is taught, preached, and believed by many today, would read more like this: "I must seek to fulfill the Lord's purpose for me; your love endures as long as I am steadfast enough and earnest enough in seeking after fulfilling this purpose." However, this is an inexplicable transposition because that is not what the verse says! The verse could not be clearer; it is the Lord that does the fulfilling of his purpose, not us. He *will* complete the good work that *he* initiated (Philippians 1:6) with his steadfast love.

If our concept of God and our doctrines will not allow us to believe that our Father is sovereign over all things, that God will indeed interfere with human will to accomplish his purpose, and he in fact did choose us as part of his grand, eternal, unchanging purpose, then we are left with no other choice but to hope that our actions are earnest enough, our prayers sincere enough, and our seeking diligent enough in our search for his will. If these fall short, then we will supposedly have missed out and have displeased our God while in the very act of attempting to please him. In one form or another, this is the teaching of much of the church today. If we are brutally and introspectively honest about this belief, does this not resemble the Pharisees who Jesus said were guilty of loading "people with burdens hard to bear"? (Luke 11:46). Few would be willing to label this as outright legalism, but have we not tied up a heavy burden and unnecessarily placed it on people's shoulders? (Matthew 23:4). Given this onerous encumbrance that we have created, is it any wonder that so many struggle to understand and dwell in the true, biblical love of our Father in today's churches, that so many Christians' lives are characterized by worry, striving, and burnout instead of joy, assurance, and stillness before our loving Father?

"Cease striving and know that I am God." These immensely powerful words from our Father to us are found in Psalm 46:10 (NASB), and they summarize the key to our confidence in our God. Furthermore, they provide us with the reason why we must understand the real God of the Bible. It is of little effect to know that he is God if we have defined that God as a feeble, ineffectual, uninvolved, hands-off, noninterfering, "struggling to outwit the devil," and "hoping maybe someone will lead a few more people to salvation" kind of God. If that is our God, we will inevitably continue striving; it is impossible to be still in confidence before that kind of God.

On the other hand, if we wholly believe our loving Father to be in complete control of everything, a God who is truly working all things according to the counsel of his great, eternal will, then that understanding can have only one result. We will abandon the human pride of self-destiny, and we will in humility naturally be still before the feet of our loving Father. Is it not a greatly more desirable and comfortable position to know that the Lord of the universe is driving in the complex, congested traffic of modern life than to think that we, the immature, amateur drivers, are striving to weave through this heavy, complicated traffic in a manner that is good enough to manage to please the Lord, who we imagine is watching and checking to see if our actions meet his "purpose"? We should instead cry out along with the psalmist, "When I thought, 'my foot slips,' your steadfast love, O Lord, held me up!" (Psalm 94:18). According to David, our Father gives us strength and "makes our way perfect" (2 Samuel 22:33 NIV). Because it is God who gives us the victory, we can be steadfast and immovable and know our labor is never in vain, as Paul told us in 1 Corinthians 15:57–58. We should note that he did not in any way suggest the opposite by saying that God's victory is dependent on our steadfastness and labor!

Yet again, we are told in 2 Thessalonians 3:3 (and in 1 Thessalonians 5:24 as well) that *because* the Lord is faithful, "he will establish us." Why do we invert the verse and preach it to the effect that "*if* we are faithful, then the Lord will establish us" when the verse says that it is the Lord who is faithful, and it is *he* who will establish us and guard us? Why is this so difficult for us to grasp hold of? Psalm 121 teaches us to rejoice that the Lord will "keep us," that he is the source of our strength and help, and that he will not allow our "foot to slip." Why would we want to resist these promises rather than rejoicing in them? We should celebrate that the Lord "preserves the way" of his people (Proverbs 2:8 NASB) instead of brashly claiming that he does no such thing! In 1 Peter 5:10, we are given the glorious promise that "the God of all grace, who called you to his eternal glory in Christ, will himself perfect, confirm, strengthen and establish you." Once again, God is telling us that he himself will establish us and perfect us—this to his eternal glory! It is God who will sustain us to the end (1 Corinthians 1:8, see also Romans 8:28–30, 37–39). Why would we not want to embrace this fact and live enthusiastically and joyfully with wonderful confidence in the affectionate purpose of the true God of the Bible, a sovereign God who is our own loving Father? Our Father's complete preeminence over his entire creation and his promises to establish us and perfect us should be our source of constant delight. As we see in the first verse of Psalm 97: "The Lord reigns, let the earth rejoice!"

Why do we resist the concept so? I have come to believe that the reasons we resist are the human propensity to want to be in complete control of our lives, the predilection to be a prideful donor rather than a humble receiver, and the nearly irresistible self-enthroning aversion to feeling and believing that our destiny is not in our own hands. And yet, if we really understood the true nature of our Father and his unconditional love for us, a great love that is backed up by his infinite power, unlimited understanding, and unbounded sovereignty, then I believe we would come to cherish the wondrous promise that it is our perfect God who determines our destiny rather than our own feeble striving. Having done that, we can finally be still and know that he is our Father.

<blockquote>
Praise him alone!
He makes everything work out according to his plan.
(Ephesians 1:11 NLT)
</blockquote>

NOTES

Chapter 1: Learning from the Sparrows

1. J. I. Packer, *Knowing God* (Downers Grove, IL: InterVarsity Press, 1993), p. 83.
2. Albert Barnes, *Notes on the Bible*, accessed January 22, 2012, http://biblecommenter.com/matthew/10-29.htm.
3. John Gill, *John Gill's Exposition of the Entire Bible,* accessed January 22, 2012, http://biblecommenter.com/matthew/10-29.htm.
4. Adam Clarke, *Clarke's Commentary on the Bible,* accessed January 22, 2012, http://biblecommenter.com/matthew/10-29.htm.
5. John Wesley, *Wesley's Notes on the Bible,* accessed January 22, 2012, http://biblecommenter.com/matthew/10-29.htm.
6. C. S. Lewis, *Perelandra* (New York: Scribner, 2003), ch. 5, pp. 51–61.
7. A. W. Pink, *The Attributes of God* (Grand Rapids: Baker Books, 2006), p. 36.
8. James Montgomery Boice, *Whatever Happened to the Gospel of Grace* (Wheaton: Crossway Books, 2009), p. 151.
9. C. H. Spurgeon, *Sermons of the Rev. C. H. Spurgeon of London,* 2nd Series (New York: Sheldon and Company, 1859), Sermon #3114, "God's Providence," p. 201.

Chapter 2: The Illusion of a Gentleman God

1. A. W. Tozer, *The Pursuit of Man* (Camp Hill, PA: Christian Publications, Inc., 1950), p. 40.
2. C. S. Lewis, *Chronicles of Narnia*, vols. 2, 5, 7 (New York: HarperTrophy, 2002) 2:200; 5:174; 7:19, 25, 36, 90.
3. A. W. Pink, *The Sovereignty of God,* (Watchmaker Publishing, 2011), p. 5.
4. Augustine, *The Enchiridion,* trans. J. B. Shaw (Washington: Regnery Publishing, 2002) ch. 98, p. 112.
5. Jonathon Edwards, *The Freedom of the Will* (New York: Cosimo Classics, 2007), pp. 1–15.
6. R. K. McGregor Wright, *No Place for Sovereignty* (Downers Grove, IL: InterVarsity Press, 1996), p. 130.

Notes

Chapter 3: *Praying to a Gentleman God*

1. C. H. Spurgeon, *The Metropolitan Tabernacle Pulpit*, vol. 25 (London: Passmore & Alabaster, 1880), Sermon 1482, "Our Change of Masters," p. 374.
2. Jerry Bridges, *Trusting God: Even When Life Hurts* (Colorado Springs: NavPress, 1990), pp. 113–114.
3. Horatius Bonar, *God's Will, Man's Will, and Free Will* (Lafayette, IN: Sovereign Grace Publishers, 2007), p. 24.
4. Augustine, *Against Two Letters of the Pelagians* (LaVergne, TN: Kessinger Publishing, 2010), bk. 1, ch. 37, p. 388; bk. 2, ch. 18, p. 399.
5. A. W. Tozer, *The Set of the Sail* (Camp Hill, PA: Christian Publications, 1986), p. 142.
6. C. H. Spurgeon, *The New Park Street Pulpit*, vol. 4 (Grand Rapids: Baker, 2009), Sermon #207, "Sovereign Grace and Man's Responsibility," p. 338.
7. James Montgomery Boice, *Whatever Happened to the Gospel of Grace* (Wheaton: Crossway Books, 2009), p. 167.
8. R. C. Sproul, *Chosen by God* (Carol Stream, IL: Tyndale, 1986), pp. 52–53.
9. A. W. Tozer, *The Pursuit of Man*, (Camp Hill, PA: Christian Publications, 1978), p. 39.

Chapter 4: *The Big, the Small, and Our Present*

1. A. W. Tozer, *The Knowledge of the Holy* (New York: HarperSanFrancisco, 1978), p. vii.
2. C. H. Spurgeon, *Metropolitan Tabernacle Pulpit*, vol. 56 (Pasadena, TX: Pilgrim Publications, 1979), Sermon #3202, "It Pleased God," pp. 292–293.
3. John Wesley, *Sermons of Several Occasions* (New York: J & J Harper, 1827), pp. 318–319.
4. Martin Luther, *Martin Luther: Selections from his Writings*, ed. John Dillenberger (New York: Anchor Books, 1962), pp. 184–185.

Chapter 5: *Our Future Is Heading Our Way*

1. David Livingston, *The Westminster Collection of Christian Quotations*, compiled by Martin Manser (Louisville, KY: Westminster John Knox Press, 2001), p. 189.
2. Jonathan Edwards, *The Works of President Edwards*, vol. 2 (New York: Leavitt, Trow & Co., 1844), pp. 513–527.
3. Albert Barnes, *Barnes Notes on the New Testament* (Grand Rapids: Kregel Publications, 1962), p. 384.
4. Stephen Charnock, *Discourses Upon the Existence and Attributes of God* (London: Henry G. Bohn, 1849), p. 290
5. Martin Luther, *The Bondage of the Will*, trans. Henry Cole (Lexington, KY: Feather Trail Press, 2009), ch. 5, sect. 9, p. 18.
6. A. W. Pink, *The Attributes of God* (Grand Rapids: Baker, 2006), p. 18.
7. C. H. Spurgeon, *The New Park Street Pulpit*, vol. 6 (Grand Rapids: Baker 1990), Sermon #343, "A Basket of Summer Fruit," p. 455.

Chapter 6: Our Loving Father God, or the Great Puppeteer?

1. Augustine, *On the Spirit and the Letter*, trans. W. J. Sparrow Simpson (Vepary, India: Diocesan Press, 1925), Ch. 52, p. 103.
2. Adam Clarke, *Clarke's Commentary on the Bible*, accessed January 22, 2012, http://clarke.biblecommenter.com/ezekiel/14.htm.
3. C. S. Lewis, *A Grief Observed* (New York: Harper Collins Publishers, 1994), p. 71.
4. Jonathan Edwards, *The Freedom of the Will*, (New York: Cosimo Classics, 2007), p. 59.
5. C. H. Spurgeon, *Sermons on Old Testament Men*, bk. 2 (Grand Rapids: Kregel Publications, 1995), Sermon 412, "God's First Words to the First Sinner," p. 8.
6. Augustine, *The Enchiridion*, trans. J. B. Shaw (Washington: Regnery Publishing, 2002), ch. 100, pp. 116–117.
7. A. W. Pink, *The Sovereignty of God* (Watchmaker Publishing, 2011), p. 16.
8. John Gill, *John Gills Exposition of the Entire Bible*, accessed January 20, 2012, http://gill.biblecommenter.com/acts/2.htm.
9. John Gill, *John Gills Exposition of the Entire Bible*, accessed January 20, 2012, http://gill.biblecommenter.com/acts/4.htm.
10. A. W. Tozer, *The Pursuit of Man* (Camp Hill, PA: Christian Publications, 1978), pp. 41–42.
11. John Gill, *John Gills Exposition of the Entire Bible*, accessed June 18, 2012, http://gill.biblecommenter.com/1_thessalonians/2.htm.

Chapter 7: Fair Is Fair, or Is It?

1. John MacArthur, "Components of Christian Invincibility," sermon preached January 2, 2002, *Grace to You*, accessed January 20, 2012, http://www.gty.org/resources/sermons/80-255/the-components-of-christian-invincibility.
2. R. C. Sproul, *Chosen by God* (Carol Stream, IL: Tyndale, 1986), pp. 103–110.
3. John Piper, *The Pleasures of God* (Colorado Springs: Multnomah Books, 1991), p. 125–126
4. Martin Luther, *The Bondage of the Will*, trans. Henry Cole (Lexington: Feather Trail Press, 2009), sections 99, 101, 102; pp. 97–100.
5. C. H. Spurgeon, *The New Park Street Pulpit*, vol. 4 (Grand Rapids: Baker, 2009), Sermon #207, "Sovereign Grace and Man's Responsibility," p. 337.
6. C. H. Spurgeon, *Spurgeon's Sermons on Christmas and Easter* (Grand Rapids: Kregel Publications, 1995), p. 126.
7. C. S. Lewis, *The Problem of Pain* (New York: HarperOne, 2001), p. 116.
8. John Piper, *The Pleasures of God* (Colorado Springs: Multnomah Books, 1991), p. 326.
9. William Tyndale, *The Works of the English and Scottish Reformers*, vol. 3, ed. Thomas Russell (London: Printed for Ebenezer Palmer, 1828), "An Answer to Sir Thomas More's Dialogue," p. 199.
10. Matthew Henry, *Matthew Henry's Commentary on the Whole Bible*, accessed January 20, 2012, http://mhcw.biblecommenter.com/matthew/11.htm.

Chapter 8: Heavenly Robots

1. Arnold Dallimore, *George Whitefield*, vol. 1 (East Peoria, IL: Versa Press; Banner of Truth, 2009), p. 407.
2. Jonathon Edwards, *The Freedom of the Will* (New York: Cosimo Classics, 2007), sect. II, pp. 5–15.
3. Augustine, *Admonition and Grace,* trans. John Murray (Boston: Daughters of St. Paul, 1962), ch. 32–35, pp. 53–57.
4. Augustine, *Enchiridion*, ed. and trans. Albert Outler (Louisville, KY: Westminster John Knox Press, 2006), ch. 28, para. 105, p. 403.
5. Albert Outler, *Enchiridion*, by Augustine (Louisville, KY: Westminster John Knox Press, 2006), ch. 28, para. 105, p. 403n229.
6. Horatius Bonar, *God's Will, Man's Will, and Free Will* (Lafayette, IN: Sovereign Grace Publishers, 2007), p. 15.

Chapter 9: Unchanging Perfection

1. Martin Luther, *The Bondage of the Will,* trans. Henry Cole (Lexington, KY: Feather Trail Press, 2009), ch. 5, sec. 16, p. 22.
2. R. K. McGregor Wright, *No Place for Sovereignty* (Downers Grove, IL: InterVarsity Press, 1996), p. 61.
3. E. M. Bounds, *The Reality of Prayer* (Racine, WI: Treasures Media, 2007), p. 15.
4. Ibid., p. 16
5. Richard Rushing, ed., *Voices from the Past* (East Peoria, IL: Banner of Truth, by Versa Press, 2010), p. 194.

Chapter 10: The God of Our Confidence

1. Augustus Toplady, *Free Will and Merit Fairly Examined: or, Men Not Their Own Saviors* (Manchester: George Parkin, T. B. V., 1774), p. 11.
2. Tryon Edwards, *A Dictionary of Thoughts* (Detroit: F. B. Dickerson Co., 1908), p. 375.
3. Ibid., p. 119.
4. John Newton, *Letters and Sermons, with a Review of Ecclesiastical History and Hymns,* vol. 2 (Edinburgh: Murray & Cochrane, 1787), pp. 158–159.
5. Jonathan Aitken, *John Newton: From Disgrace to Amazing Grace* (Wheaton: Crossway Books, 2009), p. 347.
6. J. I. Packer, *Knowing God* (Downers Grove: Inter-Varsity Press, 1993), p. 42.
7. Horatius Bonar, *God's Will, Man's Will, and Free Will* (Lafayette, IN: Sovereign Grace Publishers, 2007), p. 15.
8. Wayne Grudem, *Systematic Theology* (Grand Rapids: Zondervan, 1994), p. 679.
9. J. I. Packer, *Evangelism and the Sovereignty of God* (Downers Grove: Inter-Varsity Press, 2008), p. 115.
10. Ibid., p. 107.
11. A. W. Pink, *The Attributes of God* (Grand Rapids: Baker Books, 2006), pp. 16–18.